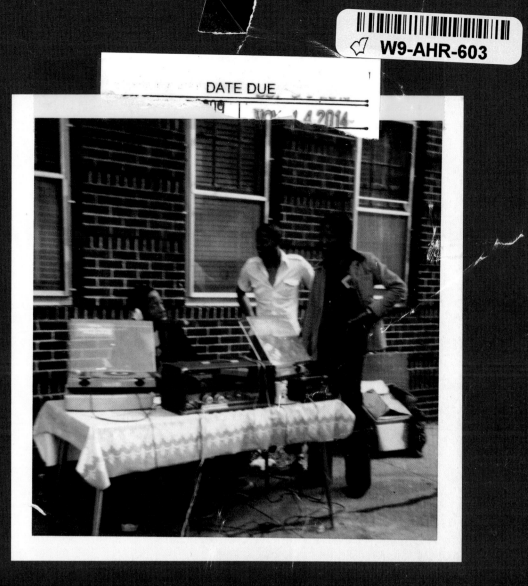

Early Brothers Disco block party with Breakout, Baron, and Jazzy Dee. Summer 1977 (Courtesy Darnell Williams)

yes yes y'all

yes yes y'all

The Experience Music Project

Oral History of Hip-Hop's First Decade

JIM FRICKE ● CHARLIE AHEARN

da capo press

a member of The Perseus Books Group

Printed in the United States of America.

Cataloging-in-Publication Data is available from the Library of Congress
ISBN 0–306-81184-7 (hc)
ISBN 0–306-81224-X (pa)

Da Capo Press is a member of the Perseus Books Group. Find us on the World Wide Web at www.dacapopress.com

Da Capo books are available at special discounts for bulk purchases in the U.S. by corporations, institutions, and other organizations. For more information, please contact the Special Markets Department at the Perseus Books Group, 11 Cambridge Center, Cambridge, MA 02142, or by phone at (800) 255-1514 or (617) 252-5298, or e-mail j.mccrary@perseusbooks.com.

Book design by Alex Camlin
Set in 9.5-point Helvetica Neue

First printing, October 2002

3   4   5   6   7   8   9   10 — 04

contents

introduction

the will to joy

The New York that spawned hip-hop spit me out, too. I came of age in the '70s, attending high school and college in the city's outer boroughs, and have many great memories of the era. But I'd be lying if I told you the '70s were a time of triumph in Nueva York. Quite the contrary. It was, at times, a frightful experience to walk the streets, ride the subways, or contemplate the future. A sense of despair and decay emanated from a poorly run City Hall, strike and corruption wracked municipal services, and the city was pervaded by the sense that it (and perhaps all big Northeastern cities) was essentially unlivable.

But in chaos there is often opportunity, in pain a measure of pleasure, and joy is just a stroke or two away from pain. The aesthetic industry now known internationally as hip-hop is a product of these blighted times, a child that walked, talked, and partied amid negativity. In Ishmael Reed's brilliant 1972 novel *Mumbo Jumbo*, he writes of an African-inspired rhythmic virus that rises to battle the rigid forces of Western orthodoxy. Unknown to all but a small percentage of New Yorkers, hip-hop "jes grew" in the damaged, insecure city of my youth, and neither poverty nor indifference nor racism could stop it. In fact, to some degree all those things helped it grow.

The twenty-first-century New York of martyrdom, national acclaim, and heroic local leadership has nothing to do with the city that nurtured hip-hop. That metropolis was an embattled, tough, cynical town that for many symbolized America's bitter rejection of the urban experience. The Republicans became the nation's majority party by railing against the excesses of welfare mothers, liberal spending, and the ills of identity politics—all of which were identified with this melting pot. Moreover, the rise of the Sunbelt states, places increasingly populated by big-city refugees, fueled an intense hostility toward New York and the snowbelt in general. The apex of this disdain came in 1975 when President Gerald Ford, who'd replaced the disgraced Richard Nixon, refused a cash-strapped city some key financial support. The once feisty (now moribund) *Daily News* proclaimed, "Ford to City: Drop Dead." The headline perfectly captured the attitude of so many Americans toward their biggest city.

The Bronx, the only one of the five boroughs physically connected to the U.S. mainland, became the symbol of all that ailed us. A brief survey of statistics from the southern end of the borough in the '70s tells a horrific tale. The median family income in New York was $9,682; in the South Bronx it was $5,200. The area suffered one-quarter of all the city's reported cases of malnutrition. The infant mortality rate was 29 in 1,000 births. There were 6,000 abandoned buildings there. In the pivotal year of 1975, there were 13,000 fires in a twelve-square-mile radius that left more than 10,000 people homeless and earned landlords $10 million in insurance settlements.

Heroin was a plague that devastated the Bronx and Harlem, yet due to the city's fiscal ills, the budget for the office of the special narcotics prosecutor plummeted from $2.4 million in 1975 to $1.1 in 1977. The trafficking was aided greatly by rampant police corruption. The Knapp Commission, whose investigation into police malfeasance was sparked by the testimony of officer Frank Serpico, issued a report in December 1972 that stated that the "problem was an extensive, department-wide phenomenon that included cops selling heroin, ratting on informants to the mob, and riding shotgun on drug deals." In February 1973 it was discovered that heroin and cocaine valued at $73 million had been stolen from the police property clerk's office.

This combination of police impotence, urban misery, and highly organized drug distribution led to the rise of Nicky Barnes, aka Mr. Untouchable, a black drug kingpin who dominated Harlem and the Bronx. Throughout the '70s, the specter of Barnes and his council of death merchants dominated crime in his communities as Reggie Jackson dominated coverage of the Yankees after his 1976 arrival in pinstripes.

While all this (and more) was happening in the streets, mayors John Lindsay and Abe Beame were indulging in accounting tricks that ballooned the city's short-term debt from $4.4 million in 1970 to $7.3 million in 1974, setting the stage for its near bankruptcy mid-decade. From the late 1970s into the '80s, a financial control board oversaw New York's budget as transit fares soared, the city's infrastructure crumbled, and white flight eroded its tax base. The South Bronx, home to Yankee Stadium, wide boulevards, and miles of burnt-out buildings, became a national symbol visited by grandstanding politicians (like future president Ronald Reagan), ridiculed in Johnny Carson's nightly Tonight Show monologues, and depicted in grim Hollywood flicks like *Fort Apache—The Bronx*.

All of this raises the question, Could hip-hop have been born in the tightly policed, gentrified, self-congratulatory Big Apple of the '90s? My guess is no. The very lack of civil control (and concern) that marked New York in the 1970s aided the culture's incubation. The sound-system battles in city parks and school yards would have been impossible in a city that strictly enforced "quality of life" crimes against loud music and after-dark use of public space. It's hard to imagine Rudy Giuliani allowing the easy entry to the subway yards that made possible the amazing train-long graffiti tags that are now celebrated on web sites and in magazines all over the world. A great many of the discos that supported hip-hop parties in the Bronx and Harlem were owned and operated by drug-related businessmen; trafficking in heroin, coke, and angel dust was both public and widespread. It's hard to imagine the casual illegality of these '70s clubs surviving the targeted, computer-driven police tactics of recent times.

The lack of employment for minority youth made gang culture and, later, hip-hop posses (where kids could be MCs, DJs, dancers, graffiti artists, or security guards) quite attractive. Much as the lawlessness of the Prohibition era aided the development of jazz, the lackadaisical criminal enforcement policies of the '70s encouraged the experimentation that was eventually organized into the hip-hop industry.

The flip side of all the grim stats of the '70s and early '80s was that none of this drama inhibited the spirit of the people. What you'll find in the personal observations, photos, and posters of hip-hop's early days that make up this book is what Hemingway termed "grace under pressure"—a will to survive through strength, self-expression, and plain old fun. Unlike hip-hop's '80s heroes (many of whom emerged from middle-class environments), the early pioneers and their audience came from housing projects, tenements, and rough areas—and didn't let any of that stifle their desire for pleasure. The will to joy proved as powerful as any of the socioeconomic forces aligned against them.

Well into the '80s, hip-hop gatherings had an edge, a balance between pain and the celebration of music and movement. Later the culture would lose that edge, would tip so that pain, as fact and subject, overwhelmed its joy. But for the people you'll meet in the following pages, that balancing act was in the party's background. In the foreground was self-expression, creativity, and love (as corny as it sounds). No one was getting rich. Most of the people in those pre-Run-DMC years made, at best, tens of thousands creating hip-hop, not hundreds of thousands and certainly not millions.

It may be cold comfort to the survivors of hip-hop's original school, but their style, taste, and culture still resonate decades later. The way they dressed, danced, spoke, and painted are still with us, sometimes submerged in commercial products, sometimes in things as obvious as the Technics turntables that have remained icons three decades later. Now remixed and recycled, their ways of hearing and seeing once represented the potent and tangible shock of the new.

At least that's how it felt to me hearing black DJs rock Kraftwerk's "Trans Europe Express" in Brooklyn playgrounds, marveling at breakers spinning on cardboard under Times Square's neon, seeing painter's caps and shell-toe Adidas emerge as high-profile fashion on Harlem streets. A shift was occurring, and you either were drawn to it or feared it. There was very little middle ground. That fear actually strengthened hip-hop. It meant parents, authority figures, and uptight people of all colors weeded themselves out from those who understood. It was a badge of honor or bad taste, depending on who was doing the pinning.

Now everyone has access. It's great business, but bad for creativity, innovation, and that intangible magic that surrounds a movement in motion. Twenty-first-century hip-hop is an industry with institutions, orthodoxies, and dogmas. That's cool. That's evolution. That's life. But this document you're holding isn't about any of that. It isn't about hip-hop today or New York today or any of that stuff. It's about a time and a place and a people that you should know about and that I, happily, cannot forget.

Nelson George
Brooklyn, 2002

the players

AFRIKA BAMBAATAA●DJ; known as the "Master of Records" and the "godfather" of hip-hop, Bambaataa spread hip-hop and his own brand of Electro-Funk throughout the world as a DJ and leader of the Soulsonic Force, Cosmic Force, and the Zulu Nation. **AFRIKA ISLAM●**DJ/MC/b-boy/right-hand man for Afrika Bambaataa and the Zulu Nation, known as "Son of Bambaataa." Spread hip-hop through the tri-state area through his pioneering Zulu Beats radio show on WHBI. **ALIEN NESS●**B-boy; originally named Kid Ness by Mr. Ness of the Furious 5 and later given the name Alien Ness by Afrika Bambaataa. Member of the New York City Breakers, Rock Steady Crew, and early member of Boogie Down Productions. **ARTHUR ARMSTRONG●**Early hip-hop promoter and owner of the successful Bronx venues, the Galaxy 2000 and the Ecstasy Garage. **BIG BANK HANK●**MC; club bouncer and one-time manager for Grandmaster Caz, recruited by Sylvia Robinson of Sugarhill Records to be a member of the Sugar Hill Gang. **BILL ADLER●**Journalist, author, hip-hop historian; chief publicist for Rush Artists Management—the promotion side of Def Jam records—from 1984 to 1990. **BLADE●**Early graffiti writer and member of the Crazy 5 graffiti crew. Active throughout the '70s and into the mid-'80s, Blade bombed over 5,000 subway cars. **BOBBY ROBINSON●**Record label owner/music industry veteran who made important blues and R&B records from the 1950s onward. Recorded many of the original hip-hop MCs and groups on his Enjoy Records label beginning in 1979, including early releases from Grandmaster Flash and the Furious 5, the Funky 4+1, Spoonie Gee, and the Treacherous 3. **BOM5●**Puerto Rican graffiti writer and b-boy (cousin of Rock Steady Crew's Crazy Legs) who began hitting tags in the Bronx in the mid-'70's as a member of the Savage Skulls and continues to paint today. **BROTHERS DISCO/FUNKY 4+1●** Developed a large following in the North Bronx toward the late 1970s, with DJs Breakout and Baron, the Funky 4 MCs (later Funky 4 + 1) and their monster sound system, the Mighty Mighty Sasquatch. Released the hit records "Rappin' and Rocking the House" and "That's the Joint" for the Enjoy and Sugarhill labels. **BUDDY ESQUIRE●** Known as the "King of the Flyer," from 1978 to 1983 Buddy created hundreds of unique, elegantly styled hip-hop flyers. **BURN!**●Brooklyn Uprocker and graffiti writer from the late 1970s. He joined Rock Steady Crew in the early '80s. **BUSY BEE**•Known as an all-around natural entertainer and master of the party rhymes, Busy Bee (aka Chief Rocker Busy Bee Starski), performed as a solo MC and with numerous hip-hop groups in the late '70s and early '80s. **CASANOVA CREW**●Security crew of Grandmaster Flash and the Furious 5 and promoter of Ray Chandler's Black Door Productions. Comprised of former Black Spades gang members and known for being particularly ruthless. **CEY ADAMS**●Graffiti artist from the late '70s and early '80s. Later a celebrated graphic designer who produced album covers for most of Def Jam's releases, including the Beastie Boys, L.L. Cool J, and Public Enemy. **CHARLIE AHEARN**● Independent New York filmmaker who wrote, directed, and produced *Wild Style*, a movie that starred many pioneers of the hip-hop/graffiti world of the early 1980s. **CHARLIE CHASE**●One of the first Latino hip-hop DJs. Charlie began as a backup DJ for disco duo Tom and Jerry, and later founded the Cold Crush Brothers with fellow DJ Tony Tone. **CHRIS STEIN**●A founding member of New Wave hit-makers Blondie and an early aficionado of hip-hop culture. **COLD CRUSH BROTHERS**●One of the most popular and original of the early hip-hop groups to come out of the Bronx at the end of the '70s. Formed by DJ Tony Tone and DJ Charlie Chase, the Cold Crush Brothers went through numerous MCs before settling on a solid lineup based around Grandmaster Caz. **COWBOY**●First MC for Grandmaster Flash, known for his ability to pump up the crowd with call-and-response rhymes like "Everybody say ho!" Passed away in 1989 after several years of crack cocaine abuse. **CRASH CREW**●Along with the Treacherous 3 and the Fearless 4, one of the most prominent of the Harlem crews. Led by MC Reggie Reg and known for their rapping skill as well as their vocal harmonies, the Crash Crew self-released "High Power Rap" in 1980 and later signed with Sugarhill Records. **CRAZY LEGS**●B-boy credited with reviving the dying art of b-boying and spreading its popularity nationally and internationally. Crazy Legs was invited to join the Rock Steady Crew in 1979 by founders JoJo and Jimmy D and later became president of the organization and its most prominent member. **DISCO KING MARIO**● Pioneering mid-'70s DJ known for his powerful sound system. **DISCO WIZ**●Latino DJ briefly known as DJ Louie Lou. Wiz worked with Grandmaster Caz—then known as DJ Casanova Fly—throughout the mid- to late '70s. **DJ BARON**●Founded the Brothers Disco with DJ Breakout in the mid-'70s. Along with their MCs the Funky 4 + 1, they ruled the North Bronx. Known for his disco beats and his ability to catch the beat without flaw. **DJ BREAKOUT**●Cofounder of the Brothers Disco/Funky 4 + 1, named for his b-boy skills. Brother of Brothers Disco promoter/manager Jazzy Dee. **DJ HOLLYWOOD**● DJ in the Harlem club scene from the early '70s, Hollywood was a major influence on the street-based DJs who would take over the scene in the late '70s. Known as the first live DJ to say rhymes over the beats. **DLB**●MC (known as the Microphone Wizard), for the Fearless 4, a popular Harlem-based crew. **DMC**●MC; formed Run-DMC with DJ Run and Jam Master Jay in the early '80s. **DOTA ROCK**●MC with Grand Wizard

Theodore and the Fantastic 5. Dota Rock first worked with Grandmaster Caz's Mighty Force, split off with MC Whipper Whip to form the Salt and Pepper MCs, and was an early member of the Cold Crush Brothers. **DR. DRE**●the "East Coast Dre"—DJ best known as the cohost, with Ed Lover, of Yo! MTV Raps. **EASY AD**●MC for the Cold Crush Brothers. **ECSTASY**●MC for the popular early '80s group Whodini. **EDDIE CHEBA**●Popular mid-'70s disco DJ/MC, known throughout the club circuit. **FAB 5 FREDDY**●(aka Fred Brathwaite). Helped create the hip-hop classic film *Wild Style* and was later the first host of *Yo! MTV Raps*. A hip-hop renaissance man who helped bring graffiti and hip-hop culture to the downtown art scene. **FANTASTIC 5**●Grand Wizard Theodore's MC crew. Formed in 1980 by Theodore after he left the L Brothers, the group quickly became one of the most popular acts of the period, developing an ongoing rivalry with the Cold Crush Brothers that only heightened their popularity. **FEARLESS 4**● Protégés of the Treacherous 3 and one of the top Harlem crews in the mid-'80s. The first hip-hop group to sign to a major label—Elektra—in 1983, they recorded popular hits such as "It's Magic," "Rockin' It," and "Problems of the World Today." **FLIP ROCK**● West Side Manhattan b-boy known for his unique flipping dance style. Joined the Rock Steady Crew and later became part of the New York City Breakers. **FROSTY FREEZE**● Legendary b-boy, in the early '80s became Co-Vice President (with Ken Swift) of the Rock Steady Crew. Known for his freezes and unique moves like the Suicide. **FURIOUS 5**●Grandmaster Flash's MC crew, the Furious ruled the early '80s hip-hop scene. With Grandmaster Flash's talent on the turntables and lead MC Melle Mel's unbeatable rhymes, the group became the most popular and recognizable group from hip-hop's old school period, producing a string of hits, including "Freedom," "The Message," and "White Lines." **G.L.O.B.E.**●MC in Afrika Bambaataa's revolving Soulsonic Force. Wrote lyrics to hits like "Planet Rock," "Looking for a Perfect Beat," and "Renegades of Funk," and later joined with DJ Whiz Kid to record "Play That Beat, Mr. DJ." **GRAND WIZARD THEODORE**●Pioneering DJ who perfected the art of needle dropping and invented the scratch. Performed in the L Brothers with his older siblings Mean Gene and Cordie-O, and later formed Grand Wizard Theodore and the Fantastic 5. **GRANDMASTER CAZ**●A multitalented performer who started out as a b-boy in the early '70s and soon added DJ-ing and MC-ing to the mix. Best known as the lead MC of the Cold Crush Brothers. **GRANDMASTER FLASH**●One of the founding fathers of hip-hop and a DJ innovator. The first DJ to master cutting the break-beat on a record back and forth, as well as cueing through headphones. With the Furious 5, became one of the most important acts in hip-hop. **GRANDMIXER D.ST.**●One of Afrika Bambaataa's Zulu Nation DJs, well known for his ability to DJ and b-boy at the same time and later renowned for his scratching skills on Herbie Hancock's hit "Rockit." **HENRY CHALFANT**●Photographer who chronicled graffiti art on the streets and trains of New York City and produced several influential documents about the artform, including the book *Subway Art* (with Martha Cooper) and the documentary *Style Wars* (with Tony Silver). **JALIL**●MC for Whodini. Worked closely with WHBI radio jock Mr.

Magic and recruited Ecstasy to form Whodini and record their first hit, "Magic's Wand." **JAZZY DEE**●Older brother of DJ Breakout and the manager/promoter of the Brothers Disco/Funky 4 + 1. Organizer of the Brothers Disco/Sisters Disco security crew, and owner of the group's sound system, the Mighty Mighty Sasquatch. **JAZZY JEFF**●First MC-ed for the Magnificent 7 with Lil' Rodney Cee, then joined the Brothers Disco/Funky 4 + 1. Later went solo with "King Heroin (Don't Mess with Heroin)" on Jive Records. **JOJO**●Early b-boy who founded the Rock Steady Crew with Jimmy D. **JOEY ROBINSON, JR.**●Son of Sugarhill Records founders Sylvia Robinson and Joe Robinson, Sr. Initiated the formation of hip-hop's first hit-makers, the Sugar Hill Gang, of which he later became a member. **K.K. ROCKWELL**●The first MC for DJ Breakout and DJ Baron's Brothers Disco/Funky 4 + 1. Later joined fellow Funky 4 member Lil' Rodney Cee and formed Double Trouble. **KEVIE KEV**●With his brother Master Rob, the original MCs for the L Brothers. Stayed with L Brother Theodore and formed Grand Wizard Theodore and the Fantastic 5. **KID CREOLE**●One of the first MCs for Grandmaster Flash, known for his never-ending rhymes and his use of the echo box. Along with his younger brother Melvin (aka Melle Mel), they formed the foundation of the Furious 5. **KOOL DJ AJ**●Early hip-hop DJ and promoter who worked with MCs Busy Bee, Love Bug Starski, and Kurtis Blow, whose 1984 single, "AJ Scratch," was dedicated to the DJ. **KOOL DJ HERC**●Jamaican-born DJ known as the "Father of Hip-Hop," credited for coining the term "b-boy," and the first DJ to extend the break-beat on a record. Most of the superstars coming out of the hip-hop scene in the late '70s and early '80s first experienced hip-hop culture at a Kool Herc jam. **KOOL LADY BLUE**●London-born promoter and one-time manager for the Rock Steady Crew who, along with Michael Holman, was instrumental in bringing hip-hop to downtown Manhattan clubs Negril and the Roxy. **KOOL MOE DEE**●MC for the Treacherous 3 who invented the speed-rap style of rhyming. Known as an MC par excellence, illustrated by his infamous MC battle with Busy Bee. Later in the '80s had a very successful solo career. **KURTIS BLOW**●Early DJ/b-boy who worked as an MC with Grandmaster Flash and was managed by future Def Jam head, Russell Simmons. Blow was the first solo hip-hop artist to sign to a major label, Mercury, in 1980, and released hip-hop's first gold record, "The Breaks." **L BROTHERS**●Popular Bronx crew from the late '70s, comprised of the Livingston brothers, Mean Gene, Cordie-O, and Theodore. Later Theodore split off from the group, taking the MC brothers Kevie Kev and Master Rob with him to form Grand Wizard Theodore and the Fantastic 5. **L.A. SUNSHINE**● MC, along with Kool Moe Dee and Special K, for the Treacherous 3, one of the most popular groups to come out of Manhattan in the late '70s. **LEE**●Graffiti artist with the Fabulous 5 crew, known for his spectacular whole car pieces. By the late '70s, his work was in galleries across the U.S. and Europe. Starred in Wild Style. **LIL' RODNEY CEE**●MC who along with Jazzy Jeff joined the Brothers Disco/Funky 4 following original member Rahiem's departure and prompting the name change to Funky 4 + 1. Left the group along with K.K. Rockwell in the early '80s to form Double Trouble.

L.L. COOL J●MC signed to the fledgling Def Jam label in 1984 at age 16. L.L.'s first record, "I Need a Beat," cemented Def Jam's status as a serious hip-hop label and catapulted L.L. Cool J into superstardom. **LOVE BUG STARSKI**●DJ/MC who began his career working with Pete DJ Jones. As a DJ, MC, or both, he worked every club in the scene and became house DJ at clubs like the Disco Fever, Harlem World, and the Renaissance Ballroom. **LUCKY STRIKE**●Former member of the Savage Skulls in the Bronx who joined the Zulu Kings b-boy crew and became very active in Afrika Bambaataa's Zulu Nation. **MARTHA COOPER**●Photojournalist who chronicled graffiti and b-boy culture in the late '70s and early '80s. Published the first known photographs of b-boys and authored, with photographer Henry Chalfant, the seminal document of graffiti culture, Subway Art. **MEAN GENE**●Early collaborator with Grandmaster Flash and leader of the L Brothers. Formed a group under his own name following brother Theodore's departure. **MELLE MEL**●Lead MC of Grandmaster Flash and the Furious 5 and major lyricist of many of their hits, including "The Message" and "White Lines (Don't Do It)." One of the most respected MCs in hip-hip with an unparalleled lyrical ability. **PEANUT**●Respected member of promoter Ray Chandler's Casanova Crew security team. Murdered during an argument while working security at the Black Door. **PEE WEE DANCE**●Early b-boy who frequented Kool Herc and Bambaataa parties. Later joined the Zulu Kings and the Rock Steady Crew. **PETE DJ JONES**●One of the top Black disco DJs in New York in the early '70s. A major influence on the DJs who would come up in the mid-'70s. **PHASE 2**●Pioneer graffiti artist from the early '70s onward and key figure in the development of graffiti as an art form throughout the '70s and '80s. He was also known for his DJ skills and the hundreds of flyers that he produced for the hip-hop scene during that period. **PISTOL**●One of the first graffiti artists on the scene. Contemporary of innovators Blade and Phase 2. First artist credited with a 3-D piece. **POPMASTER FABEL**●B-boy with the Magnificent Force who joined the Rock Steady Crew in the early '80s. A renowned choreographer, teacher, and hip-hop historian. **RAHIEM**●MC for the Brothers Disco/Funky 4 who left that group to join Grandmaster Flash and the Furious 5. Known for his amiable personality and his excellent singing voice. **RAY CHANDLER**●Pioneering hip-hop promoter who ran the Black Door club/Black Door Productions and booked Grandmaster Flash and the Furious 5. Known for his imposing stature, no-nonsense attitude, and his hiring of the notorious Casanova Crew as his security. **REGGIE REG**●Lead MC for Harlem group the Crash Crew, which became popular in the early '80s. **RICHARD SISCO**●First MC to perform with Charlie Chase and what would become the Cold Crush Brothers. Produced many flyers for hip-hop jams in the late '70s and early '80s and briefly teamed up with DJ Wanda Dee. **RICK RUBIN**●Cofounder with Russell Simmons of Def Jam. Responsible for launching the careers of countless hip-hop acts, including Run-DMC, L.L. Cool J, the Beastie Boys, and Public Enemy. **ROBERT FORD & J. B. MOORE**●Music journalists for Billboard magazine in the late '70s who documented the hip-hop scene and later collaborated with Russell Simmons on the lyrics for Kurtis Blow's smash hits,

"Christmas Rappin'" and "The Breaks." **ROCK STEADY CREW**●Legendary b-boy organization founded in 1977 by JoJo and Jimmy D. Revived by Crazy Legs at the beginning of the '80s, the Rock Steady were instrumental in popularizing b-boying worldwide. **RUN-DMC**●Multi-platinum hip-hop act from Hollis, Queens, consisting of MCs DJ Run (brother of Def Jam's Russell Simmons), DMC, and DJ Jam Master Jay. Their rise to superstardom coincided with the decline of the original Bronx-based hip-hop culture. **RUSSELL SIMMONS**●Cofounder with Rick Rubin of Def Jam. The quintessential hip-hop entrepreneur, Simmons was responsible for launching the careers of most of the big hip-hop acts of the '80s, including Kurtis Blow, Run-DMC, L.L. Cool J, the Beastie Boys, and Public Enemy. **SAL ABBATIELLO**●Disco Fever club owner active in Bronx civic culture. Abbatiello and the Disco Fever were featured in the classic hip-hop film *Krush Groove*. **SEQUENCE**●First all-female hip-hop recording artists, with members Cheryl the Pearl, Blondie, and Angie B. Formed in 1978, they released several hits for Sugarhill Records, including 1980's "Funk You Up." **SHA-ROCK**●The most celebrated old school female MC and "+1" with the Funky 4 + 1, Sha-Rock inspired a whole generation of female MCs and later formed Us Girls with Debbie Dee and Cosmic Force member Lisa Lee. **SOULSONIC FORCE / COSMIC FORCE**●Afrika Bambaataa's revolving member, Parliament/Funkadelic-inspired Zulu Nation crews, who produced hits such as "Zulu Nation Throwdown," "Planet Rock," "Looking for the Perfect Beat," and "Renegades of Funk." **SPECIAL K**●MC for the Treacherous 3, along with Kool Moe Dee and L.A. Sunshine. **SPOONIE GEE**●Nephew of Enjoy Records owner Bobby Robinson, and an original member of the Treacherous 3, known for his sexually themed hits "Love Rap" and "Spoonin' Rap." **SUGAR HILL GANG**●Hip-hop act put together by Sugarhill Records' owner Sylvia Robinson and son Joey Robinson who produced, in 1979, the genre's first hit record, "Rapper's Delight." **SYLVIA ROBINSON**●Owner, with husband Joe Robinson, of hip-hop's first big label, Sugarhill Records, the company responsible for the Sugar Hill Gang's "Rapper's Delight," and for launching the careers of many of the acts from the late '70s and early '80s hip-hop scene. **TONY TONE**●Sound man for DJ Breakout and the Brothers Disco who, as a DJ, paired up with DJ Charlie Chase and formed the Cold Crush Brothers. **TREACHEROUS 3**●The most popular of the Manhattan-based groups from 1979 through the early '80s, producing hits for Enjoy and Sugarhill Records, such as "New Rap Language," which featured the speed-rapping of MC Kool Moe Dee, "The Body Rock," and "Feel the Heartbeat." **VAN SILK**●Hip-hop promoter and manager from the late '70s to mid-'80s, later producing the first pay-per-view hip-hop programs such as "Sisters in the Name of Rap" and "Rapmania." **WANDA DEE**●One of the first female DJs on the hip-hop scene in the early '80s. **WHIPPER WHIP**●MC who began his career with Grandmaster Caz, formed the Salt and Pepper MCs with Dota Rock, was briefly a member of the Cold Crush Brothers, and then joined Grand Wizard Theodore's Fantastic 5. **WONDER MIKE**●MC with the Sugar Hill Gang whose voice introduced the first hip-hop hit, "Rapper's Delight."

South Bronx, 1981 (© Charlie Ahearn)

ROCKING:

gang culture and the beginnings of hip-hop

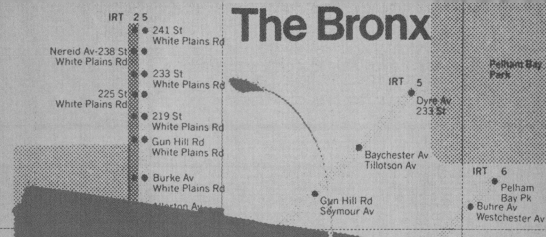

The Bronx

IRT 2 5
241 St White Plains Rd
Nereid Av-238 St White Plains Rd
233 St White Plains Rd
225 St White Plains Rd
219 St White Plains Rd
Gun Hill Rd White Plains Rd
Burke Av White Plains Rd
Allerton Av

IRT 5
Dyre Av 233 St
Baychester Av Tillotson Av
Gun Hill Rd Seymour Av

Pelham Bay Park

IRT 6
Pelham Bay Pk
Buhre Av
Westchester Av

Westchester Av Sq.

The street gangs which rose up in New York in the late '50s and '60s seemed to explode in numbers around 1970, carving up areas in the Bronx and Brooklyn into warring territories. By the early '70s, gang violence and drug dealing had become such a problem that new laws were passed making it easier to incarcerate drug- and gang-related offenders. Many people in the affected neighborhoods had tired of the drugs and violence by this time as well.

Hip-hop culture rose out of the gang-dominated street culture, and aspects of the gangs are still defining features of hip-hop—particularly territorialism and the tradition of battling. As hip-hop grew in the '70s, prominent DJs claimed specific territories as their own, and "crews" that derived either directly or in spirit from street gangs guarded the DJs, their equipment, and their territories. These DJs would battle for supremacy and territory.

The art and the dance associated with hip-hop culture—graffiti and b-boying or breaking—also have their roots in gang culture. Gang members "tagged" their territories to identify them and tagged rival territories to provoke those rivals. These "tags" were taken up by "writers" who were not affiliated with specific gangs and developed into an art form that found its most spectacular expression in rolling murals on the city's subway cars. At the same time, battle dances were refined as an alternative to violence, though they were sometimes only a prelude to it.

ART ARMSTRONG: Rap was territorial. It came from the gang wars; I don't know if a lot of people know that many of the rappers came from the gang wars of the '70s. Some became DJs, MCs; some became security. So it melted over into rap music, protecting their territory. So that's basically how it started.

LUCKY STRIKE: To be down in the streets back then you had to be down with something. To get respect, to survive. If you weren't a part of nothing, you'd be constantly harassed. Kids asking you for money. Taking your sneakers.

AFRIKA BAMBAATAA: There was a lot of street gangs at the time: the Black Spades, the Savage Skulls, the Savage Nomads, the Javelins, the Royal Charmers, the Seven Crowns. Little wars could start if you just looked at another person or woman wrong, or you stepped on somebody's sneaker or their shoe, or if you just made a bump or touched a person at the wrong time or the wrong place. Or even if you said certain words that another group didn't like—that could have led into a full-fledged war, and violence could have sprung up all over the Bronx, and it could have spread into Manhattan and then into other parts of the city, because the Black Spades, the Savage Nomads, and the Savage Skulls had chapters throughout the whole city and even in other states and towns.

LUCKY STRIKE: Being in the Savage Skulls was more of a unity thing, the second family that I never had. When I first joined, I didn't really know how to go through the Apache line, and that really freaked me out 'cause that was one of the first stages to become a member. An Apache line is when you got ten people in one line and ten people in another line, and when you go through, they beat you. You had to go through I guess to show your courage, to prove to them that you want to be down with this family.

The final stage was when you had to play Russian roulette. That was the scariest thing that I ever went through. Sometimes I even have nightmares. I can't believe I did it. There were a couple of people that had got shot, and they were left in those abandoned buildings, and the cops never realized what it was until people started speaking up and saying it was gang-related.

BOM5: I grew up with the Savage Skulls. My cousin was a warlord and hey—when you grow up in a neighborhood that's all gangs, you got to join. It's a part of your life. I became a Savage Skull, a "Baby Skull" in 1972. I was nine years old. They used to call me 174 Spider. That was my name. They gave me the name Spider cause I was short and fast. I used to go in and out, steal from Woolworth's, Macy's, whatever. And I put the 174 for where I lived. But I wrote 174 Spider (not Spider 174, as most graffiti writers would have done it). I felt my block was me, and that came first. I never said I was a graffiti writer; I was just writing. I was in a gang.

DJ DISCO WIZ: I grew up in the Bronx. Born and raised in the Bronx, half Cuban, half Puerto Rican. I got involved in gangs early on in the Bronx because that was the scene in the early '70s—gangs pretty much dominated the city. In my era, the prominent gangs were the Savage Skulls, an all-Latin gang that I was affiliated with; the Supreme Bachelors, which also was a Latin-based gang; the Black Spades and the Black Assassins, which were the gangs that Bambaataa and the Zulu Nation came out of; and the Golden Guineas. Those were pretty much the dominant gangs at that time. We basically stayed in our own area, because that's the way it was—it was a pretty rough time in those days.

BOM5: Savage Skulls were strictly Puerto Ricans. They were smaller than the Black Spades, but they were the most notorious gang in New York City. They were the worst gang. You wouldn't even want to step to them. Me being part of that, going home I had to take my bandanna off, my jacket off, because of my parents, but they knew something was going on.

6

DXT (D.ST.): I lived in the Bronx, "where the people are fresh," in the Eden-Wald projects off 233rd Street and Baychester Avenue. There was heavy gang activity in the early '70s; at Bronx River, the Soundview neighborhood, was the rival gang. There were two gangs there: one was called InterCrime and the other was called the Uptown Organization. There were two jackets: InterCrime's was the planet Earth with a knife stuck through it, and Uptown Organization's was the picture in the police department where they do target practice with a gun. Bambaataa was Black Spades. I was pretty young then, and I was terrified of those guys because they were always beating somebody up.

I remember one day we had after-school basketball in the gym until 8 or 9 p.m. We were playing in there, and this guy comes in and forces everybody to stop playing. He says, "Yo man. The Spades is coming and everybody in here is fighting!" I was terrified. My brother was there, and he said, "Go home." I went home, but I remember hearing police cars all over the place.

Gang members c. 1972. They knew how to spell "Roman,"
they just ran out of "A"s (Bill Schwarz)

BLADE: Golden Guineas would actually come down to fight with the Savage Skulls, and the Savage Skulls would go fight with the Black Spades, and while all those morons were out there blastin' each other's heads off, the rest of us were out there painting and having a good time. All the graffiti guys are just stealing paint and having a good time, and all these guys are knifing each other, beating each other up—as long as they didn't see you with the spray paint. Gang guys would chase graffiti guys to catch them, take their paint, and spray all over them.

BURN: I used to go to John Jay High (Brooklyn), and all these writers used to hang out there. They used to dance and smoke weed. The term was rock, burning and jerking. That's bullshit about how dancing took the place of fighting—they were gangs, they always fought. Gangs had their dancers, their graffiti writers, and their stick-up kids! It all started with the gangs, all over—Bushwick, Bedstuy, East New York, Coney, every block had dance crews and they rocked.

BOM5: The famous Smiley 149 (RIP), he was my cousin's friend. Smiley was an original Savage Nomad. I always call him my grandfather in graffiti; he's a forefather. A lot of people talk about writing in the '60s, but I know of only one person who was writing in the '60s. Smiley was his gang name, so he was already in there with the Savage Nomads, who were a brother/sister gang to Savage Skulls.

My cousin was always coming to pick me up—he was five years older than me. He told me, "Yo, if you want to survive in this neighborhood you got to stick with me." He told me everything that I know about fighting, and since I was really good with art, they told me, "Hey, you're going to be the one putting up the name"—a quick skull and crossbones and SS with lightning lines. I used to do it all over. I never used spray paint. I used a can of paint and a brush, and I'd dip it in and write 174 Spider (Savage Skulls) all over the place, and to this day I got a tag left in the Bronx.

LEE: The Fab Five [a graffiti crew] were painting trains since 1971. They were an off-shoot of some violent gangs—the Savage Skulls, the Puerto Rican Bros. They had balls. They had no fear. They carried pistols and pistol-whipped people. They were vicious, but I thought that was kind of cute. They were like protective brothers to me.

Base I was one great writer, and he was a great acrobatic dancer, too, with flips. He'd spin on the floor. He'd come off, flip his hat, and stuff it in your face. People were intimidated. Black guys from the Hill or the Avenue would come down to battle. They were the best. Suave with white hats, bell-bottoms. I was burning, too! People'd be cheering.

ALIEN NESS: The b-boying didn't start at the Herc parties. You could take the b-boys back to the outlaw gangs of the late '60s, '70s. They were the original b-boys, and it was part of their war dances. That's why the competitive level is always going to be there with the b-boy. It's not just entertainment and flash; there is a competitive level, and that comes from its true essence and its roots, from the competitive levels of the outlaws.

BOM5: Even when I was in a gang, we played "Apache"…"Bongo Rock" on a phonograph hooked up to a lamppost outside. We'd bug out. Go wild. Some people called it a bite off the Bus Stop, but it was faster. We were already top-rocking. Gangs were already doing it, man. They had a lot of famous Puerto Ricans in gangs that won a lot of contests back in the '70s top-rocking.

JORGE "FABEL" PABON: The first groups I ever saw dance were actually outlaw gangs. Back in those days we had the Black Spades, the Savage Nomads in the Bronx, the Ching-a-Lings. In my neighborhood, you had the Savage Samurais on 123rd to 117th. Back then those gang members wore leather vests, similar to Hell's Angels, with the name on the back. They had younger brothers called the Young Samurais, and then they had even younger guys who were the Baby Samurais.

    The first b-boys I ever saw were the Baby Kings—the youngest members of the Spanish Kings—and they were about my age. I was eleven or twelve, and I was seeing some of the most incredible dancing. The style of dance was different from b-boying, where one guy went out and then you had to go out and burn him with better moves. With the outlaw dance they would do it at the same time; they would sort of dis the guy they were battling with a series of moves, and then they'd flash their colors. They'd open their vests and then turn around and show you their colors and then walk away. Then you'd have to come out and burn that. And it didn't always turn out a peaceful outcome.

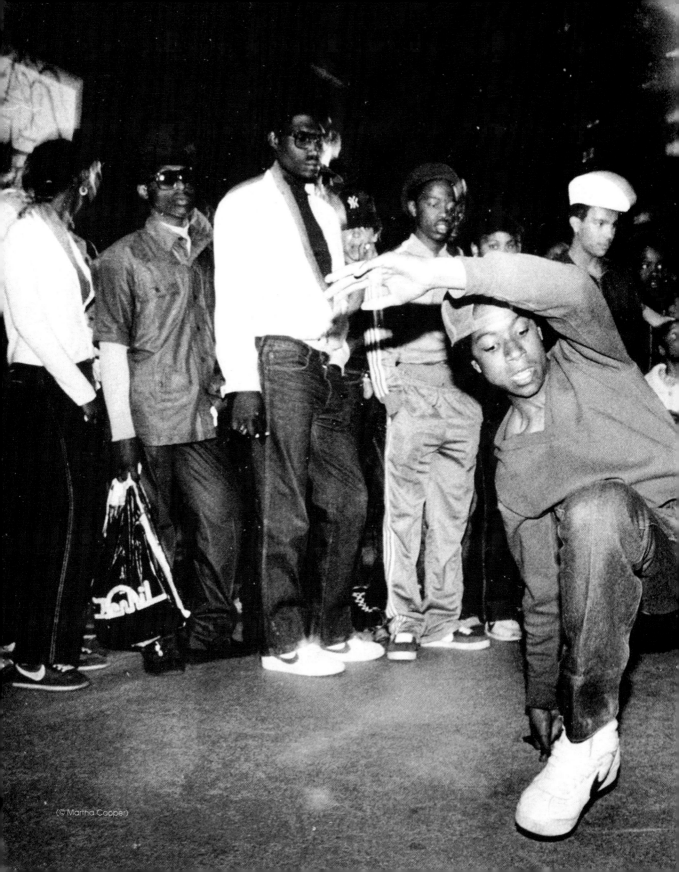

DJ DISCO WIZ: A lot of people from my era say that the gangs really never left, that the gangs became crews. I could validate that, but when I'm talking about street gangs, I'm talking about the ones that were ready to bust you up. When they transferred into crews, they more or less made the transition into hip-hop. They weren't out looking for trouble. They were more or less partying and making sure nobody came in there and wrecked their party.

BURN: All the gangs would fuckin' rock. They would hustle and they would rock. You're a gang member and you go to somebody's neighborhood to dance and you got fifteen people lined up behind you ready to kick ass. Much tension. If I go in there and dis you, your friends are going to jump me. Some get mad 'cause they got burned, but the real ones, they got respect.

DXT (D.ST.): People have this misconception of b-boys. All of us were b-boys. Kool Herc was a b-boy. The dance was just a small part of it. The b also stood for breaking, or boogie boy or from the Bronx. Breaking also referred to people who would show up for parties and knock people out. "Yo, why you always come around here breaking?" We never called it hip-hop; we called it b-beat music.

FROSTY FREEZE: DJ Breakout and Baron were b-boys before they started playing their music. Most of those guys were b-boys before they became DJs and MCs, you know? Mr. Ness, Rahiem, K.K. Rockwell, and those guys.

FABEL: The original style was very different from what we see now. There were no spins—maybe a one-shot head spin, or a butt spin, but it was based more on flavor, finesse, freezes, footwork, top-rocking. The drop—how you get from being on top down to the ground—that was just as important. Going into your footwork, how you went into your freeze, and how you came out of your freeze, and how you came back up to your feet. All of those things were vital and sometimes made the difference between losing a battle or winning a battle. We took things very serious back then. There was a lot at stake, like your whole neighborhood laughing at you. There was no money involved, but it was more from the heart, you know?

WHIPPER WHIP: Your b-boys be doing the moves, mostly up-rock. There was no backspin at that point. We had the Zulu Kings; they were b-boying—Afrika Islam, Monk, Sinbad, a bunch of other guys—they were all dancin', and they were Zulu. Everybody had their own little sections, and everybody had their own little crews. So as far as the b-boys, it was all one package: we'd have the DJs—at that point there were no MCs—and then there would be the b-boys. The b-boy was here before the MC. They were dancing and there was graf being done before all hip-hop.

PISTOL: Graffiti...it was like a virus. They had no way of controlling it; every subway line was completely covered. We had our way with it. We just saw it as art and a way to get recognition.

Lindsay—he was the mayor—he assigned this cop named Schwartz as the head of the taskforce to catch graffiti artists. Everybody had these tales of escaping Schwartz. He lived to try to catch the top artists, and if you were caught by Schwartz, it was almost like an honor. It was like a press conference—they would take pictures of him with his catch like he went deep-sea fishing or something and caught a big catch. They had to make an example. But there was just no way they could stop it.

BLADE: Back then it was about doing as many single hits as you could on the red train or the flat black train. SUPER KOOL 223 was on every red train that I can remember in '72. Every time a red or black train pulled into the station, Phase 2's name was on it—El Marko 174, Staff 161, insides and outsides. Insides with markers and outside with Red Devil spray paint with a Jiff-foam cap on it—you started taking oven cleaner caps and putting it on top of the spray can. It made it fat, and you could actually combine colors.

PISTOL: We had this thing called Writer's Corner, which I helped to originate. That was a place where you would go after school or during school, where we would watch our work go by and compare notes and see who was doing what. It was just a train station stop. We all hung out at the last bench on the left side going uptown—you would get off the train and you would see like thirty kids just sitting at this bench.

BLADE: We all sat down on the Writer's Bench in the summer of '72 with Phase, Little Hawk 149, King Kool 156...all those guys were down there. Phase used to sit down there at the concourse at the Writer's Bench with this really cool outfit like Super Fly, and he would draw styles for writers in their black books. The one he drew for me, I actually put that piece exactly on the train. At the time he was the man. '73 Super Fly outfit—the coolest hat. You had to have the bell-bottoms and Playboy shoes! Suedes. Everybody dressed that way. It was just cool.

PISTOL: Phase was one of the greats. He was an innovator, a visionary. He was an original kind of thinker, that guy, with his art. He totally had a very unique way of writing his name. Very brilliant guy, very colorful character. I like to think of him as the Miles Davis of the movement. I'm the Hendrix; he's the Miles. That's how our personalities were.

BLADE: By the end of '72 to early '73, you could actually see a development: the letters got bigger, and people expanded. Bubble letters came along around '73, which was invented by Comet, Jester, and Phase 2. You know, each one of them debate it, but that's the first people you saw do that. And then by the end of '74, you saw pieces with 3-Ds, with clowns, with designs, making characters.

PISTOL: All the letters were flat and very one-dimensional, so I came up with this thing called the 3-D. I don't know—anyone could have done it, but I did it first, and I really worked it out. The piece I did was in 1973.

Super Kool 223 piece from piecebook c. 1973

LEE: In early '73, I started looking at the trains. Graffiti was making a big change in color, composition. The names weren't tags anymore. They were more colorful, more constructed with 3-D incorporated, geometric shapes, stars. I said, "Wow! Who's doing this?"

There were whole cars by '74, monumental masterpieces. Blade, Cliff, Vinnie, and the Mighty Whiteys, The 3 Yard Boys. Tracy 168 was big. Early in '75, I went to his house in the Bronx, and he showed me his photo albums. Sixteen whole cars on the 7 line. I was blown away.

PISTOL: It basically got larger. I mean there used to be two or three pieces on one car. And then it got where one guy, like Blade, just did an entire car. That took like—I don't know how he was able to spend all that time down there.

BLADE: Things just expanded and got bigger until by 1975 the whole train was just covered with colors. And characters: Woody Woodpecker pointing out your name, cool stuff like that.

LEE: Blade had his "Dancing Ladies" train running on the IRTs. I was so moved by his happy, suggestive mood with these gorgeous, sexy girls...they got sexy eyelids and long thighs. "Wow! I want to do something like that!"

HENRY CHALFANT: I remember seeing a train by Blade that had women on it who moved in a very kinetic and wonderful way as the train moved. I remember seeing early Lee pieces, but that was a little later, toward the mid-'70s. Through those early years, it was trains like that one by Blade that really inspired me to do something about it. I felt a real urgency to document it. It was more than just calligraphy; it had become mural painting.

20

Casanova Fly and DJ Louie Lou at the Webster P.A.L., 1977. Notice the haloed b-boys and hustle kids gettin' down. (Courtesy Luis Cedeño)

(© Henry Chalfant)

2

THE FOREFATHERS:

b-boy and dj culture in the bronx

The popular music world was changing fast in the early '70s. Following a period when rock, rhythm and blues, soul, and funk coexisted on popular radio, radio stations were splitting into segregated formats. On the R&B side, groups like the O'Jays, the Spinners, and Harold Melvin and the Blues Notes were paving the way for the disco sound, and club jocks—disc jockeys who played regularly in clubs rather than on the radio, like Grandmaster Flowers in Brooklyn—were making waves and taking gigs away from live musicians. These things were leading inexorably to disco downtown. There were discothèques uptown in the Bronx, too, featuring DJs like Pete Jones and John Brown, but they played for the "mature audience." Young kids had fewer entertainment options. They gave house parties and sometimes rented community centers in the projects to throw larger parties where they charged admission to cover expenses and make a little extra money. The story of hip-hop begins here, with a young DJ of Jamaican descent trying his hand at throwing parties.

As Kool Herc, followed by Afrika Bambaataa and Grandmaster Flash, developed a new way of spinning records, there was one similarity between their parties and the parties downtown on the burgeoning disco scene: the action was on the floor, not the stage. The action in the Bronx was dominated by the b-boys, and the DJ's job was to keep the party going and periodically create the musical space for the b-boys to take over and do their thing. The percussion breaks—where most of the band drops out, leaving the drummer and percussionists to carry the music—were the parts that the b-boys liked, and the hip-hop forefathers developed a way to extend those breaks, alternating between the same section of the song on two records on different turntables. As DJ Disco Wiz said: "The main hip-hop entrepreneur was Herc. Then Bam gave an African flavor to it, and once he did that it was off the hook. Flash cut it up, and that took it to a different level. Then Theodore scratched it. That started it—the evolution of hip-hop."

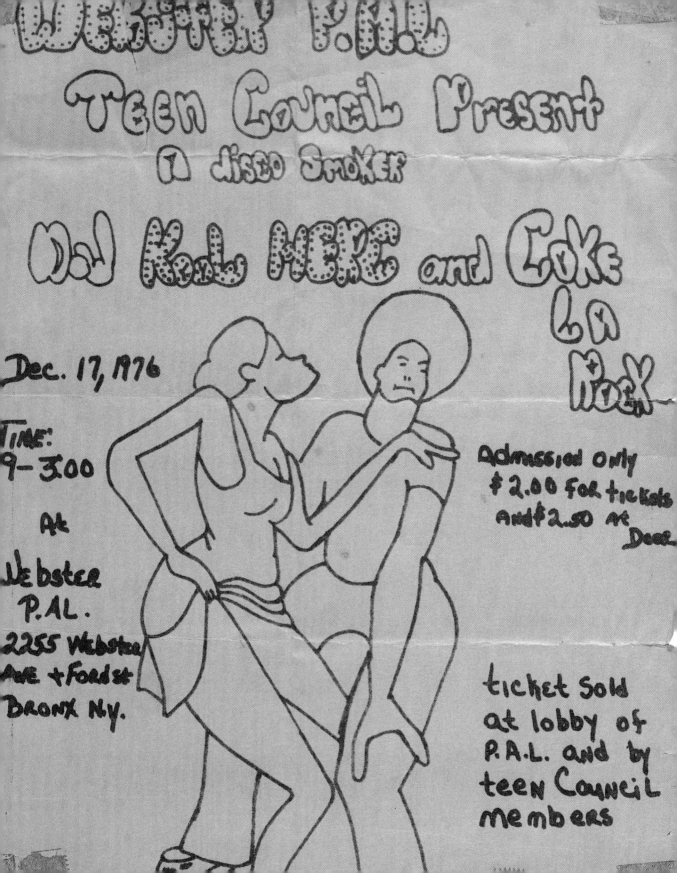

beginnings:
kool dj herc

KOOL DJ HERC: I came to the States in 1967 from Jamaica; I was twelve years old. My mother was studying for nursing in New York, and she used to bring back records from Motown, Smokey Robinson. And James Brown came to the island one time. "I Feel Good" at the time was a hit record, and I fell in love with that record. Also Jamaican music was a big influence on me, because there was a lot of big sound systems they used to hook up and play on the weekends. I was a child, ya know, lookin', seein' all these things going on, and sneakin' out my house and seein' the big systems rattling the zincs on the housetops and stuff.

When I first came here in '67, I was listening to a lot of white stations...DJs like Cousin Brucie. So I was singing a lot of white music—until I got turned onto WWRL (New York's top Black music station), surfing the stations, picking up the Temptations and different groups.

As it went along I started to go to parties and stuff, and checkin' out the vibes of the scene. And I started to dance. I'd go over to a place called The Puzzle. The DJ there, John Brown, used to go to the same high school I used to go to. I would go there basically for break-dancin'. I used to run with a graffiti crew called the Ex-Vandals. It was Phase 2, Super Kool, Lionel 163, Stay High 149, El Marko, and Sweet Duke, a lot of graffiti artists. We used to meet up there—it was like a meeting ground. We'd all talk about where we tagged, where we bombed, and all that, and we used to dance. A lot of those graffiti artists also was break-dancers, you know, just free stylin'. The word, "break-dancing" didn't come up 'til I started to play.

[In the early '70s] the gangs came up and started to terrorize the clubs in the Bronx. Started smacking up girls, starting feeling them up, disrespecting them, robbing people's coats and stuff, so it shut the discos down. At the time, graffiti vandalism was getting out of hand, and I had a strict father so I couldn't run with that too long, before MTA start bangin' on my door, arresting me. And after I've been arrested, my father gonna put an ass-whippin' on top of that. So I took a chance and put Kool Herc on an index card (announcing a party), chargin' 25 cents to get in for the ladies, 50 cents for the fellas. I had heard a lot of gripe on the dance floor. "Why is this guy not playin' this music?

An early Kool Herc and Coke La Rock party at the P.A.L.

Why's he...you know, F-in' up?" And I was agreeing with them. So I took that attitude behind the turntable, giving the people on the floor what they were supposed to be hearing. You know? So it was like "Whoah! There's somebody who knows what they doin'!" So I was the guy who kind of resurrected the music again, on the West Side, a place called 1520 Sedgwick Avenue. 1973.

It was like a speakeasy: "Hey, 'cross town on the West Side there's a guy named Herc, Kool Herc, giving parties, man. And it's nice, ya know? Girls is there, ya know. You could do your thing. All he asks is—don't start no problem in here, ya know. He's a big guy, man." 'Cause I have friends, ya know? I'd tell 'em, "Look, you got a problem, take it down the block." Ya know? I don't care, "You want to smoke your weed? Take it down the block. Don't hang in front of the building."

DJ DISCO WIZ: You had a sense that something was going to happen, because everybody was going with this disco trend, but we wasn't feeling it. It wasn't for us. We weren't socially accepted at disco joints; we were pretty much segregated. I was looking for an outlet to express myself. I was young, thuggish, and just looking for something to do besides getting in trouble, so we used to throw house parties: one turntable, three-room apartment full of people...just tore down, and that was basically it.

When Kool Herc finally hit the scene, we started getting the buzz that something was different. The funk that he threw on turntables, and the soul that came across with the African beats, was something that I related to. I could feel it. When I heard the beats and the bass thumpin', it was something that really blew me away, more so than any other music I'd ever heard in my life.

KOOL HERC: At the time, my friends wasn't running with no gang. The gang members asked us to join the gang—some of the division gang members wanted us to be division leaders—but we wasn't going for that because we respected each other, and we just said, "Look, we don't need that." They respected us; we respected them. We didn't need no colors to be on our back to be recognized or put fear in people's heart, stuff like that. When they come to the party, they know if they mess with us, we was gonna have our business. If you step to me, you're gonna have problems.

So even the gang members loved us because they didn't want to mess with what was happening. You know? They come in, keep to themselves. Not only that, a lot of Five-Percenters (a splinter group of the Nation of Islam) used to come to my party...you might call them "peace guards," and they used to hold me down: "Yo Herc, don't worry about it." So we was just havin' a good time.

Everything was fine. The girls was there. I had just bought a Reverb echo box, so we was experimentin' with that, throwin' it out, ya know? "Herc...Herc...Herc... Herc...Herc...Herc," you know, "what...what...what...what...what...what", "the joint... joint...joint...joint...joint...joint...." We just playin' around having fun with it, calling out our friends' names. At the same time people was jealous of that: "Well, why he callin' your

Happy birthday Herc 1980. Lil' Rodney Cee, Tony Tone, KK Rockwell, Breakout, and Kool Herc (Courtesy Angelo King)

name out?" "Well, he don't know you. Ya know? When the party's over, you're going to go back to your neighborhood and we still see him. So he call our name out. Until you get to know him, then he call your name out."

DJ BARON: I was going to Herc parties in '74, '75 when he was still doin' the Community Center in his building (1520 Sedgwick Avenue). I used to live on Undercliff Avenue, and Herc lived on Sedgwick Avenue. I had an older brother named Dimitri who used to hang out with Kool Herc. I was too young so I was like a tag-a-long. To get into the parties free I used to help move Herc's equipment.

Herc started with PA columns and guitar amps. All DJs in the Bronx started like that. There was no mixer, no power amps—it was a guitar amp and speakers. He used to switch from turntable to turntable on a guitar amp, from channel one to channel two. That's how mixing started out. As he did parties and accumulated his money, his set got better.

KOOL HERC: I was giving parties to make money, to better my sound system. I was never a DJ for hire. I was the guy who rent the place. I was the guy who got flyers made. I was the guy who went out there in the streets and promoted it. You know? I'm just a person who bring people together, like an instrument, an agent who bring people together and let 'em have fun. But I was never for hire. I was seeing money that the average DJ never see. They was for hire; I had my own sound system. I was just the guy who played straight-up music that the radio don't play, that they should be playin', and people was havin' fun. Those records, people walk from miles around to get 'em 'cause they couldn't get 'em, they wasn't out there no more. "Just Begun," Rare Earth, James Brown, the Isley Brothers—they just love it. Ya know?

Sometime people would make a mistake and give a party on my date. And they would stop their party at two o'clock and tell the whole party, "I'm goin' to see Kool Herc. We're goin' to finish the party at Kool Herc's party." I look out the window and see like twenty or thirty people headin' towards the little recreation room. So I gave a block party, and that showed me that this thing got bigger than what we thought it was going to turn out to be.

GRANDMASTER FLASH: There was this guy Clive Campbell, who went by the name of Kool Herc, that used to play music. And the word went around—just word of mouth—that this guy was coming out in the park, that you had to go see this guy. This guy would bring this setup outside to what was called a block party. And he'd have these huge speakers, this huge, huge setup. And he'd be playing this particular type of music that they weren't playing on the radio.

At the time, the radio was playing songs like Donna Summer, the Trammps, the Bee Gees—disco stuff, you know? I call it kind of sterile music. Herc was playing this particular type of music that I found to be pretty warm; it had soul to it. You wouldn't hear these songs on the radio. You wouldn't hear, like "Give It Up or Turn It Loose," by James Brown, on the radio. You wouldn't hear "Rock Steady" by Aretha Franklin. You wouldn't hear these songs, and these are the songs that he would play. And I said to myself, "Wow, this is pretty interesting, what he's doing here."

KOOL HERC: We couldn't come back to the recreation room so I went out looking for a place, and I found this place called the Twilight Zone on Jerome Avenue in between Tremont and Burnside. And at the same time, there was a club called the Hevalo. The Hevalo used to be called "Soulsville." I used to give out flyers up there. I used to promote my parties, and they used to chase me away from the door. "Get outta here. Don't give no flyers out!" I say, "Yo, man, one day I'm gonna be up in there. I'm going to be up in there one day."

So my first (indoor) party I gave away from the recreation room, away from 1520, was at the Twilight Zone. And it rained. But it so happened from the start that anytime it rained on my party night, it's the best night. And this night—the first time playing—it rained. It rained. We looked out the window, and it was nothing but umbrellas on the sidewalk. And the place was packed. And everybody left from the Hevalo and came down to the club.

[The guys that ran the Hevalo] was like, "What's going on? What's happening?" They heard, "Kool Herc. He's playing down the block." "You mean that guy that always come up to give the flyers out? That we chase away?" So like a week later, I got a phone call: "Herc, we wanna talk to you." It was the Hevalo. "Okay. I'll hear what you have to say." This was, I think, in '74–'75. And so I start to play weekly. No more three weeks or a month for me to give a party—now you gonna hear me every weekend.

But some nights it'd be packed...less money; some nights it'd be less people...more money. So I said, "Hold up, Coke." That's my man, my partner. He used to come out and play. He used to grab the mic and start to throw out his poetry and stuff like that. I said, "Coke, man, I'm going to hold the door down tonight. I'm going to see where this money's going." And I stood there and I see what was happenin': everybody was sliding through one side [not paying]. I stood [at the door]. "So look man, right here man [points to the right], right here." And we saw our money that night. And after that they would say, "Kool Herc and Coke La Rock is makin' money with that music, up in the Bronx." We was recognized for hustlin' with music.

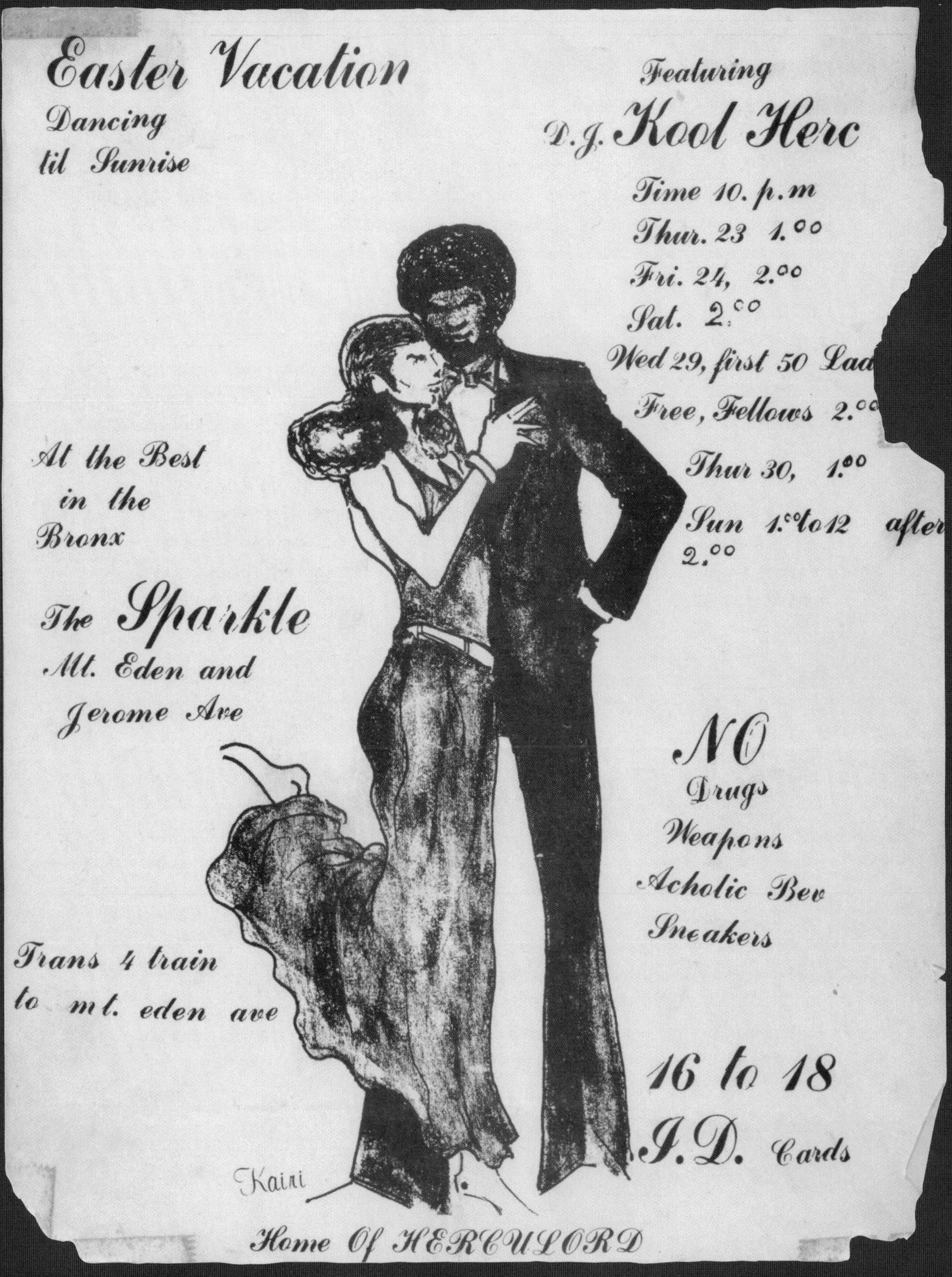
Easter Vacation
Dancing
til Sunrise
Featuring
D.J. Kool Herc
Time 10. p.m
Thur. 23 1.00
Fri. 24, 2.00
Sat. 2.00
Wed 29, first 50 Lad
Free, Fellows 2.00
Thur 30, 1.00
Sun 1.00 to 12 after
2.00
At the Best
in the
Bronx
The Sparkle
Mt. Eden and
Jerome Ave
NO
Drugs
Weapons
Acholic Bev
Sneakers
Trans 4 train
to mt. eden ave
16 to 18
I.D. Cards
Kairi
Home Of HERCULORD

TONY TONE: 1974–1975, I was working at a record shop called 3 Stop Record Shop on University, which is maybe four or five blocks from Jerome Avenue where the Hevalo was. At the time, I was going to Stevenson High School, which is all the way on the other side of town. After school I used to go to the record shop and work, and I started hearing about this guy Kool Herc and this place called the Hevalo. My older brother and my God-brother used to go there, so they was telling me about it. I was taller than both of them even though they was older than me, so they said, "Well, you probably can get in." So we all would go. They would walk in first, and when I came in last the guy wouldn't question it, 'cause I was taller than them. So I walk in the Hevalo, and it's dark, and the music is pounding—I think he was playing "Melting Pot"—and it's like...running through me. I'm only sixteen. I'm feeling the music, I'm feeling the heat of the club, and I'm walking around watching people just enjoy the music, and I'm saying, "OK, OK." The next day I was like, "I'm going again!"

I worked in the record shop, so I used to know all the records...but I didn't know the records that Herc was playing. So now it's grabbing me, now I'm trying to order them for my record shop, but I can't find them 'cause they're not records that are selling right now—they're older records, jazz records, whatever. Now every weekend I'm in the Hevalo. Sometimes I go and they would ask me for I.D. and I would just walk out. I'd wait about twenty minutes and then go back in there and try and look older and then they would let me in.

DJ BARON: Herc used to have music people never heard before. Beats. Herc's speakers were the ultimate at the time. The main person on the microphone was Coke La Rock. He was the MC and he was a DJ. Herc had his thing, and they went back and forth. Then there was Timmy Tim and Clark Kent (DJs). Sau Sau, the Nigger Twins, Tricksy were his break-dancers. Sau Sau was double jointed; he could do impossible moves that nobody else could do.

PEE WEE DANCE: When I was sixteen, I moved to the Bronx, to Mt. Eden and Jerome. I tried to get into the Hevalo on Burnside and Jerome. I was too young, but I snuck in there, and I started dancing so they wouldn't put me out. Everyone said, "Let him stay," and I kept dancing. I felt in my heart that I couldn't be beat. My main competition was Sau Sau and Tricksy. To this day, I haven't seen moves that could fuck with them. They was goin' off.

RICHARD SISCO: The hippest music out was what Kool Herc was playing—"Apache," "Mardi Gras," "Just Begun"—these certain records that everybody was b-boying off of. What propelled it was all the b-boy action. That was what drove the music forward.

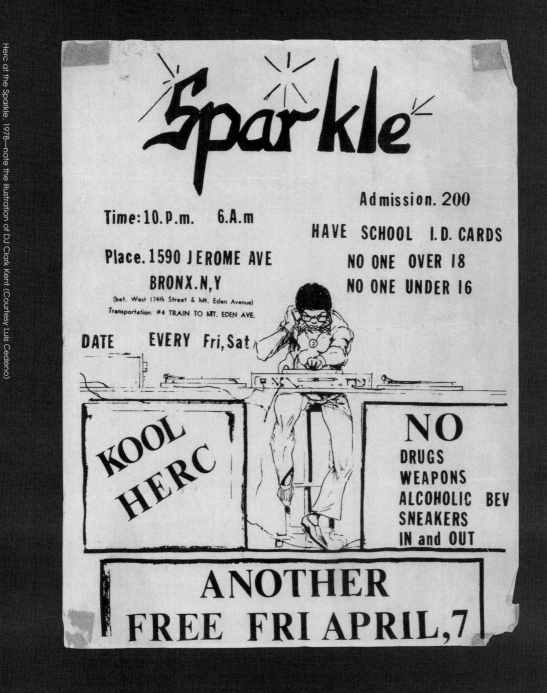

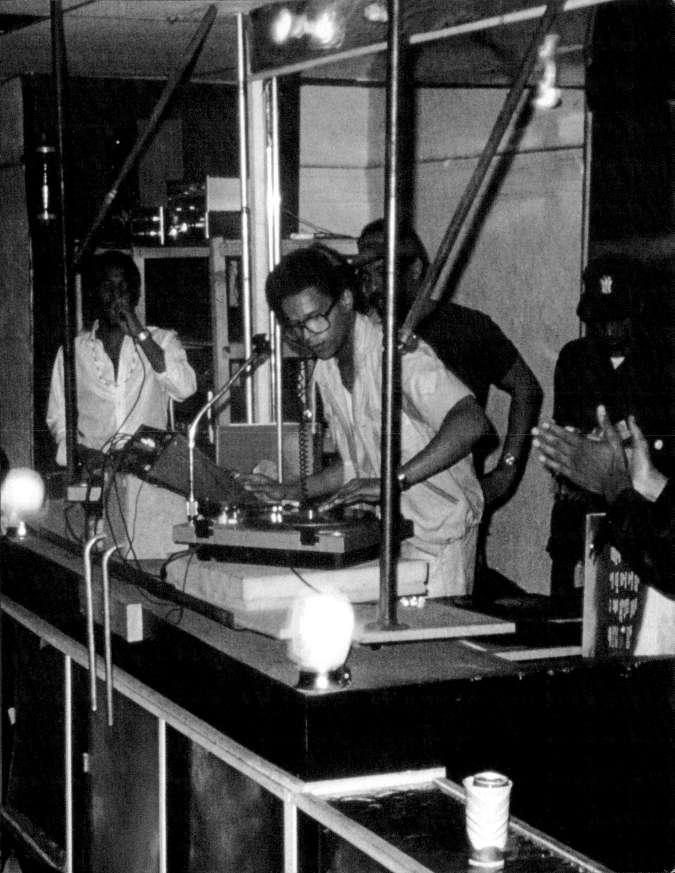

GRANDMASTER CAZ: The turning point—which made me go from pedestrian to driver, I like to call it—was in 1974. I went to a party, a indoor party, at a club called the Hevalo, and I saw this DJ named Kool Herc. He was the DJ. I mean he was it. Everything that I heard and saw all came together that night when I saw him DJ-ing. I saw how it's really done and what it's really about, how he had all the b-boys dancin'. I said, "Now that's what I wanna do. I mean, I did the dancin', now I wanna be the one who makes people dance." That night in 1974 when I went in that club and I saw Herc, I knew from that day on that's what I want to do for real, you know? Not as a hobby. I wanna be a DJ.

TONY TONE: I was introduced to it all in the Hevalo—the break-dancers, the hard bass, the jazz breaks—all that, it was all there. Today it's a parking lot, but I can picture how it used to look. I could draw out the floor plan...maybe 400 people could get in there. When you came in, you would walk through a set of doors—security, where you paid was there. They would search you, and then you go through another door. On the left-hand side was a seating area...one step up to a seating area, and on the right-hand side, a bar, and then all dance floor. The DJ booth was over in the corner. Other DJs used to use the DJ booth—Herc would never use the DJ booth. Herc would bring in his own sound system, 'cause he was credited as having the strongest, loudest hip-hop sound system at the time.

It was a party atmosphere. If it was drugs, I didn't realize it. I mean—there was some drinking, but as far as drugs, it wasn't out in the open.

KOOL DJ AJ: When I first saw Kool Herc, I was about eighteen years old. I used to attend a lot of parties, and at that time Kool DJ Herc was number one in the whole Bronx. I was like a follower—I used to take my girlfriend, and we used to go to his parties. I used to just watch him, and he used to do a lot of amazing things. It was much different from the disco of the day...he played a lot of breakin' beats. He used to play a lot of records that you couldn't buy in the store. He played a lot of James Brown, Melvin Sparks, the Incredible Bongo Band, Baby Huey, a lot of real interesting breakbeats. But I didn't go to a party really to concentrate on Herc that much—I went to a party to party.

See, in the South Bronx we really had nothing to do. There wasn't no movie theaters—everything we did was like something just to make a little bit of excitement in the area. Shooting cans with a water pump was exciting in the area, you know what I'm saying? And then when people seen Kool DJ Herc, it was like some excitement, and it drew a crowd. I just took notice, and it was interesting.

DJ DISCO WIZ: P.A.L. was the Police Athletic League, which is a sponsorship from the Policeman's Benevolent Association that sponsors athletic programs. The one that we used was on Webster Avenue in the Bronx on 183rd Street. It was called the Webster P.A.L. I used to box at the P.A.L., and that's how I got to hear Kool Herc. Kool Herc used to practice and DJ on the weekends in the P.A.L. on Webster Avenue. I first heard Kool Herc's sound check and heard of his parties through friends and acquaintances. I went to his party and was blown away by what I saw. I went with Caz; it was in the athletic room in the P.A.L., which was the center. We're talking maybe 400–500 people and Herc on top of the stage with these huge speakers on each side. And he's a massive presence to begin with, in the middle there....

It was just something for a young guy like me; I can still remember how awesome that was. The music that he played was definitely funk, but the way he cut it and the cuts that he used—sound bites and things that I've never heard before in my whole life—it was something that definitely opened the door for me. I never heard a DJ before; maybe disc jockeys on the radio, but they just slapped a popular tune on. This was my first initiation into what a DJ was, and I saw the best. It was overpowering. For a young guy like me, it was an awakening.

MELLE MEL: The first Herc party I went to was at the P.A.L. on Webster. There were three or four of us in the gym drinking beer, high on weed. I was fourteen or fifteen years old. There was this slow-motion thing...people were dusted, smoking angel dust (PCP). The acrid smell was in the air, the smoke was visible, floating on this one level, flashing in the red strobe light. It was illin', a hostile atmosphere, people getting high in the bathroom.

When we came in, they wanted to see what circle we would dance in. I got punched in the eye; I had to battle one of the Nigger Twins. He used this spin move. Clark Kent was a DJ, but when he wanted to burn somebody he would dance. They all rapped but not on the beat. Coke La Rock was Jamaican. Timmy Tim was the smoothest: "The sounds that you hear hear hear...(heavy echo vibes) deaf to your ear ear ear...'cause you have no fear fear fear...'cause Herc is here here here ...." "We're going to give you a little taste of the bass...(turns off the treble). We're going to hit you with the highs...."

DJ BARON: Some of the main parties was so jam-packed you couldn't move to get in. One time we was in the Executive Playhouse, in a Herc party. Somebody had an argument with somebody in the party and pulled a gun out. Everybody's doing the Bus Stop, and when the shot went off, everybody's moving toward Herc's speakers. His speakers fell and everything. Herc had to pull his stuff out [Baron mimics drawing a gun]. "Yo! Y'all got to go that a way!" That's when all hell broke loose. Everybody ran out, and it was crazy!

Kool DJ Herc with DJ Tony Tone, at the Ecstasy Garage, late 1970s (Courtesy Angelo King)

A packed jam at the Celebrity Club, 1980 (© Charlie Ahearn)

THE T-CONNECTION DISCOS' DOWN WITH...

THE HERCULORDS

CLARK KENT

JAY CEE

SWEET 'N' SOUR

KOOL HERC

TONY D'

AND IT'S KOOL KYLE" THE STARCHILD "

" GRAND WIZARD THEODORE "

MASTER ROB, KEVIE KEV, STARSKY

IT'S ALL HAPPENING THANKSGIVING DAY

THURSDAY, NOV. 22, 1979 · THE T-CONNECTION

2 TRAIN or 55 BUS to GUN HILL ROAD

LADIES FREE BEFORE 10pm · DAMAGE 2$

3$ ALL AFTER 12pm · NO WEAPONS

phasetwo·

TONY TONE: Herc had his Herculoids: him, Clark Kent/Superman—Clark Kent and Superman the same person—and I think he had a guy named Kryptonite, and the Nigger Twins. The Nigger Twins was Kool Herc's break-dancers. They all was known as Herculoids.

There was a cartoon called the Herculoids. Since his name is Kool Herc, he took on the name of Herculoids from that. And his system was named the Herculord—it's huge and can't be touched. Powerful. I guess Herc got his name from Hercules, 'cause Herc was big. I have pictures where I look like an infant standing next to Herc.

KEVIE KEV: I went to mad Herculords parties in the P.A.L. on 183rd. You standing in line to pay with your fresh green Pumas, fresh green mock-neck sweatshirt with your name on it. You got on sheepskin. You go in and you get searched. It's so dark inside, but its so cool 'cause it's so many fly people there, and you are a part of this. Herc's dropping James Brown, like (he sings), "Clap your hand, hunh, stomp your feet," playing "sure shots"—that's what we was calling the dope records. It was all over when he played "Bongo Rock"..."Apache," that took us out.

You feeling yourself 'cause you and your friends all looking dope—Mom sent you out looking real fly. The beats is coming out so loud. It only costed two, three dollars to get in, but it was packed. Clark Kent was on the microphone, Timmy Tim . . . but when they turned over, they never cut on the beat; they never scratched. But they was the first playing two turntables, just playing them. B-boying was going on. It was a Black thing—I saw no Puerto Ricans around this time. We was in the Bronx, those b-boys, they was Black and they was goin' off! It's a whole 'nother rhythm.

RAHIEM: I used to break-dance. I'd hear the music on tapes from people in the neighborhood, but I had never actually gone to a hip-hop party or anything. The very first party that I went to was DJ Kool Herc, and he was playing at the Webster Avenue P.A.L. on 183rd Street and Webster Avenue in the Bronx. I remember when I walked in how electric the vibe was...I wasn't even old enough to get into the party; I had a curfew, and my mom was like, "You can go to this party but you better be home by 11:30." We were there in the middle of the floor, and I was just watching people dancing, and the kind of music that Herc was playing was really conducive to this style of dancing. No one was getting on the floor—b-boys at the time were not doing floor moves—it was up-rocking. I remember this guy El Dorado Mike, the Nigger Twins. . . . The people who were on the floor were the best b-boys at that time, and I remember going home and practicing the moves that I saw them doing. My next door neighbor M&M was doing the same dance steps that these guys at the P.A.L. was doing, and I was like, "OK, I'm gonna get serious about this dancing thing."

A birthday party for the big boys, 198

SHA-ROCK: The atmosphere was awesome, cause Herc had a system, and if you were really into music and into the hip-hop scene, that was everything. You had to have the system to cover the music, because that s why a lot of people go they go for the bass. Just to hear the bass was like everything, and that s what made me rebel: to hear the bass. You know? Whether or not it was right or wrong, I just went to hear the bass. The music. James Brown...all these different types of music that you could break-dance to. Herc, he ll get on there and say like one or two words, and then he ll have like the mirror ball going around, and Clark Kent would get on there and rhyme for a minute.... Herc wasn t like a rapper or anything like that; it was just a sound, his music, his system. The music that he played was just like no other.

KOOL HERC: Little did anybody know that this thing was going to turn into a world-wide phenomenon, billion-dollar business and all that. Cause I wasn t looking at it like that back then. I love my music, I love my sound system, and I just love to see people havin fun. Period.

afrika bambaataa
& the mighty zulu nation

AFRIKA BAMBAATAA: I grew up in the southeast Bronx. It was an area where back in the late '60s, early '70s there was "broken glass everywhere," like Melle Mel said in "The Message." But it was also an area where there was a lot of unity and a lot of social awareness going on, at a time when people of color was coming into their own, knowin' that they were Black people, hearing records like James Brown's "Say It Loud—I'm Black and I'm Proud," giving us awareness. Hearing people like Sly and the Family Stone telling you to "Stand!" "You Can Make It If You Try," "Everyday People."

Seeing all the violence that was going on with the Vietnam War and all the people in Attica and Kent State, and being aware of what was going on in the late '60s, with Woodstock and the Flower Power, the Love Power movement...just being a young person and seeing all this happening around me put a lot of consciousness in my mind to get up and do something; it played a strong role in trying to say, "We've got to stop this violence with the street gangs."

Basically the Bronx was looking for something new. The gang scene was starting to fade out because a lot of the women was getting tired of all the gang-banging and drugs that were coming into the community. You had the police crackdown on the gangs, and you also had religious organizations and Black leaders trying to speak to the gangs, trying to bring down gang activity. Hearing the teachings of the Nation of Islam made a lot of people get up and try to get the drugs out of their community, and seeing a lot of the struggles that was going on all around the world through television gave a lot of hope to this area to do something for itself.

What I did is I took all these elements from all these great leaders and teachers that we had at that time and said I will start a group called the Zulu Nation—from seeing a movie back in the early '60s called Zulu. Just to see these Black people fighting for what was theirs against the British, that always stuck in my mind. I said when I get of age, I will start this organization and put all these ideologies together in this group called the Zulu Nation. So what I did, with myself and a couple other of my comrades, is get out in the street, start talking to a lot of the brothers and sisters, trying to tell them how they're killing each other, that they should be warriors for their community.

44

And when we started this music called hip-hop, which didn't have a name at the time, it brought a lot of the elements of these different movements together. We still had little spots of violence here and there, you know, at parties and stuff, but a lot of time you had people who was coming together to kick the drug dealers out of the area—we used violence against a lot of the dope pushers and all that. We went from a negative thing to a positive thing.

★　★　★

Before the father, Kool Herc; myself, the Godfather; and Grandmaster Flash even started DJ-ing, there was a lot of disco DJs happening, as well as a lot of radio jocks. You know, you had Jocko, we had WLIB with Eddie O-Jay, we had Gary Byrd, who was on WRL, Cousin Brucie on WABC. You had Murray the K doing his shows at the Brooklyn Fox. You had the Apollo Theater with all the MCs there...all these different people who was doing what we call jive-talking rap, and then as they got into the disco era, it was the disco style of rappin'. We just took the different forms that was happening, what they was doing, but then we started adding new rhymes, and Herc came in with the beats.

I started DJ-in' in 1970. Not with the two turntables and the mixers: you went and got your mother's set or your father's set, and you would come down to a recreation center, you would put up your speakers and turntable—that's the kind where you put five records on there, and then the needle would go back and the record would drop. You had one guy that was set up on this side of the room, and I was set up on another side. We had a flashlight, so if he was playing the Jackson Five, "I Want You Back," when his record was going down low, he would flash at me, and that would give me the time to put on "Stand" or "Everyday People" by Sly and the Family Stone. And that's how we started DJ-in' back and forth, before they came with the two turntables and a mixer.

In the early '70s, we was already indoors in many of the community centers in the area. One of the first DJs that came out of the Black Spades organization was a guy by the name of Kool DJ D and his brother Tyrone, and they had a MC by the name of Love Bug Starski. Then Kool Herc came out from the West Side of the Bronx, and he was doing these beat-type records, whereas on our side of the Bronx we had the disco era still going strong. But after awhile we got tired of hearing the Hustle and disco records—we wanted that funk. We was missing the James Brown, the Sly, the Mandrill, Earth Wind and Fire, so we kept that funk alive with the break-beat sound. When that break come on, the b-boys hit the floor, start doing their different dances.

We was young entrepreneurs, when we didn't even know we was entrepreneurs. We would rent out the gymnasiums for parties. A lot of times we couldn't rent certain places, so we had to get an adult to do it for us, but we were still more in control of what was happening. We'd have to get out there to make a flyer—sometimes we'd get these flyer makers that made some extraordinary flyers, and you had the other ones that made the cheap type of flyers. But the thing was getting out there and doing promotions, hitting all the high schools or the junior high schools, hitting all the different communities, walking up and down the street doing hand-to-hand contact, leaving flyers in record stores, and if you got on the bus, sticking it up on the bus signs—you'd cover over the advertising signs. It was a lot of work.

master of records

DJ BREAKOUT: Bambaataa used to play the wildest records in the whole entire world. He played stuff like Bugs Bunny—it's got a beat on it. Everybody was break-dancin' to that.

AFRIKA BAMBAATAA: I was looking for beats all over the place. I even had people who used to follow me in the stores, because a lot of times we had spies from other DJ groups. I had a broad taste in sound, and I was checkin' all into the rock section or the soul sections or the different African sections or the sections of the Latin records. Back then you didn't have the stores where you can listen to records or turntables where you could put the record on, so the cover had to grab me. If the words sounded funky or if it had a certain way they wrote it, I would say, "Well, this must be funky. Let me take it home." Sometimes you got some records that was a piece of... but then you had some that was just great—I heard the sound and I said, "Well, this is funky here." It had a nice break-beat, or the groove was kicking, or the patterns was right, so that's how I try to pick records to put on my audience.

AFRIKA ISLAM: I heard Afrika Bambaataa play at Bronx River Center, and the only thing he lacked was somebody that would be behind him, working with him, who knew the technical aspects of it in order to build a better sound system. (Afrika Islam took over that role.)

His music influenced me because he listened to the same music I listened to. Everything from rock and roll, J. Geils, "Honky Tonk Woman" by the Rolling Stones, all the way to James Brown, Funkadelic, Sly Stone, R&B, funk. And that's what I came up under, so I knew where my allegiance was, you know? My allegiance was definitely to the music and the record. The techniques, the more technical style came from Flash, and as far as sound systems, that came from Herc. That's the way it was.

AFRIKA BAMBAATAA: The Bronx River Community Center was one of the original hip-hop big spaces—hundreds of people could fit in at one time. Then we had another place called Junior High School 123, which we renamed the Funky 3. We used to always give tribute to James Brown, Sly and the Family Stone, and then later on to Uncle George Clinton of Parliament-Funkadelic for bringing us the funk. Everybody was

46

known for certain records they brought out, and that made your audience come to see you. My audience was the most progressive of all, because they knew I was playing all types of weird records for them. I even played commercials that I taped off the television shows, from Andy Griffith to the Pink Panther, and people looked at me like I was crazy.

You could be playing records with your group, and other people is sneaking up, trying to get next to you, to see what you was doing. So I used to peel the labels off or put water on there and take the cover off so they couldn't see.

VAN SILK: An Afrika Bambaataa party was totally different from a Grandmaster Flash party, because Bam played more obscure records. I'll be honest with you: I hated going to Bam parties. Bam would be playing the break-beats and then would jump off and start playing some calypso, or playing some reggae, or playing some rock. I was like, "What is Bam doin'?" But Bambaataa's mind-set was that hip-hop was an open field of music. He'd take an Aerosmith record, "Walk This way," and slow it, or speed it up.

AFRIKA BAMBAATAA: It might just be slammin', the people sweating, breaking, everything. And I would just stop in the middle of the thing and throw on "Sweet Georgia Brown," and then everybody'd just start doing that basketball-type dance. I would tell them, "I want you to take it back to the day when your mama and papa used to dance," and started playing a lot of the '60s records, and you would see people trying to do the Monkey, the Jerk, the Twist, and all these other type of dances. So when you came to an Afrika Bambaataa party, you had to be progressive-minded and knew that you was going to hear some weird type of stuff.

bronx river center • zulu nation headquarters

DJ BREAKOUT: I used to go to Bambaataa parties and start break-dancin', and I started likin' music. I just went to the parties. Everybody was scared to go to Bronx River; they said, "Don't go to Bronx River or you wind up in a fight." I used to take a cab down there. I just liked to break-dance. I'd hear that old record "Apache" and I used to go crazy. Just danced. I'd go home, have sores on my knees, sneakers all dirty, messed up. That was b-boying...that was it.

K.K. ROCKWELL: Breakout took me to Bronx River. A real b-boy party. They had some kind of ceremony on stage with the Black Spades. They was doing a lot of talking, and I was scared. I thought they was gonna kill everybody in the place. They was giving tribute to some members that had got killed.

My cousin came up from Brooklyn and we took her to a party, and I said, "Do y'all do this in Brooklyn?" She was like, "Kevin, we don't do nothing like this in Brooklyn!"

LOVE BUG STARSKI: My grandmother lived like four blocks away from Bronx River, and we used to be in the Spades—in order to walk in that neighborhood I had to be in the Spades. So I met Afrika Bambaataa and Kool DJ D, and DJ Tex and all them, who were old school DJs, you know? People don't even mention them anymore.

WHIPPER WHIP: Nobody wanna go to Bronx River, 'cause you hear all the rumors. "Never go to Bronx River, man. You gonna get shot!" It's true, 'cause usually after every show Bam would throw, you'd hear gunshots throughout the projects in Bronx River, and it's a mess. You never know who or what's getting shot. I mean, due respect, because I'm a Zulu King, but at that time I was like, "Nah, I'm not going to Bronx River." That was the one place. Brooklyn, Queens, I'd go anywhere, but for some reason the Bronx River Park, where Bambaataa played...I mean, I finally broke down, I went quite a few times, and I've heard the shots and witnessed all kinds of beatdowns, but then it's like what can you do?

You can never label who was responsible for that, due to the fact that you're in projects. When you in projects, it could've been any fool that wants attention. Bam's crew, they were Zulus so they were his thugs. It was always fine with him and his, but when you're leaving there, you're leaving. You're not with Bam; you're going with whoever you came with, so smart people leave a little before it's over, stuff like that.

SHA-ROCK: You had your fights, you had your shootings or whatever, but it wasn't really bad because people mostly went for the music, for the beat. There was nobody that can come into a Afrika Bambaataa party and start any trouble, because you had the Zulu Nation that made sure that there was no trouble whatsoever. And it wasn't just one person—we're talking about...people would travel from Jersey, from all over, that wanted to be a part of the Zulu Nation. So if you went to a Afrika Bambaataa party, you expect to be safe, because nobody was starting any trouble at a Afrika Bambaataa/Zulu Nation party. That was a good atmosphere, and I think that's what a lot of groups wanted—people to feel safe and come in and just listen to the music and everything. That's basically what it was about: it was about the music.

Bambaataa at Bronx River Center
(© Lisa Kahane)

The Zulu Nation present their 3rd Annual Disco, Tribute to......

SLY STONE

Donation   (Free Records)
$1.00 with flyer $2.00 without flyer
Bronxriver Comm. Center
1619 E. 174 th St. Bronxriver Houses
Come in peace   9: PM - Until

"Soulsonic Funk Sounds by''
D.J. Afrika Bambaataa
Zambo & MC. Mr. Biggs   FRI. NOV. 10,

Art: Jamal T.

Zulu Nation Sly Stone tribute
at Bronx River, 1978

DJ DISCO WIZ: Bam was more of a big brother to us; he never advocated that gang mentality. He definitely made a transition out of that. But you knew that you couldn't go into a party and try to wreck anything. Nobody rushed Bam's party. Bam's parties were respected, and he never had a thuggish element in there. But you knew that you couldn't go in there messing around like you could in a lot of other parties.

LUCKY STRIKE: We didn't really go to Bronx River 'cause at that time you couldn't really fly colors (wear your gang vest), 'cause there was just so many gangs on different blocks who didn't want you going through their block with colors. That was disrespect to them.

Then my friend Blue—who was part of the Savage Skulls—got found in the gang clubhouse murdered. We didn't know what happened, but I believe it was gang-related. Somebody from another gang must have ransacked the clubhouse. That made me see everything, see life. After his funeral, I just dropped my colors. Then I bumped into a couple of friends of mine who introduced me to the Zulu Nation. There was a guy who was running Chapter Two (of the Zulu Nation); his name was Trouble. What he talked to me about in the Zulu Nation was finding yourself, who you are. I got to see what they were all about when I went to one of their meetings in Bronx River. I met a lot of people that day. Everybody was really cool. They were teaching me things about my own culture that I never knew and things I never learned in school.

BOM5: Bambaataa was giving out flyers—he was giving a party at Bronx River. I got the flyer and my cousin was like, "Oh that's some trap! That's some bullshit." He [Bambaataa] wanted to squash all this beef with the gangs. "It's going to be a party. Everybody's welcome. Leave your gang colors home. It's all about Peace, Love, Unity. Come learn about your brothers." I wish I still had that flyer; my cousin ripped it up. He was a [Savage Skulls] warlord. "I don't trust them Black Spades! That's a set up!"

But I went to the center. It was free for everyone. My other cousin came with me and we just went in. Once you see some Spanish people in there, you know there must be some peace going on! I met Bambaataa. They shook your hand! It was funny. My cousin says, "See. Looks like things are changing!" I didn't see no colors in there, no vests on. Before when you went by Bronx River, you'd see the gangs lined up, leaning up against the fence. Masses. You knew it was a gang.

Thank God for Bambaataa realizing there was too much violence going on. Bam was like my mentor. I knew Bam when he was riding around on his bike writing graffiti. He wrote Bambaataa 117.

BUSY BEE: I started over at "The River," Bronx River projects. Bambaataa had a whole mob of these motherfuckers, dressed in ski jackets and ski hats and goggles. I didn't really know what it meant to be a Zulu; then I found out Bam was the chief head. Mr. Biggs was Bam's permanent MC. Zambu was the DJ, and Bam was the Overseer, and there was Baby Bam—Afrika Islam—who was a b-boy. I worked with Bam for a while; I picked up a lot from Bambaataa.

NUBIAN PRODUCTIONS PRESENTS

JUNGLE ROCK CITY

featuring D.J. AFRIKA **Bambaataa** MASTER OF RECORDS

Original D.J. **JAZZY·JAY**   D.J. **RED·ALERT**

Soul Sonic Force M.C.s

Mr.Biggs Pow·Wow Hutch·Hutch

Lisa·Lee Ice-Ice Master·Bee Master Ice

the ALONG with **FUNKY4** plus 1 more

KEITH·KEITH K·K ROCKWELL

SHA·ROCK

JAZZY·JEFF LIL RODNEY·C

THE T·CONNECTION

3510 White Plains Rd.

Time: 9 p.m. until 6 a.m.

Sat. Mar. 15. "1980"

Donation $3.00 b/4 12 & 2.00 with School I.D.

The Zulu Nation   COME IN PEACE

AFRIKA ISLAM: I was in the Zulu Kings, Zulu Master break-dancers, carrying records, finding beats, writing lyrics, DJ-ing...whatever it took to keep the Nation strong. I was his right-hand man. I was a spokesman, but he was the power. I did what needed to be done without question, because it was a peace mission, to bring the culture, the hip-hop culture, together from the break-dancers to graffiti artists to the DJs to the MCs, to all come together as one unit. That's what mainly got me that title Son of Bambaataa, because I was always around the man.

VAN SILK: Bam's a very influential, very strong, very community-conscious person. Bam is more like a father figure to a lot of young kids in the neighborhood he came from, in Bronx River. He was the type of person that would get the summer jobs for kids, all the city summer jobs. Without the help of Bambaataa, we would have been in a lot of trouble.

RICHARD SISCO: Bam always used to talk about positive things for the Black race, so there was nothing scary about it or nothing. But knowing that some of the Zulus were original Black Spades, I think the first division, it was like a lot of street justice involved in the Nation. But it was good for those wild kids that don't have no direction. Bam gave them good direction and gave them some self-respect. I think that was the most beautiful thing about the Nation. It got out of hand when it got large, but the nucleus of it was a thing of upward mobility to give somebody something to keep their head up—self-esteem—because in this world we're living in there's not too much for a Black man out here to have any self-esteem about. Everything seems to be geared toward an education, college-wise, and there's a lot of other things, like being a master of your own history and being a master of yourself. So the direction Bam was taking was beautiful. There was no fear in my heart for the Nation because I knew it was a positive thing, but it would need time to work itself out to be at the level of something like the NAACP or something like that. But it was a good move.

grandmaster flash

GRANDMASTER FLASH: I grew up in the South Bronx. My family hails from the Barbados, which makes me East Indian. It was somewhat of a melting pot of music in my house—my father was deep into Artie Shaw, Glenn Miller, Miles Davis; one of my sisters was into Tito Puente, Eddie Palmieri; I had a sister that was into Michael Jackson, Sly and the Family Stone, the Motown sound—so I was around all these various styles of music.

From what my big sisters tell me, I must have been in my single digits, and I got interested in this object called a record. My father had his prize collection of records. He knew I loved whenever the stereo was turned on—when I was a little baby I used to get in the center of the room, and I used to start dancing. But he would say to me, "Listen, don't ever touch my records."

I used to watch where he put these prized records—it was a closet near the front door. So when my father went to work, I would go grab a chair out of the kitchen, against my mother's instruction and my bigger sisters saying, "Don't go in there touching Daddy's records," and I used to drag this chair to this closet, just high enough for me to turn the knob, and then get down, go in there, get a record. And I would crawl over to the stereo, and I would just put any record on, and I would start dancing.

So early on my father used to say, "If I catch you in there, I'm going to give you a beating, give you a spanking." My mother was able to protect me, up to a point, because every time he told me, the next day, when he went out to work, I would grab that same chair from the kitchen and grab that same knob, open the closet, go in and get a record, and turn on the stereo.

So after awhile, the yelling started turning into serious beatings. Like beatings, beatings, beatings, to the point where I was like almost unconscious. My pop used to really bust my behind, and that used to cause a lot of problems between my mother and my father. I guess, in some reverse sort of way, I learned the value of a record because he used to bust my behind for me so much.

Later on, in the years when I was able to get a little job, I went out and got me a messenger job, and I started buying my own records.

And in my early teens, I had this habit of wanting to know how the internal workings of things operated. Like I would take apart my sisters' radios, hair dryers. I'd go behind the washing machine. I'd go in my mother's stereo in the living room, you know? And I was getting beat for all these things, so in me doing this, my mother decided to send me to technical school. And since I was so intrigued with the internal workings of these electronic items, I then started learning the actual technical terms for these particular items, to the point where early on in high school, we had assignments where we had to build amplifiers.

So I was able to understand how you diagnosed circuits, how you use a signal generator or ohmmeter, you know? I had somewhat of an electronic knowledge of how these things work. My mother sent me to school to be an electronic technician. But for whatever reason, I guess I must have got sidetracked.

* * *

My thing was, to every great record, there's a great part. This is what we used to call "the get down part." This is before it was tagged "the break"; it was called "the get down part." And this particular part of the record...unjustifiably, was maybe five seconds or less. This kind of pissed me off. I was like, "Damn, why'd they do that?" You know? So in my mind, in the early seventies, I was picturing, "Wow, it would really be nice if that passage of music could be extended to like five minutes."

There were two heroes that inspired me to do this. One was Kool Herc. Kool Herc was playing the type of music that I loved so much, this obscure, funky, funky, funky music. But Kool Herc, although he's an incredible individual for what he's done, didn't so much concentrate on taking duplicate copies of the record and making a break extended in time. He wasn't too much concerned with that. He had the massive bass, the massive system, so I guess that was not one of his considerations.

On the other side of town, there was this other DJ that went by the name of Pete DJ Jones. Now Herc was playing this great music, but the style, the way he was playing it, didn't really turn me on. Pete was playing the sterile disco music, but the thing about it is that before he would let the record end, he would blend in the next record on time. So I was saying to myself, "Well, if I can figure out how to take the music that I love, where the break is so short, extend them particular sections, and make them as long as I chose to, that would really be the way to go."

GRAND WIZARD THEODORE: Flash discovered how to play the break part on beat. He went to a radio station, and the DJ had a pair of earphones, and he could listen to the record before he played it! He went home and said, "There's got to be a way to hook the cue to the mixer so I can hear the record before everybody else hears the record." So he experimented, bought some books. He went to Samuel Gompers Vocational.

GRANDMASTER FLASH: From that point, my electronic knowledge had to come into play. I had to build these small amplifiers to drive the headphones, and then I would put these on the mixers. I had to create what I called a "peek-a-boo" system. It allowed me to pre-hear the music in my ear before I push it out to the people. And what it involved was a switch attached to an external two- or three-watt amplifier on the outside of the mixer, just enough to drive the headphones. Once I came up with the peek-a-boo system and I was able to pre-hear and take these five-second drum breaks and kind of segue them all together, then I just went out and just got "x" amount of duplicate copies of hot records and played just the break. I would cut the break and then, with the duplicate copy, cut the break again to just keep it going. Just the break. I used to play the break with what's called a backspin or the "clock theory" [reading the label of the record to spin it backward to the place where the selected segment began]. Now I was able to play the break of all these songs in succession, back to back to back to back to back.

scratch creator

GRANDMASTER FLASH: I had created a new style of DJ-ing, so to some degree I was ridiculed by all the other jocks that was doing the other style of DJ-ing, saying that I destroy records and that what I'm doing is not a good style.

At that time I had a partner; his name was Gene Livingston. I really wanted him to learn this technique so that we could go out as a team and introduce this new style of DJ-ing all throughout the city. I tried showing him over and over and over again, count-less times, and he just could not understand what it was that I was doing.

While I was trying to teach Mean Gene there was this little kid that was also in the household...

GRAND WIZARD THEODORE: I have a older brother, his name is Mean Gene. Him and Flash were partners; they were like a team together. I have another brother called DJ Cordie-O who had a partner whose name was Disco Bee. When I was twelve, I was watching Flash and Gene doing parties. I used to help them carry their equipment, help them hook their speakers up.

The first block party I ever went to was in 23 Park—Flash and Gene, before he had any MCs. The mic was just used for "This record goes out to..." "We going to start slowing it down so you guys better start picking out some girls...." Back then Flash used to play a lot of disco records. It wasn't really hip-hop all night. They used to have a segment when they would play Van McCoy records, the hustle record, Donna Summers, KC and the Sunshine Band. Flash would need a record, and I'd pull it out for him.

My brother and Flash used to keep their equipment inside the house where me and my other brothers and sisters and my moms lived, on Boston Road and 168th Street. Cordie-O and Disco Bee had their equipment in another room. When they'd leave, I would go in the room and start foolin' around with records, playin' this and playin' that, getting familiar with this record and getting familiar with that record. Just basically playin' music.

I'd go to Downstairs Records, down in Manhattan (it was in the subway at 42nd Street and Broadway) to pick out beats for them. They had a pinball machine down there, and if you got a certain score you'd get a free 45. I was the "Pinball Wizard." The guy would always be playing records behind the counter. I'd be playing pinball and keeping track of what he'd be playing. So when my brother would be throwing parties on the weekends, they'd have extra records to play.

GRANDMASTER FLASH: This little kid used to go to his mother's stereo, and where I had to repeat the break by back-spinning a certain amount of revolutions and repeating it over and over, he used to pick up the needle and just drop where it's supposed to go on one turntable. I coined the phrase "needle drops" for him.

THEODORE: I used to love the break part. I used to hate to wait for the break to come around—I used to skip to the break part with my thumb. You watch the grooves, the thickest grooves are where the break part comes in. When the record rolls around at a 360-degree angle, you can pretty much see where it starts. You say, "Here it comes." I made sure that I picked up the needle at a certain point. I watch the record go round and round, then bam! It comes right in. I did it so many times that I came to do the needle drop. I developed a technique, and I didn't know what I was doing. I got this down to a science. I used to astonish myself.

GRANDMASTER FLASH: I found that so amazing. I would say to Gene, "Your little brother has this unusual rhythm. I don't know where he got it from, but he has this rhythm where he can physically, on one turntable, pick up the needle and just drop it down and have it on time." Gene owned the majority of the equipment that we used—I didn't have nothing, okay? And Gene used to be threatening, saying, "Listen, if I hear that my little brother's on the set, man, we're going to break off, and you're going to go about your business. I don't want my little brother touching none of my stuff."

So what I would do is, when Mean Gene used to go to work, his little brother Theodore used to come into the room and he used to watch me. I used to get a milk crate for him to stand on, and I would do something and he would emulate it. His timing was impeccable, his nerves was of steel. And this was a little kid! So for quite some time, it was me and Theodore's secret that I was allowing him to touch the turntables.

I would try to convince his brother. "Listen, I just got this feeling"—I couldn't really tell him the truth—"I got this feeling that this little kid here can really make us look good. If we could put this little guy out in the streets along with our DJ crew, he would really help our reputation." Gene was totally against it.

After awhile, I refused to keep it a secret. I'm like, "Listen Gene, your little brother is incredible on these turntables. His timing...everything that needs to be done as far as follow through and how to DJ, he knows how to do." So one thing led to another, and he got his debut in the park. I said, "Theodore, come on." Got that same milk crate...the crowd lost their mind. They already knew what I could do, and to see this little teeny guy on a milk crate do what I do, was so incredible!

THEODORE: First time I got on the turntables was at 63rd Park. Flash was like, "Yo, Gene, your brother plays pretty good. Let's let him get on for a minute." Gene would never let me touch the turntables and he said, "Naw, he's too young!" Gene left to get something for Flash, and Flash put me on and everybody was like, "Wow, this kid is really good!" Later when Gene found out, he was really pissed.

GRANDMASTER FLASH: It was kind of the end of his big brother's reputation, but it was the rise of his reputation. It was like, "Flash has this little guy with him that's incredible on the turntables!" To see this little guy do this and have the crowd at a frenzy was proof enough that this style of DJ-ing can become something. And then, on top of that, Theodore came up with this style of adding a rhythm to the rub, which was later coined as scratching.

THEODORE: I was always in my house trying to think of new ways to be different. I wanted someone to close their eyes and say, "That could only be one person—Grand Wizard Theodore—playing that record." One particular day I was in the house practicing, and the music was a little bit too loud, so my moms came and banged on the door and said, "If you don't turn that music down, you're going to turn it off." And she had the door open, and while she was talking to me, I was still holding the record, and the other record was still playing. And when she left the room, I thought about what I was doing; I was trying to make a tape and I was like, "Wow, this really sounds like something." I practiced with it and perfected it and used it with different records, and that's when it became a scratch.

Back in the days, Grandmaster Flash invented this way of rubbing a record, but he usually just rubbed it once and just let it go. What I did was give it a rhythm; I made a tune out of it, rubbing it for three, four minutes, making it a scratch.

Before that, a DJ would have his earphones on, and I could see him moving the record back and forth, but the people couldn't hear him moving it back and forth. What I did was, I just switched it over so the people could hear the record going back and forth, and it made a beat out of it. The first time I ever played it for people was at the Sparkle on Mount Eden. I wanted to do something different with this record "Johnny the Fox," by Thin Lizzy. I'd play the drum part over and over. People were like, "Whoa!"

Disco Bee and Love Bug Starski at the Ecstasy Garage, August, 1980 (© Charlie Ahearn)

the scene
is set

AFRIKA BAMBAATAA: By the mid-'70s, it was getting strong, with hundreds of people coming to each jam. I mean, you could have Kool Herc going to the West Side, Grandmaster Flash could be playing in the South Side of Bronx, I'd be in the Southeast Bronx, and then you had DJ Breakout and the Funky 4 up in the North Bronx. And each of us would have a jam-packed party with hundreds of people all over the place. You had to have teamwork and organization to get that going on, and that led to other people becoming producers and promoters.

SHA-ROCK: Hip-hop was a part of everybody's life back then. Herc started it with the music and everything, but then you had different DJs from different parts of town that would take over and represent from their area. That's how it worked. Flash had downtown Bronx; Bambaataa had a certain area in the Bronx. And then you had the Funky 4 uptown in the Bronx. There's a lot of other people out there. You had Disco King Mario and DJ Hollywood that was a part of Manhattan. You had Disco Bee...there were all different people that were representing from their area in town. It was all different DJs.

AFRIKA BAMBAATAA: Grandmaster Flash brought the quick-mixing into the hip-hop culture. Then you had the scratching and the needle dropping of the Grand Wizard Theodore, and that's when the whole movement started changing to another direction.

Chief Rocker Busy Bee and Grandmaster Caz clocking DJ Love Bug Starski at the Battle of the MCs at the Ecstasy Garage Disco, August, 1980 (© Charlie Ahearn)

MCS TAKE THE STAGE:

the rise of mc crews

Summer 1976: Bicentennial celebrations are held in communities across the country, and disco rules the clubs and the airwaves. Downtown the disco DJs are focusing on seamlessly weaving together increasingly formulaic disco records, keeping the polyester-clad dancers sweating on the dance floors. Uptown the DJs are working out the new techniques developed by Grandmaster Flash and Grand Wizard Theodore, creating a sound that is the antithesis of disco's endless groove, although it should be noted that most of the new DJ crews have one DJ who specializes in b-boy or break-beats and another who specializes in mixing records not unlike the downtown disco DJs.

Some interesting things happen as this new DJ culture establishes itself. First, the virtuosity of Grandmaster Flash and his followers begins to draw attention away from the b-boy and b-girl circles down front. The "two turntables and a microphone" setup is augmented by a mixer, headphones, and often an echo chamber to add an otherworldly flavor to the MCs' voices. A new style of MC-ing appears that further draws the attention from the floor to the stage. The MCs begin to involve the whole audience in the party.

The gangs are also beginning to fade at this time, which hastens the decline of the b-boy crew. The legacy of the gangs and their territories lives on though, in the regional aspect of the DJ crews; the dominant DJs each rule a specific territory and have gang-like security crews to help maintain this order. New groups develop new followings in different parts of the Bronx. Grand Wizard Theodore and his brothers put together a popular crew; DJ Breakout and DJ Baron emerge from the North Bronx with a crew to be reckoned with. More DJ crews than we can name appear, and the focus falls increasingly on the intricate routines developed by the MCs out front. Older promoters and club owners also began to see the potential to make some money from this new music.

Dez and crew DJ-ing at a park, East Harlem, New York, 1984
(© Henry Chalfant)

f you weren't in the Bronx in the '70s or early '80s, the phrase "Park Jam" might conjure up an image of rolling grass with bushes and trees and a DJ party. In fact, the "parks" referred to are asphalt playgrounds surrounded by chain-link fence, as shown here. The numbers usually refer to public schools. "63 Park" is the schoolyard for IS (Intermediate School) 63, on Boston Road between 169th and 168th Street in the Bronx.

GRANDMASTER FLASH: I was like totally wack on the mic. I knew that I was not going to be an MC, so I had to find someone able to put a vocal entertainment on top of this rearrangement of music. After so many people tried, the only person that really passed the test—and I think he was one of my lifesavers, with his technique—was Keith Wiggins, who, God rest his soul, has passed. His name was Cowboy. Cowboy found a way to allow me to do my thing and have the people really, really rocking, you know? So we were the perfect combination for quite some time.

MELLE MEL: It just seemed like Cowboy came out of nowhere that day at 63 Park. Flash just had this open mic, and anybody could grab it. Me, Scorp, and Kid Creole were in the middle of the crowd dancing—me and Scorp were like Flash's dance team. Suddenly I heard all this yelling, and Cowboy was on the mic telling people, "Throw your hands in the air and wave 'em like you just don't care!" The basic crew down with Flash at that time was Mean Gene, Cordie-O, Disco Bee, and E-Z Mike.

Before Cowboy lived on Boston Road, he used to live over at Bronx River. He was a tough thug type. He was in the Black Spades with Bambaataa.

BUSY BEE: Cowboy's name was Keith before they called him Cowboy. They called him Cowboy because he had the bow legs and he walked like an old cowboy.

GRANDMASTER FLASH: Theodore, my partner in DJ-ing early on, he branched off and created his own crew, which was called the L Brothers, so it was basically myself and Cowboy for a minute. I had to get my own partners, assistants, and stuff of that nature, so Disco Bee came into place, and then E-Z Mike came into place. We would go through doin' little block parties here and there, you know? We would just generally do things in the Bronx.

I'm not sure how we made the decision, but there was another person who wanted to get down with the group. His name was Nathaniel Glover—Kid Creole. Kid Creole had this gift of never ending rhyming, so when he kind of auditioned for me I was like, "Yes, you're in." He was just so good at what he did.

G Man and his crew DJ-ing at a park, Bronx, New York, 1984 (© Henry Chalfant)

KID CREOLE: When I met Grandmaster Flash, it was '75...something like that. He lived in the Mott Haven section, and we grew up in the Morrisania section of the Bronx. Flash used to come out for parties, and back in those days it was word of mouth, so we used to hear Flash was coming out. It was 23 Parkhurst Forest playground. And he used to bring his equipment out—little makeshift turntables and makeshift cueing that he built himself, and go out there and play records that we never heard before, with the break in it. He used to extend the break. One thing about Flash, at those times, he was extremely revolutionary; before him, everything was mixes and disco. That's when the disco era was just starting to form. So when the record would change, you heard, "Boom, boom, boom, boom, boom"...the next one would come in, "Ba-boom, ba-boom, ba-boom, ka-boom, ka-boom..." and then the other record would fall off even, "Boom, boom, boom, boom." So you had to almost wait for a minute to dance, because nobody really had a technique to bring one record in while the other record was going out, for it to be like a uniform thing. And Flash was doing that back in the early '70s. Extremely revolutionary. We'd just stand around and watch, you know, and eventually we got up the nerve to go over to him and say, "Yo, Flash, can we get on the microphone?" And that's how we met him.

BUSY BEE: Grandmaster Flash was the first thing as far as rap that I ever heard. And I heard it in the Bronx, in the backyards, in the schoolyards. Flash was like a super of a building, or he had a little power with the super in the building, to where he could come out in front of the building, set up a table, and use the electricity from the light pole on the street corner. This must have been '77 because it wasn't even the Furious at the time; it was Grandmaster Flash and just two MCs.

GRANDMASTER FLASH: It was Cowboy, Creole, and myself. Shortly thereafter, Creole got his brother interested. His little brother was into break-dancing. He was pretty good, I might add. His name was Melvin Glover, and he was known as Melle Mel.

The Kool Herc style at the time was basically freelance talking, not necessarily syncopated to the beat. The three of them—Cowboy, Creole, and Mel—came up with this style called the back and forth, where they would be MC-ing to the beat that I would play. I'll take a sentence that hopefully the whole world knows: "Eeeny meeny, miny mo, catch a piggy by the toe." So they devised it where Cowboy might say "Eeeny meeny," and then Creole would say, "Miny," and then Mel would say, "Mo." So they would kind of bounce it around.

Visually, it was an incredible sight to see. I'd keep the beat steady—I think probably the first song we did it to successfully, where we wanted the people to just stop and just look and just listen, was a song by Cymande. It's called "Bra." It's a funky beat but it's real quiet. And they used to just do this thing, and it was so incredible.

KID CREOLE: When we first started rhyming, Flash would have guys on the microphone who'd just get on there and say his name, haphazard, no real talent being displayed. And my brother...I don't know, somehow or another he got in his head that he was going to try to make up his own rhymes, and that's what he did. And when he did that, it spurred me to do it. We used to go back and forth, where we used to like take a rhyme and split it up, you know, that kind of thing.

74

"One, two, this is for you, you, and you,

three, four, cuts galore is what we have in store."

Back then, what inspired me to write...my brother inspired me a lot. There was no real outside force that made us write rhymes, because nobody was writing rhymes. So it was self-motivation. After a point, everybody started writing rhymes. My brother and I first started writing rhymes, and then everybody in our neighborhood who wanted to do the same thing that we was doing started writing. Then they became our inspiration. To crush them. And anytime we heard somebody say a rhyme that we thought was butter, then that made us go back over there and write something that was similar to that. So that if we ever went to battle that person, we'd have something like him, to crush him with.

WHIPPER WHIP: Flash at that time was just Flash and the 3 MCs; Rahiem wasn't part of the group yet, and neither was Scorpio. They were the first MCs that I ever really saw, and to see them do their thing, it was like, "Well, I got a lot of homework to do" [laughs]. Each one of them had their own aura. Mel was just an incredible writer; Mel would rock a crowd. Kid Creole, he just rocked that echo chamber like no one else; he was like, "Creole (ole), Solid Gold (gold), the Prince of Soul (soul), playing the role (role)." It was just incredible. And then Cowboy was the guy who just hyped up the party, "Say ho!" and had everybody scream. So each one of them had their own little thing.

KID CREOLE: When we used to rehearse, most of the time it was in the street, or Disco Bee had an apartment over there on 169th and Fulton Avenue; we used to go up there and practice rhyming and workin' out our little routines. We wasn't calling ourself the Furious 3; we was calling ourself just the plain old 3 MCs. Me and my brother would say rhymes together, and we'd finish saying our little routine, and Cowboy'd just get on the mic and charge the house. When we first started rhymin' there was no crowd response involved, because the people that we looked at was Kool Herc, Timmy Tim, Clark Kent, and Coke La Rock. And they said phrases; they didn't say rhymes. They would say, "On down to the last stop." "More than what you paid at the door." Stuff like that. And when we started writing rhymes, we put sentences together. We really didn't have any concept of crowd response. If we tried to say something like this:

> He tried to rock the spot
> with a cheap cheap rhyme
> the rhyme was a joke
> the sucker went broke
> and he died and went to heaven in a little row boat

To say, "Hoooooo!"...that wasn't in our mind. We had no concept of doing that. So after we said our rhyme, we just...was finished. And then Cowboy, in his mind, he had a concept of, "Yo, we need to try to get the crowd to do this."

the ORIGINS of the MC

With the emergence first of Cowboy and soon after of Melle Mel and Kid Creole, the Bronx street scene was developing a distinctive style of MC-ing. But a smoother style of rapping DJ presided over the turntables in the clubs of Harlem and the Bronx. The style of DJs like DJ Hollywood and Eddie Cheba was closely tied to the mellow vocalizing of radio DJs like Jocko Henderson. To a certain extent, these DJs existed in a parallel universe to "street" DJs like Herc, Flash, and Bambaataa, but the two schools were aware of one another and influenced each other.

Although these older DJs usually played in clubs with age restrictions and dress codes, they couldn't resist trying to capture some of this new younger audience, so they would often hire DJs and MCs from the street scene and play all-ages affairs. Many young MC wannabes got their first taste of rapping listening to Hollywood at the Apollo Theater. As hip-hop grew, there were MCs like Love Bug Starski and the young Kurtis Blow who bridged the gap between the mellower Harlem club scene and the rougher Bronx street scene.

AFRIKA BAMBAATAA: Rap always has been here in history. They say when God talked to the prophets, he was rappin' to them. You could go and pick up the old Shirley Ellis records, "The Name Game," "The Clapping Song," Moms Mabley, Pigmeat Markham, when he made "Here Comes the Judge." You could pick up Barry White with his love type of rap, or Isaac Hayes. You could get your poetry rap from Nikki Giovanni, Sonya Sanchez, the Last Poets, the Watts Prophets. You could get your militancy message rap coming from Malcolm X, Minister Louis Farrakhan, Muhammad Ali. A lot of time, the Black people used to play this game called The Dozens on each other, rappin' about your mama or your father, and stuff. And you could go back to the talks of Murray the K, Cousin Brucie, and all the other radio stations that was pushing the rap on the air or pushing the rock and roll. So rap was always here.

Godfather's Prod. Inc.

Presents

"A Night with Cheba"

Disco With
THE AWARD WINNING VOICE OF
Eddie Cheba

Featuring:

Easy "G" & the Cheba Crew
SHARLENE ★ SHARLETTE ★ STELLA
SANDY ★ MUFFIN ★ JEANIE
"LISA"
"Bobby Bob" "Blue Boy D"
&
"DR. LOVE"

Star of "371 Club", Small Paradise
Now Appearing On Station
WFUV 90.7 Every Sat., 10 - 12 A.M.

Saturday, November 18, 1978

At the New

"T" Connection

3510 WHITE PLAINS ROAD, BRONX, N.Y.
Right Off Gun Hill Road

From 10 P.M. until ???

TICKETS $5.00 ◄ ► TICKETS LIMITED

For Information Call:

320-1397 ● 653-1126 ● 881-0493 ● 654-8374

Curt

Bob

PRODUCTION

PRESENTS

D.J. Hollywood

'Theoredore' Flash
you better run
we have called No.1
so cut, mix and rhyme
as best you could
Then come listen to Hollywood.

Guest Attraction

Also Appearing

Super Added Attraction

M.C. La-Shu-Bee

**And
D.J. Doctor
U.S.A. Inc.**

D.J. Starski

D.J. Young Blood &
The Crus_____w

Place : 164 W 129 St. [3rd building from 7 ave.]

Donation : $3.00

Time : 9 : 00 P. M. - ??

Date : [Fri.] 5-18-79

All D. J.s Guaranteed to Appear

Chuck

Design and produced by Carl D.

"If you really wanna get right to where the MC-in' part came about in hip-hop, I would give that to DJ Hollywood. Going to see Hollywood, he didn't really rap like we did, but he had his chants—"Hollywood, I'm doing good, I hope you're feeling fine"—making the crowd scream and stuff like that. There's different versions; there's scatting and all of that, but still I'd give it to Hollywood, Pete DJ Jones, Love Bug Starski, and that clan." ● **WHIPPER WHIP**

GRANDMASTER CAZ: When I started out as a DJ, MC-in' as an art hadn't been formulated yet. The microphone was just used for makin' announcements, like when the next party was gonna be, or people's moms would come to the party lookin' for them, and you have to announce it on the mic. "So and so, your mother's lookin' for you at the door." You know, that kind of thing. So different DJs started embellishing what they were sayin'. Instead of just sayin', "We'll be at the P.A.L. next week, October this and that," they'd say, "You know next week we gonna be at the P.A.L. where we rock well, and we want to see your face in the place," little things like that. Up until then, the DJ was preoccupied with DJ-in', and he had whoever was in the crew, the record guy or whoever was down, to start talkin' and make the announcements. Different groups started gettin' their own personnel to do that so that it started growin' from there. I would make an announcement this way, and somebody would hear me, and then they'd go to their party and they add a little twist to it. Then somebody would hear that and they add a little bit to it. I'd hear it again and take it a little step further 'til it turned from lines to sentences to paragraphs to verses to rhymes.

Pete DJ Jones at Fordham University, 1979

SAL ABBATIELLO: DJ Hollywood at that time was more of a dressed-up type—he wore a sports jacket—and he had June Bug who was a young Hispanic DJ. Hollywood had this little crew with him, five or six people, and they would repeat everything he would say. It was all rehearsed; if he would say, "Holly," they would say, "Wood," but it was loud, five or six of them screaming at the same time.

Pete DJ Jones had all these kids under him. He would go down to Savoy Manor, the Audubon, all these big wedding places and put four, five DJs in there: Hollywood, Love Bug Starski, Flash, Eddie Cheba, Reggie Wells. Pete was more of an older R&B type of DJ who was a grown man. He had money, he had a job. He would get these different rooms, and he would put all these DJs in there on the same night. Thousands of people would come. He was doing it like once every three months, on holidays, sometimes on a Saturday.

LOVE BUG STARSKI: Flash introduced me to Pete DJ Jones, and I worked with Pete DJ Jones for about four or five years carrying equipment and filling in with him when he was too tired to play. We played all the clubs, like Superstar 33, Nell Gwynn's, Leviticus, Justine's, places like that.

Pete DJ Jones was big on the mature club side. Flash, Mario, Bambaataa, Kool Herc, Breakout from Uptown, and Grandmaster Flowers from Brooklyn, that was the only heavy hitters that was out back in those days, besides Eddie Cheba and Hollywood.

VAN SILK: Hollywood was the first person inside the clubs doing the DJ-ing and talking over the microphone. He was doin' the Wolfman Jack-type style they used to do back on the radio; he had his little sayings with his crew, the Hollywood dancers, and the whole nine. The clubs that we couldn't get in was the clubs he was playin' at.

What Hollywood was doing was more disco. He came through the Pete DJ Jones era, which came from Grandmaster Flowers, who was a DJ out of Brooklyn. Hollywood, Eddie Cheba, and Reggie Wells, along with Love Bug Starski came through that older club scene, as opposed to Kool Herc who was from the streets. But Hollywood was still young enough to be able to connect to the hip-hop scene, and he would always work with younger DJs.

BUSY BEE: Disco King Mario was a DJ known for sound. He was a perfection nut! He set those standards to where a system is supposed to sound like a system: you got bass, mid-range, and highs. I didn't know nothing about this, but I learned through Mario. He'd say, "Hey Starski, when you talk on this mic you're going to sound so vicious!" That's what he used to say [laughing]. "Oh, so vicious!" And I'm saying, "Yeah Mario, yeah, put it down!"

Herc had a system, too, but Mario had one of them systems where he'd stack it. If you come to the show, it was like you're listening to a building play! A big building, and you're sittin' in the middle. Two turntables and a big old wall of system! Just how I'm talking to you now—that's how I sound on that microphone. And it wasn't just loud, it was perfect loud. You can hear the voice, the strings of the guitars...you heard the music! With Mario's system, you could be the worst DJ or the worst MC in the world, but you was on the best system in the world.

RICHARD SISCO: Kool Herc had his MC—Coke La Rock—but if you want to say the first "rhymer," Cowboy definitely was the first guy in the Bronx that put it together. He used to go on like, "A one-two, y'all," and "Yes, yes, y'all," all that kind of stuff, and then he'd start to say a little rhyme. That was the first.... We said, "That's funky, man, you checking that out?"

Yes, Yes, **my** Mellow, Back By Popular Demand

N.Y.'S #1, DISCO KING MARIO
AND C. C. CREW
WITH SOUNDS BY

BX.'S #1 COOL D.J. NICKY DEE
D.J. RONIE RON & D.J. DESIE
THE VOICE OF D.J. STARSKY
D.J. JOEY DEE & D.J. DANNY
VS.
D.J. C. D. LA ROCK & D.J. ISLAM

J. H. S. 123
1025 BRUCKNER BLVD. AT MORRISON AVE.

FRIDAY, MARCH 10, 1978
8 P.M. UNTIL

C.C. Dues: $2.00 with Flyer - $3.00 without Flyer

Only If House Is Packed Back To Back,
Freak N' Freak Contest - One Hundred Dollars
WHEN YOU DANCE TO THE RHYTHM OF THE BEAT
EVERYBODY DO THE FREAK

VAN SILK: The credit given to Kool Herc as the godfather of hip-hop should be spread to a couple of other people such as DJ Hollywood. That side of Hollywood and Eddie Cheba was more like the commercial style. Herc was more like the underground side, but as far as Hollywood bein' called a godfather of hip-hop, you can't take that away from him. Hollywood played a big part—there's two sides to the story.

REGGIE REG: Hip-hop was in the Bronx for like five years before it came to Manhattan. And the way hip-hop came to Manhattan was through the high schools. A lot of kids from the Bronx would have these mix tapes of Flash, Bambaataa, Kool Herc, the L Brothers. In Manhattan, we ain't heard nothing like that. We was more into what they would call the R&B DJ, like Hollywood, Eddie Cheba, Reggie Wells. Not the real hip-hop DJ that has a lot of rhymes and stuff. The first time we experienced that was in high school when we listened to a Grandmaster Flash tape, and we heard this guy doing these scratches and cutting and then the MC with the echo chamber. This was when it was the 3 MCs: Cowboy, Melle Mel, and Kid Creole. We kind of copied that.

Disco King Mario at JHS 123, with Busy Bee (Starski) and others, 1978

"*I was one of the brothers from Brooklyn that was comin' uptown when uptown didn't respect Brooklyn. I was down with the party set with Grandmaster Flowers, Maboya, and DJ Dagger. I got inspired to come uptown and check out Hollywood and them when they was at the 371 Club. DJ Hollywood and June Bug on the turntables, they would take over a crowd and have complete control.*" ● **JALIL**

Keith Keith and Jazzy Jeff chill outside the Black Door, the original club spot for the Grandmaster Flash crew, 1980 (© Charlie Ahearn)

BLACK DOOR PRODUCTION
PRESENTS

EASTER-WEEK-END
with
"GRAND MASTER FLASH"
DISCO BEE - 3. M.C's
KEITH-KEITH, MELE-MEL.
KID CREOLE

PLACE- ATMOSPHERE BY SCALES
809 Southern Blvd. Bx

DATE: MARCH 24,25,1978

ADM. LADIES #3.00 - Gents #4.00

TIME .10 PM UNTIL ?

ABSOLUTELY NO SNEAKERS

----

ray chandler & the black door

RAY CHANDLER: It all started one very cold winter night when we were walking along Boston Road in the Bronx and I seen a whole lot of young kids, like a posse situation, in a school yard—PS163 by 169th Street. At first I thought it was a fight or something. Then I see one guy with turntables, and some other guys were saying something over microphones. I had a chance to talk to the young man on the records, and he introduced himself to me as Grandmaster Flash. I asked him, "Why you out on the street in this cold weather?" They said they didn't really have a place to go.

At that point I had a little club that I was putting together down the block, and I hadn't really opened it up yet. I was still fixing it up. It was going to be a social club for adults.

GRANDMASTER FLASH: We were outside doing block parties, and Ray Chandler came to us and said, "Why don't we try it inside for $1 a head?" This place must have been the size of maybe four large bathrooms, you know. Held I'd say a hundred people and it was packed. From there we did lots of parties in gymnasiums and community centers, but we had a home base—the Black Door. Eventually we called our production company Black Door Productions.

RAY CHANDLER: Phase 2, he would come to the parties. I found him through DJ AJ who told me about this guy who was a good artist. I decided we could make some flyers and advertise to the various schools. Phase 2 asked me, "What are we going to call this production?" As we stood outside, it came to us, "Well, the door is black, so let's call it the Black Door."

KOOL DJ AJ: Back then I used to open up for Grandmaster Flash, 'cause I was a member of the Black Door Productions. The Black Door was a disco in the South Bronx, on Prospect Avenue.

WHIPPER WHIP: Getting in the Black Door was a little job, 'cause you'd have to go through security, and they were real selective. And the thing about it was, it would get crowded quickly, 'cause any party Flash played would draw a crowd, because Flash was no joke. And these weren't huge venues; they were small. So you'd have to wait outside, unless you had clout. The average person would wait quite a while to get in there. They get that up at Studio 54 or something, I don't know.

K.K. ROCKWELL: I used to listen to Flash tapes, but I was too young to get into his parties at the Black Door. But one night, when I was in ninth grade, I was hanging around the front door, and I noticed that nobody was around so I snuck downstairs. It must have been around 2 a.m. The funny thing was that once I got in, they announced, "OK. We locking the door. Ain't nobody leaving until 6 a.m." That way they could keep the party nice and crowded. And I thought, this is my chance. I'm staying.

The "freak" was out—real nasty dancing—guys and girls would be on the floor going wild. And I was on the floor, too! They held a freak contest, and this guy from the Casanova Crew won the money and champagne, and they made a soul train line going all around the room. They was yelling, "Casanovas! All over! Casanovas! All over!" When they finally opened the door, it was bright sunshine outside. I thought I was in for it, but when I got home all my mom said was, "I just can't keep yelling and yelling at you. I'm worn out."

RAY CHANDLER: My first encounter with the Casanovas was at a big party. There was a group of about sixty young guys outside, and they called themselves the Casanovas. Their slogan was "Casanovas All Over!" The first one I met was a gentleman by the name of Hootenanny, and he had a large medallion. He said, "We're the Casanovas, and we're not going to pay any money to come in. We come to all the parties free." I found that to be a little funny because I knew that wasn't going to happen. I explained to them what would happen if they bum-rushed the door to get in, because I had guys working with me that was in law enforcement. I started making package deals. "I'll let twenty of you in for "x" amount of dollars, thirty of you for "x" amount." Thereafter they would come to the parties every weekend.

We became like one big family. I gave them jobs. There were times when I would give them the door, and they would have to pay all the expenses so they could split the profits amongst themselves. They'd have to pay Flash. It was their night.

RAHIEM: I had heard Flash, and at that time, they were the 3 MCs: Melle Mel, Kid Creole, and Cowboy. I heard them on tapes only. I had never seen them, and when I listened to Flash's cuts on tape, I didn't have a clue as to the mechanics behind what he was doing. I mean, it sounded like a pause-button tape to me. Back in those times, guys would make pause-button tapes: they'd play a portion of a record, then pause the cassette player, take that portion back, and take it off pause and let it go again. So when I first heard Flash, I thought it was trickery, not actual turntable skills.

I remember the first time that I actually saw Flash cutting; it was at a place called Benjamin Franklin High School. It was totally dark in this place except for the lights coming from his two Technics turntables and a little lamp in between them. But they had a light on him, and when he started doing his thing on the turntables, I remember everybody stopped what they were doing, and they ran—I mean literally ran—to the front of the ropes, and when they could actually see, it was like, "oooh, aahhh."

At that time, I hadn't even heard of Theodore yet. Flash was the only one that I knew of who did that. With all due respect to Kool Herc, he played music totally different from the way that Flash played it. When you went to a Herc party, you would see the b-boys doing their thing, break-dancing or whatever, but there was always a lull, or a pause in the action because Herc wasn't a turntablist. Herc let his records play until you heard, "khhhhhh, khhhhh, khhh" (makes the sound of a needle hitting the end of a record). Every now and then at a Herc party, you might hear that. Or every now and then at a Herc party, you would hear what we call the "wack" part of the song, where-as Flash is such a hyper person, I don't think that he could wait until the record got to the end; he had to do something. I think that's the reason why he...I'm gonna say...why he invented scratching, OK? There are other people who say other things, but Flash is the only person that I know who was scratching at that time.

KOOL DJ AJ: Grandmaster Flash was the guy who dethroned Kool Herc. He did it on a show where it was a battle between Kool Herc and Pete DJ Jones. I think it was at the Executive Playhouse. At that time, Herc still had his little following and Pete DJ Jones had a following, so they collaborated together. They battled together, and Pete DJ Jones had always hired other people to play on his set. He needed somebody else who had skills, so at the battle he put on Grandmaster Flash.

Pete DJ Jones came on first. Pete DJ Jones didn't have an MC back then. He was the MC. He was a little bit disco, but it was a hip-hop audience, and they wasn't feel-ing him that much. Then he put Grandmaster Flash on, which was something different, 'cause he was quick-mixing and spinning around and doing a lot of amazing feats which you ain't never seen no DJ do.

Kool Herc was like the man who had records; he played a lot of break-beats. Herc was great, but Flash was a DJ. He had skills. He had finesse. He was fast. He amazed Kool Herc's audience. It was like Flash had skills and Herc had the records, but maybe people was really more into the skills because they had heard all the records already. So that's how that battle went on. Flash did his thing in front of Kool Herc's audience, and after that show, Flash just snatched up all their following. It was so amazing—I mean he did it so fast that you didn't even believe it. It was like, "How could a DJ do that? I gotta go pay to see Flash again to see if he could do that same quick-mix he did that night when he played with Pete DJ Jones and Kool Herc." It took maybe two or three weeks, but Flash snatched up all that clientele. Maybe people was a little tired of just hearing break-beats; they wanted to find something new. And I think they found something new in Grandmaster Flash.

the dixie club

GRANDMASTER FLASH: We had the Black Door for awhile, and then we outgrew that. We then got in contact with this man from Jamaica who owned the club down the block on Freeman Street, which was called the Dixie Club, and this was our new home base, and whenever we weren't touring the city, you could catch us there almost every weekend. And this place held maybe two or three hundred people.

RAY CHANDLER: These fellas came from a neighborhood they called "The Nine," which was 169th Street and Washington Avenue. They decided they was going to stick us up. Keep in mind that we knew all of them. But they decided that night that they was going to rob us. We was making too much money.

But what happened was, I was in the Dixie Club that same day. We was cleaning up, preparing for the night, getting it ready. And one of the guys that was involved in the stickup team came banging on the door in the afternoon. I thought he had come to borrow some money. I'm telling him, "Look. Go away." "No man. I got to talk to you!" He came in, and with tears in his eyes he started telling me, "They gonna rob you, man! They gonna rob all y'all and do some damage to y'all. But I love you, man. You're like my father. When I came out of jail, you the only one who gave me a job, you know?" He went on to describe exactly what was going to happen. "They said, 'We got to take big Ray out first. We got to take out his partner Charles. We got to take the Casanovas.'"

To get in the Dixie Club, you come in from street level, and you go up steep steps, and when you got to the top, there was a door where the party was held. So we had the doors closed, and all these teenagers was in there dancing without knowing that at any moment there could be drama at the door. They came up the steps, and I knew all of them! I seen a shotgun protruding out of the guy's coat. But we took them with the element of surprise. We had Casanovas at the door and the rest of them inside. I had my other people in law enforcement—they didn't know about these guys in the law enforcement. They were surrounded. I was like, "I never thought you would do that to us. You come to all our parties and we treat you like family." It ended with no violence. They were sent to jail. Some of them were already on parole; automatically they went back to jail.

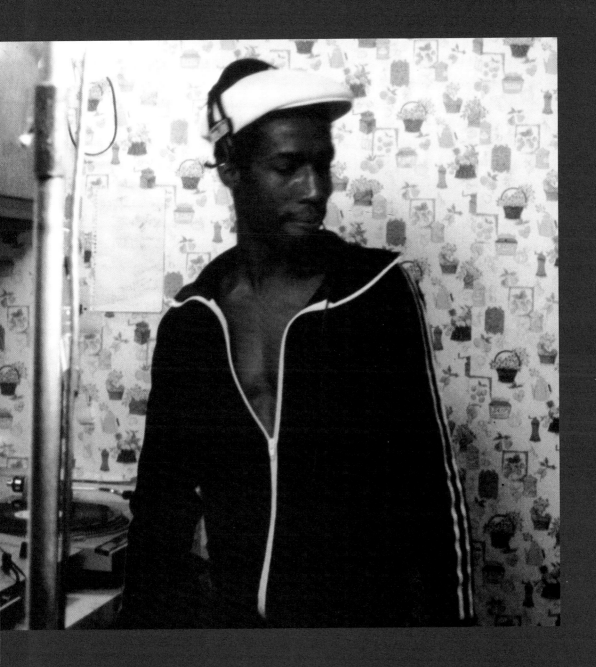

Flash in his kitchen DJ lab (during *Wild Style* shoot), 1981 (© Cathy Campbell)

CREWS
SECURITY &
VIOLENCE
at PARTIES

DJ DISCO WIZ: To be a DJ in those days, you had to have 'em really big, because it was rough. Economics was tough, so for you to bring out a system to a park or to a center was a big thing in the '70s. I mean people use the word "player hatin'" now. People don't know what player hatin' is. Player hatin' was real in those days, because people were struggling. No one had any kind of means, so to see some young cats doing something like that, believe me, it was very risky. People were going to jams and pulling out guns and shooting up the place; people were getting bum-rushed or being robbed. So you needed that element of respect, even though you didn't advocate violence.

"A lot of guys would get stuck up for their shit. A van would come in, and they just packed it in. All those people who'd be there with the DJ? They were just young guys. What would they do? They used to have battles for equipment set for set. Niggers would go talking that shit, but they wasn't prepared to give up their set. They just thought they were going to win. Then when they lose, yo, they take your shit. They pull a gun or just muscle it. 'Yo, I'm taking this.'"

● **GRANDMASTER CAZ**

KOOL DJ AJ: DJs used to battle: you would bring your sound system, I would bring my sound system. It would go by sound, it would go by records you played, it would go by how you made the audience react. But it was hard to get DJs to battle back then because there was always a conflict. You had to bring your gang of people, and they have their gang of people, you know what I'm saying? You had to bring your gang for protection, because my system might have cost like $15,000, which I paid out of my pocket, and if you didn't have no gang behind you, you might've lost your system in the South Bronx. You know what I'm saying? You might've came up out of that venue and got stuck up. Really it wasn't like your gang; it was your crew—people who came out of your neighborhood, who knew you, who would get in free every time you did a show. You'd shout their name out, you made them celebrities along with you. So those was the people that you dealt with. That was your crew.

Sugarhill convention breaking, 1981 (© Charlie Ahearn)

Celebrity Club after the gunshot, 1980 (© Charlie Ahearn)

SHA-ROCK: A lot of different incidents would happen when you go to a party, but mostly I think that a lot of people had security for their own reasons. It was just—you're supposed to have security, so just in case something happened, the MCs and DJs didn't have to go out there and take care of the problem. And the security was there to protect the environment, you know?

WHIPPER WHIP: Every big group would have a crew. We had the Nine Crew doing security; the Casanovas was Flash's main security, and you didn't want to mess with those guys [laughs].

CHARLIE CHASE: A lot of bad things did happen. Not at every party—it's not fair to say that something always happened...I mean, you have to understand: you're in a park—the bodega is right down the corner, man. You go pick up your Colt .45, which at the time was hot. Or Old English 800. People have too many to drink, they have a little bit of a disagreement, or they're actually battling—the b-boys never really started any trouble, it was just the other knuckleheads that were with them that started the problem. It did get to a point where I didn't want the reputation that Flash had, because at one point, everybody was saying, "It's dangerous to go to a Flash party." And I didn't want that to happen to me.

RAHIEM: Every time Flash played "Listen to Me" by Baby Huey, there was some kind of violence. Oh man, I don't know what it was about that song, whether it was the lyrics to the song or what. I do remember there being a—how can I explain this—it's like this music kinda brought you down. It was a up-tempo song, but it was a dark song. "Give It to Me" [singing the version of the song that the stick-up kids sang]...I can't even remember all of the words to the song, but I can tell you this: the words were not violent enough to

where, when they played it, it incited some kind of violent act. It wasn't that kind of a song, but I think just the overtones of that music just brought about a certain mood, and every time...I mean, Pow! They let off shots. It's crazy.

WHIPPER WHIP: Back then when Bambaataa would play "Give It to Me," it was like "step aside." Sheepskins, your shoes, you got your stuff taken. At that time, it wasn't gold chains; everyone was wearing silver. So you wearin' silver chains, and you see everybody sticking their stuff in their shirts, 'cause they know! They know it's time to get up outta there [laughs]. That was such a great record. It's a classic, but that's what went down when Bam played that. Or Herc—Herc used to play at a place called Monterey in the Bronx. Real tiny, tiny place for such a huge system. It was the Monterey Center, and when he played that, you'd just clear out. You know what you gotta do.

GRANDMASTER FLASH: One night Cowboy, God bless him, was on the mic. There was a loud, "Pow!" I thought my crossover blew up. Cowboy fell back right into my arms. He pulled his shirt up, and he was shot! While he was on the mic. One of the other MCs, the bullet went right through him. He kept rocking; he didn't know it. Cowboy went to the hospital. Ray Chandler had a special relationship with the local police so nothing happened.

KEVIE KEV: You definitely had to be tough coming up out there. If you was rolling anywhere around hip-hop, you'd have to be around adults, man, 'cause you fourteen or fifteen, and you able to get in, you better remember you around twenty-year-olds and guns go pop.

The Casanovas—Crazy Eddie, Peanut—were family. Big Man and Little Jay and all them. These brothers was real fly. Like Hootenanny: thing I noticed most about him was that he had this real fly gold chain around his neck. He had pieces of

> *"They were playing joints like [sings] 'Do you want to see it? Do you want to see it? I'm going to do it for you!' [singing "The Breakdown (Part 2)," by Rufus Thomas]. And then they'd show their guns at that record. Certain records were played; certain things were done."* ● **KEVIE KEV**

---

medallions that was six down the front like stuck together with a good six across to make a cross from like thirteen medallions. But these was like their emblem—when you seen that, you know Casanovas was in the house.

GRANDMASTER CAZ: The Casanovas were the biggest cats out there. All ex-Black Spades. They just changed their name; they never changed their game! People would be mortally afraid of these guys.

THEODORE: Every time Flash gave a party, the Casanovas did security for him. It was either beat 'em or join 'em. They'd get in for free, and then at the end of the night, they usually got a couple hundred to split up amongst their crew.

RAY CHANDLER: When we'd give a party, we'd have U-Haul trucks; sometimes we'd have fifty or sixty Casanovas in the trucks 'cause wherever we went it was like a family. They would have their run-ins with rival people. They would have to beat people up. My job was always to keep them in check. They would tell me, "So and so disrespected my girl! So subsequently we had to whip somebody's ass, you know."

From my understanding they did have a lot of members that were originally Black Spades, and they turned into Casanovas. I got them out of many situations, squashed many a beef with other gang members.

peanut

RAY CHANDLER: Peanut was a very little guy, but he had a heart as big as a building. He would keep the other Casanovas in line. If he said, "Ray said to go home," they'd listen 'cause he was so loved and respected by all the Casanovas, by all of us. He wound up getting killed one night. That was one of the saddest things, and that got me to start looking at the whole rap picture.

There was an argument that night at the party, the night Peanut got killed. This guy came back with a shotgun and shot little Peanut right there in front of everybody. Now everybody in the Bronx is looking for this guy. The thing was, he said he wasn't hiding. He was armed. He said he was going to kill the Casanovas.

Casanovas, gang members from all over the city, Brooklyn, Queens, all they wanted to do was to get the perpetrators that killed Peanut. This was one of the most dangerous times in this business 'cause my job was to keep the peace. They were hunting for this guy. Police were looking for this guy. Homicide detectives were looking for this guy.

The Casanovas was extremely upset, and through the help of the leaders—Tiny and Bambi and Cletus—we had meetings. Everyday we had to talk to the guys. Holy war was going to break out. But the guy who killed Peanut was captured and convicted.

DJ Baron on the turntables, with Pookie D (front) and Kimoni at Eden-Wald Center, Fall 1977 (Courtesy Darnell Williams)

the brothers disco:
dj breakout, dj baron,
& the funky 4 mcs

DJ BREAKOUT: Before I was a DJ, I was a b-boy. I used to break-dance, and I used to have "Breakout" on the side of my leg. I used to spray paint it. I had three names—I had Breakout, I had Crip, I had T—but my friend told me to pick Breakout. I kept dancin' and dancin'. I said, "Watch, I'm gonna be famous one day. Watch, I'm gonna be famous."

K.K. ROCKWELL: I always lived a dual life at home. I'd be "Yes ma'am. No ma'am." I was so nice. Then as soon as I got outside, I'd be down for the crown with my gang. We grew up kind of wild. As soon as we got outside, we'd be fighting like we was in some karate flick, kicking and chopping at each other. Everybody had like these two sticks with a nail holding the rope or chain (nunchucks), and we'd pretend we were Bruce Lee. There was a dude in seventh grade in full colors: MC boots, denim jacket with fur on top that said Seven Immortals with a knife going through it. We'd go to the Kung Fu flicks. They were open 24 hours. Once I fell asleep in there 'til the next day.

Later b-boying was the thing. We'd go to the park. The only reason my mom let me out of the house was because Breakout was older, and he lived up the block, and she trusted him. Everybody would come around to watch us dance, 'til one day a real b-boy, who'd gone to the real parties, showed up and danced. He burned us so bad. I went to Breakout later and said, "Yo, we got to learn how to do that!" I felt like I had to protect my neighborhood from dudes like that coming around.

DJ BREAKOUT: I kept dancin', kept playin' hooky from school to go to parties and dance. Then I started buyin' the music, buyin' the records, and then I became a DJ. I had an old turntable. I had another turntable that had a radio on the bottom of it. So I took the wires, and I ran 'em together, and one would play, I'd cut that one, grab this one, and play the next record. There was no mixer. I just kept playin'. I built me a speaker up with a strobe light in it.

When I started DJ-ing, I practiced a lot at home, and friends used to come over. I'd play one record for like two hours, just keep practicing, holdin' the beat, catchin' it. Now they spin back the record, but we was droppin' needles, usin' our hands to move it over. No spinnin' back. You gotta be that quick to catch the beat before the bad part come on, 'cause the beat only lasts like a couple seconds.

Say there's a lotta singin' on the record, and then the singin' stops and the beat comes on. You gotta make that beat last for a long time to keep the b-boy keep dancin', 'cause once the words come on, he stops dancin'. So you gotta be able to catch that same beat, hit it, hit it, again and again. I'd buy a whole album just for one little beat. I'd be searchin' all over, every record shop in Manhattan, for one beat.

K.K. ROCKWELL: Breakout would be, "Yo! I got some fresh beats. Let's go up to my crib." He'd play his new records, and I'd practice my new rhymes over them.

TONY TONE: I met Breakout in high school. One day we sitting in class, and this kid named Fox came to me 'cause I was DJ-ing with this crew called Unity Productions. Fox told me that he needed a DJ to battle Afrika Islam at JHS 123. I was like, "I don't know..." Breakout was nudging me saying, "I'm a DJ, I'm a DJ, I'll do it." I was saying, "I don't know you as being no DJ," but he convinced me, so I gave Fox my word that he could do it. Breakout took me to his house that day, he showed me his equipment, he showed me his skills. He battled Afrika Islam that night and won. So from then I was just hanging with his crew.

AFRIKA ISLAM: I remember my first battle was against Breakout, November 4, 1977, at Junior High School 123. It was me, Busy Bee Starski, and Rahiem started off together.

DJ BARON: My family moved to the Bronx in 1972, when I was fourteen. On weekends I used to go to Kool Herc parties—he'd give parties out in this building that was on Cedric at 1520, in a little community center. I was fascinated at how he played his music.

I was always wanting to be a DJ after I heard Herc. I used to go to little social clubs and put my little 45 records on the system and call it DJ-ing. I was collecting records— my project was finding all the records that Herc had. I'd practice at my house, and when I got enough records to go ahead and go out and play, that's what I did.

K.K. ROCKWELL: In eighth grade I had a friend—the Amazing DJ Baron. I became the "Voice of K.K." I was so little I had to stand on a stool at the parties. I was just saying stuff like, "K.K. is in the house, cooling out without a doubt." We'd talk to the b-boys— "B-boys, are you ready?" "To my mellow"—or do little rhymes we got from Herc parties. "Back and forth, forth and back. Two words to the wack: Stay the hell back!"

DJ BARON: My brother Kimoni was in karate class with Breakout. Breakout lived uptown, in the Gun Hill Road area, and I lived southwest. After I graduated from high school, we got together and started practicing. We started with raggy homemade speakers. I don't know who made them. Eventually we got nerve enough to go out and do a little party. Our first pay party was at Minisink in Harlem, a community center down on Lenox and 143rd Street. It was just two of us, playing the records that Herc was playing. We sounded terrible, but there was a lot of people in there. That was our first break. After that, I started building my sound system.

DJ BREAKOUT: I had met Baron at a party. He said, "Well, I got some equipment, too." So we put all our equipment together, and it came to be the Brothers Disco. Then K.K. Rockwell came along—that's before the parties started—and he said, "Yo, I could talk for you." I said, "I don't need you to talk." He said, "Yes, come on. I could get the crowd goin'."

DJ BARON: Herc came to see us first time in Breakout's backyard. He used to live on Needham Avenue, and there was a school down the block called 73 schoolyard. He came there, and we had our little speakers. It sounded nice. He was like, "Yeah. You're doing a little something."

DJ BREAKOUT: Then my brother came along, said, "What're you doin'? Let's get some real stuff." I said, "This is real stuff." He said, "This is garbage!" So he took me out and bought me some equipment. He said, "I'm your manager now. Let's go" [laughter].

JAZZY DEE: This was back in...like '77. He took my mother's stereo apart, started DJ-ing in the schoolyard, puttin' speakers in milk crates, and whatever he could do. I was not a part of it. At this time I was attending my first year in college. I got my student loan, and he came to me and asked me can I help him. I thought about it, and then I talked to DJ Baron. Me and DJ Baron went down to a guy with a discothèque store. Baron explained to me that the guy loved countin' money, so we got like $500 in singles. We went down to the office, and we was just pickin' out stuff we wanted, and then we gave him a lot of singles, and we left him there countin'. And that's how we got started.

adding mcs

DJ BARON: Our first MC was K.K. Rockwell. On our flyers we would put "Baron and Breakout and the voice of K.K." Then it became Baron and Breakout and K.K. featuring Busy Bee Starski, because sometimes Starski would come to our parties, and he would be MC-ing, too. Busy Bee Starski's style was really impressive. He had a storytelling type of rhyme. While I'm playing the beats, he goes on and on and on.

BUSY BEE STARSKI: I went from Disco King Mario to Breakout. He didn't have no rappers; he just had K.K. K.K. was alright. He had a voice, but he was a shy type of rapper, where you would have to push him. Whereas me, I grab it: let's go! You know?

What made me want to rap with Breakout was that he had a wild style of cuttin' his records, and I liked that. If Breakout was rockin' his beats, he'd dance behind that turntable. He would be on them turntables rockin' and dancin', man! That's hard to do—to dance and play and follow your MC at the same time. That's incredible. I said, "Look at that! I would want to get down with that."

K.K. ROCKWELL: This is how serious it was: Breakout would be playing the music; the music would get Breakout so excited that he'd forget and leave his set and throw himself down on the floor. I'm supposed to be on the mic, and I'd be break-dancing, too! The record's just spinning on its own, and we're both down on the floor. That's how pure, how real it was! We would have our dungarees rolled up high, so you could see our white socks moving in the dark.

BUSY BEE: Breakout would say, "Hey, Starski, I'm playing here tomorrow night. You want to do this party with me?" If I said I wanted to help him, he would let me help him. I would say, "Yeah," and he would put me on the flyer, and we did that. It wasn't like I really was down.

TONY TONE: It was K.K. Rockwell by himself for a while; then Busy got down for a little while, and then Busy left. Busy has always been a floater.

DJ BREAKOUT: Our first big party was Evander Child High School. That's where we really started moving up. That was the first time we played with Bambaataa—Bambaataa was on one side, and we were on the other side.

JAZZY DEE: My brother was tellin' me to try to get Evander High School. We walked into the principal's office about 7 o'clock in the mornin'—me, DJ Afrika, Bambaataa—and he had like eight or nine Zulu Nations with him. We stayed there until 11:30. The principal said there's no way in the world I'm going to give my school to you kids. We all went home.

    That night I laid out a three-piece suit. I got up at 6:30 the next morning, put on the suit, put on a tie, walked into the principal's office, and had his school in forty-five minutes. We got the school from 6 o'clock to 12 o'clock. From 6:30 to ten minutes to 12:00, people was lined up back to back. The police department came. The fire department came, saying the gym floor's goin' to fall in, that you can't let more people in. It was my first dance. I waved the contract in their faces and said this school belongs to me [laughter]. The school got fined for it, and they didn't give another party for a long time.

BUSY BEE: It was Breakout and Bambaataa, and I was rappin' with Breakout at that time. And Bambaataa needed some help with Breakout and Baron, I'm tellin' you [laughing]! So Bambaataa had to call and ask Mario. He needed an amp. Mario said, "What happened?" He said, "I'm going to battle Breakout." He said, "Oh yeah? Then you need the MacIntosh [amplifier]. You need this."

DJ BARON: Afrika Bambaataa was on one side of the gym, and we was on the other. The place was jam-packed. But Bambaataa had one up his sleeve: Disco King Mario had loaned Bam a power amp. We were going back and forth, and all of a sudden you couldn't hear us no more [laughs], 'cause Bam borrowed this amp from Mario and blew us out of the water, just drowns us out totally. We lost the battle, but we made our money, 'cause it was our party. So the next day, we went out and bought a BGW power amp, and we couldn't be touched then.

"attention..
attention..
attention..."

The Brothers Disco

presents

"A Disco Dance at Evander"

Featuring The Sounds of:

DJ

Breakout

DJ

Baron and the Breakout crew! (This is no battle.)

DJ AFRIKA

Bam Baataa

and his Zulu Nation And Lambo

Friday January 27th

Also Featuring the Voices of:
K.K. and Casanova Starsky

Fee

$3.00/xx

"Freak" To The Beat!

Directions:

Take the 2 train to gunhill and white plains rd.
walk east 4 blocks to evander

* come on out *

From 7 PM To am

a Jazzy-De production

Drawn by Mark Fisher 18.

Fashion
is on!

the mighty mighty sasquatch

TONY TONE: I started putting their system together, and they realized that I knew what I was doing, so I just became one of the members. I was their hook-up man. When we first started, it was two bass speakers, raw horns, and a guitar amp. And it was loud; it was loud and fairly clear. But Herc had a real system. Your biggest night was when Herc finally agreed to battle you. Then you knew you had to come correct, and maybe with some luck in your pocket, 'cause Herc's sound system was no joke.

So people started trying to imitate his system. Everybody had their own little section of town that they ruled, and at the top of the mountain is Kool Herc. We have to climb the mountain. So we made some money, and we went and bought equipment. We found out about crossover power amps; we tried to get more professional. We put the Mighty Sasquatch together. Now Herc got competition.

DJ BARON: You can ask anybody: We had the cleanest sound anywhere. We had unique equipment—we had garbage can speakers. Everybody knows about those garbage can speakers. They were like Electrovoice speakers going in the opposite direction. It made a lot of noise, but it was just the uniqueness of a garbage can as a speaker. It was called Mighty Mighty Sasquatch.

TONY TONE: We had 15-inch speakers made out of 55-gallon steel drums. They laid on the floor, and they had 6-inch legs that shot 'em up. The speaker faced down so that you could get a bass reflex, and it would shoot out—you could hear it for at least ten blocks. Everybody was so amazed that we got steel drum speakers! I never seen 'em anywhere else. They had a long throw. They sounded real good. If I was crazy, I would have a pair made today.

BUSY BEE: Those garbage cans poured out sound! Crazy! I couldn't believe that! They were oil cans! When they pulled out their system, and you see these garbage cans...[laughing]...you said, "Hey, whatcha gonna do with that?" You know what I'm saying? They go to put them up, and you go, "Stop playin', yo!" And then you hear the system, these sounds come out these speakers. You go crazy! They sounded perfect!

DJ BREAKOUT: We played in parks. We played in gymnasiums. We played a lot of high schools—Stevenson High School, Leamon High School. That's how you get famous. You go in a park and you play. And people keep hearing about your names and it goes around.

DJ BARON: We used to do the block parties, so people could know about you every-where you go. We used to do block parties uptown in Cedar Park—that's in my neigh-borhood, right off of Sedgwick. That's a famous park. Herc was the one who played in there first, and then everybody else played in there. If you didn't play Cedar Park, you weren't happening.

BUSY BEE: Early on, we did the streets, the backyards, the schools, and stuff like that. The janitors—that's how we got into the schools, because the janitor cleans up when school is out. So if you can find a janitor that was cool, you can say, "Hey listen, I've got twenty extra dollars for you to let us use the gym at night, and we'll clean it up after, no problem." But the janitor didn't know that 200 people were coming to the gym that night [laughing]! We would help him out at the end of the night with the soda cans and stuff, and we'd clean up. That's how we got to play the 123, Evander High School, the high schools and the junior high schools that we mostly played in during those eras. The janitors let us in.

TONY TONE: When we used to do the high school parties, we would go and talk to the dean or the councilor, and they would say, "Well, if you get one of the janitors to stay, then it's okay." So then we would talk to the janitor and say, "Listen, how much?" We would offer him money to stay, so we could have a party there. It wasn't all that much money—you know, buy them a little beer and stuff. But then again we was only charging $3 for a party. Sometimes we would have dollar parties. We was kids, and that was a lot of money we was making.

In the high schools, you would set up right under the basketball hoops, facing each other. If it's in the lunchroom, you just face each other—any battle, you face each other. The battle consists of who got the clean sound in their set, who got the strongest set, whose DJ is better, and whose MCs is better. So you got to show and prove in differ-ent areas. It would be like, "OK, you play for an hour, I play for a hour, you play for a hour, I play for a hour." Then sometimes it would get to, "Why you playing? I'm tired of waiting. I'm gonna turn on. If you can't be heard, that's just your luck. You gotta go out and buy more equipment."

birth of the funky 4

TONY TONE: In '78 it really started picking up momentum. We start trying to organize as a business, giving people separate jobs: "You on security, you help Tony with the sound system, you're flyer people ...." We tried to organize and really make it a company-type situation.

DJ BARON: As we grew, as we built the system up, then we started out with another MC; that was Keith Keith. Then Jazzy Dee discovered Sha-Rock. She was a part of the Sisters Disco. Sha used to hang around. Sha was shy, but one of the girls encouraged her to be an MC, "Oh, your voice sounds good, you ought to get on the mic." So eventually she learned to rap.

SHA-ROCK: I grew up in the Bronx. My family were music fanatics—I grew up on James Brown, Marvin Gaye, and Tammy Terrell, Diana Ross. I started getting into the hip-hop music around '76. I attended a school called the Evander Childs High School. That's when I ran into DJ Breakout. He used to come up to the school all the time, I guess just to look at the girls or whatever.

I would sneak out and go to the clubs or go to the P.A.L. where Kool Herc used to perform a lot. I even was a break-dancer back then! I wouldn't say I was a tomboy, but I had more guy friends than women friends, so I would learn from them. I would watch Breakout, I would watch other guys that would get out and break-dance. Breakout was the ultimate break-dancer. He would do things that you couldn't even believe. He would spin on his head. He would do this thing where he jumped up and down and played like he was dead, and it was awesome. Breakout was an excellent break-dancer. That's where he got his name from.

I was in the ninth grade going on the tenth grade when I began to get into the MC-ing and all of that. DJ Breakout and DJ Baron were like, "OK, come and audition to be an MC." And I did, and from there it went on.

DJ BREAKOUT: Sha-Rock said, "I can talk, too." I was, "Well, no, you can't. There never was a girl MC." And then she started practicing.... So we had the first girl MC, Sha-Rock.

SHA-ROCK: When I started, there was no female MCs. Back then, there was no one to pace yourself behind; we were all testing it. My mom was worried about me being a female out there, but once she saw that this wasn't something that would lead me into the wrong direction, she was alright with it.

BUSY BEE: When Keith Keith and Sha-Rock came along, I felt it was cool. I can go on. There was no hard feelings, because Breakout is my friend today, still.

SHA-ROCK: The whole Brothers Disco/Sisters Disco thing came about when Jazzy Dee wanted us to have security. With me being a female out there, I just had to be safe. The guys—Brothers Disco—were for the men in the group, and the Sisters Disco were for me. It was like an organization. They would make sure that everything was protected, make sure that everything went well, that nobody that was a part of the group was harmed. If it meant lifting speakers, that's something that they did—carry speakers. And they was like our crowd pleasers—they would get the crowd hyped. They knew all our rhymes, so they would be out in the crowd getting the people started.

TONY TONE: Sisters Disco, they was like Sha-Rock's security. They watched Sha-Rock's back. You carry your own girls, they cheer for you, and if it's a problem with the women, let the women take care of it, 'cause the guys don't want to get involved in women's stuff.

Brothers Disco took care of the guys. Big Tommy, Iron Mike, B. Herin, Artie Choke, everybody had their names, their killer instinct names. Artie Choke was a little guy with a big temper. Big Tommy was Big, and Lancer was in control of the security.

JAZZY DEE: The Brothers and Sisters Disco was just family. We slept together—I mean, not sexually-wise, but just hangin' out. And people followed us. There was people that started with us in the beginning and went to just about every party we gave. They followed us wherever we went. They was a part of us.

filling out the funky 4

K.K. ROCKWELL: Baron brought this guy over to Breakout's house to try out for the group. Rahiem had his own style. He could rhyme and make you laugh at the same time! I'd never heard anyone as good as Rahiem before.

RAHIEM: I met a guy named Theron Johnson. He was down with another hip-hop pioneer D.St., who had a group called the Infinity 4. Theron introduced me to James Latimore and his cousin Eugene, and together we formed Master Plan 2 and the Phase 1 Crew. Our thing was giving house parties. And when I say house parties, I mean we gave a party in the same house over and over again; we didn't travel around to different houses. That's where I honed my MC skills.

Brothers Disco—Big L, DJ Breakout, Little Rod, and Jazzy Dee—at
Edenwald Center, 1977 (Courtesy Darnell Williams)

Brothers Disco—Artie Choke and DJ Breakout at
Edenwald Center, 1977 (Courtesy Darnell Williams)

The Brothers Disco Security—Artie Choke, Black Black, Alccapone, and Iron Mike—Boston Secor Projects party, Fall 1977 (Courtesy Darnell Williams)

Members of the Sisters Disco: Cheba Girl, Lisa Lee, Busy Bee, Yvonne, J-Little, Bronx, NY, 1978 (Courtesy Darnell Williams)

Theron Johnson lived on Undercliff Avenue in the Bronx, where DJ Baron lived. He told me about a battle between the Brothers Disco and a group called the Little Brothers. This battle was on a Friday night at a place called Boston-Secor, a community center. That was the very first place that I met the Brothers Disco.

I don't remember exactly what any of Breakout's MCs sounded like at the time, because I was too taken by the atmosphere. The Little Brothers had their sound system up full blast. They had like a bunch of Peavey columns, and the party was kinda live—it was packed. They had some girls walking around with picket-style signs saying "Little Brothers," and I remember saying to myself that this was kind of like a spectacle, you know?

Breakout was listening to music in the headphones, and his sound system wasn't on yet—they were getting a sound check while the Little Brothers were doing their set. Breakout had a row of tweeters [high-frequency speakers] on strings going the width of the stage, and when he turned up the tweeters, it was deafening—high and loud, like a million bees in your eardrum at one time. Breakout is testing the highs in their sound system, and just by him turning up the tweeters, you couldn't really hear the Little Brothers' sound system. That wasn't good for them. So Breakout said on the mic, "Little Brothers, feel the highs," and the highs was kicking! Then he said, "Now here's the mid-range." He had some Electro-Voice horns on stands; they really projected the mid-range. Any record that he played, it was like the people who made that record were right there performing in your face. And when he turned up the bass, it was...you couldn't hear Little Brothers at all.

This guy Richie T, he was one of Breakout's MCs at the time, but it was unofficial—he was Sha-Rock's boyfriend. He was on the mic, and then I remember K.K. being on the mic. Then Baron got on the turntables, and I got on the mic, and wow! I didn't really have a lot of rhymes, but the rhymes that I had, I guess they were really effective at that time.

After that night, it was pretty much sealed: I was a member of the Funky 4. They officially gave me my white Brothers Disco sweatshirt with the black letters on it, and I was walking through the party with my Brothers Disco shirt on that very same night. I remember it was wild; there was angel dust in the air, marijuana...people were really gone that night. I saw this guy holding on to the walls, feeling his way through the party like he was blind, and I said to myself, "Wow, this hip-hop stuff, it's really exciting" [laughs].

Initially, when I got in the group, I was added because DJ Baron needed an MC, because the MCs that was in the group didn't say Baron's name; they said Breakout's name.

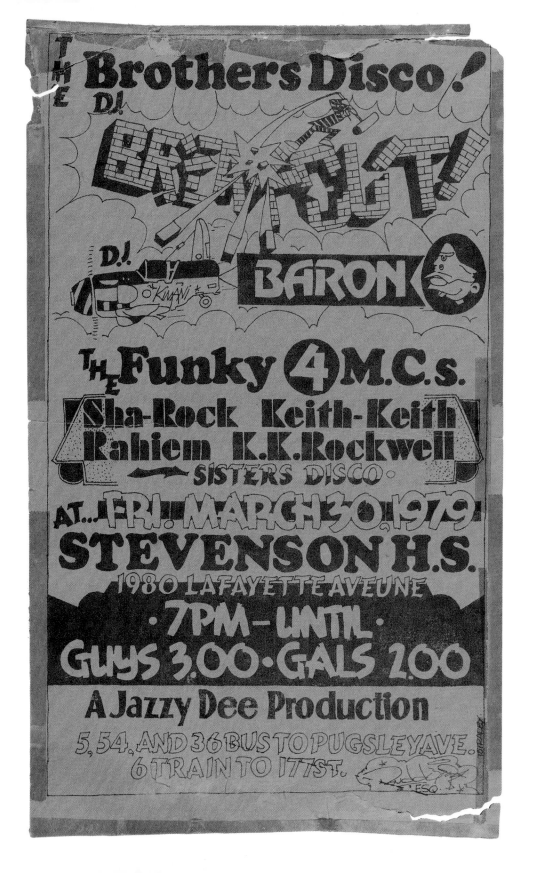

Brothers Disco at Stevenson High School, 1979.

DJ BARON: When I was playing my music, nobody would rap to my music. In the beginning, they was rapping to Breakout, so I got frustrated, I said, "I'm gonna get my own MC." So here comes my brother, and he found me an MC. He said, "I want you to hear this guy." It was Rahiem. Rahiem had the style I liked, like K.K., just keeping on and on and on, no stopping. A good flow. So I said, "When I get on, you rap." Rahiem was my own personal MC. That's when it became the Funky 4.

SHA-ROCK: We was the original Funky 4: DJ Breakout, DJ Baron, K.K., Keith-Keith, myself, and Rahiem. Jazzy Dee got us the shows, the parties, and put everything together. We started playing in parks, different clubs, and it was just exciting. I would sit home and just write or listen to the different beats, and I'd be like, "OK, I wanna rap to this song. This is gonna be my song." So I basically just lived, ate, slept, and drank hip-hop. If we weren't listening to music, the different beats that they had, we were writing. Or if we weren't writing, we were thinking of new steps to perform, different ways to go out and do what we had to do when it came to us battling another group at that time.

RAHIEM: We almost immediately started doing routines. I was a pretty good mimic; I could take other people's songs, sound like whoever, and they liked that. So I would add my little singing thing to the routine; then we'd kick rhymes.

Sha was very smooth in her delivery. She was intelligent; she put her words together cleverly. K.K. was more harsh. I guess it was because of the raspiness in his voice more than anything else. I think that K.K.'s actual skills as an MC were not as great as Sha or myself. I don't feel like this was personal opinion, because our audience pretty much gave us the feedback of who was who.

JAZZY DEE: We just kept givin' parties. We gave a lot of parties at the T-Connection. We was in head-on competition—we had the uptown, Flash had the South Bronx, and the L Brothers had like right in the middle, you understand? Whenever we played—if all three of us played the same night—the crowds separated. If we played uptown, we had uptown; if Flash played, he had downtown. If only one of us played, everybody from the Bronx came to us. If nobody played uptown, everybody went downtown to Flash.

RAHIEM: The first few months was really exciting, because not only did we do parties in the area of the Bronx that we were from, but we ventured off and did parties in places like Queens, Far Rockaway. We had battles out there in Queens and Brooklyn. We were going outside of our domain and getting a chance to see what it was like and how people received us in other places.

DJ BARON: We were huge uptown, and Grandmaster Flash was huge downtown, and it was a battle going back and forth like that. As time went by, we played at the P.A.L., T-Connection, and a lot of block parties. We used to go into other people's territories and destroy 'em. Like the L Brothers. We went into the L Brothers' territory and just ripped them apart. They used to play in a park called 63 Park off of Boston Road and 169th Street. It's not really a park; it's a schoolyard. We came in their park and destroyed it. It was just word of mouth. No flyers, just talk. "Breakout and Baron and the Funky 4 are playing 63 Park." Because of our sound, you know, "Sasquatch is in the house." The L Brothers was there. It just blew them away. It just killed them. They never seen so many people in the park in their life.

JAZZY DEE: The Funky 4 was the first ones that used mic stands in front of the DJs. All the MCs used to stand back behind the DJ; I brung out four mic stands, and I put them out in the front of the DJs. As things went on, I started feelin' their rhymes more, understandin' 'em, and that's how I started usin' the echo chamber. I just started messin' with it, and it came to me how to make it echo when they get to a certain part.

SHA-ROCK: Jazzy Dee knew everybody's rhymes, but because I was the female, he mostly put the echo on my voice. My thing was like, "OK, when I go on, what you do is you echo this part." He knew when to turn the echo chamber on to make what I'm saying double up, to mesmerize the crowd while they're listening to me.

DJ BARON: When Sha-Rock got on the mic, she blew people out of the water. Sha-Rock represents the women. She didn't have a lot of rhymes, but she was female, and her voice was unique. Sha-Rock always had an echo. That brought out Sha-Rock. When she came on, everybody came to the front. "Shaaaaa Rock ock ock." People went wild. She was the core of the group.

SHA-ROCK: I was a kind of star at a young age. I was touring at an early age, sixteen, seventeen years old, going to different places. Hearing someone say, "I know you. You're Sha-Rock. You're good on the mic," that was a good feeling, but you take it with a grain of salt because we were all just experiencing this, just being a local celebrity, within our community. You get used to the idea. As a teenager, you just dealt with it.

I started b-boying when I lived on Grand Avenue in the Bronx. I used to go up to the Bronx River projects to Bambaataa's jams. He had a lot of Zulu b-boys. Back then, the Puerto Ricans wasn't catching too much rep; it was mostly dominated by the Blacks. ● **JOJO**

B·BOYS

JOJO: People would come over to school during my lunch break to battle me, so I never ate lunch. I ate b-boys for lunch! I'd come out and battle somebody and then go back to school. One day I came out, and Cisco was out there with his box, and Abby from TBB (The Bronx Boys), he came with this dude, "Little Spinner," talking, "This kid's gonna serve you!" I came out, and I toasted him.

We did a routine—"the shoe shine"—which was bugged. I spin around, and he'd throw his leg up...boom! We'd both spin down to a baby freeze, end it to a backspin to a bridge. That was the first time they seen a backspin on that side of town. Not to mention I had a big afro! My shit was out like this [holds his hands out from his head]!. We bet $2 a man on the contest, and we burned them. Crazy Legs as a little kid was in the audience 'cause he used to be in TBB.

BOM5: The guy I learned from in the beginning was Simmons from the Zulus. Simmons was a Black Spade and all that, and they had Bo and Robbie Rob; they were all from the Bronx River, and they were all cool with me.

In '75, when the gangs was fading out, you had the Nigger Twins getting busy doing their thing. But by '76, they started slowing down, and that's when the Puerto Ricans started taking over. That's when I met Spy. Spy was the most famous b-boy ever. To me, there's no b-boy that comes close to Spy. He was "the man with a thousand moves." He had his own crew—CC Crew. They were from Burnside Avenue in the Bronx.

JOJO: Spy ran the CC Crew—which stood for the Crazy Commanders—and there was a DJ called DJ Cisco who used to come around. He was a karate instructor. He knew I was always taking niggers out right and left. He came up to me and said, "I know a Puerto Rican crew that's on your side of town that said they were number one." I was like, "Yeah?" So we went looking for the crew. We seen these kids in the hallway: "We're looking for the CC Crew!" "What are you?" "B-boy JoJo and Easy Mike."

A whole army of kids come downstairs. They lined up in two lines, and Spy and Shorty Rock came down through the troops. They came right up to Mike. I looked over at Cisco and said, "Box!" He had that shit cued up on "Apache." We started battling in the hallway courtyard, inside with a marble floor.

Shorty ran up to Spy and put his hand down, and Spy flipped up in the air and did a full twist. And because they did a flip with a twist, they claimed to have won. I said, "OK. You want to settle this? Y'all won in the air, and we won on the floor. A flip? That's not even b-boying! That's gymnastics!"

Doze, Mr. Freeze, and Frosty Freeze watch
Ken Swift in action. (© Martha Cooper)

"Spider" breaking move, 1982 (© Martha Cooper)

JOJO: Zulu Kings, they was sort of dying out when they saw Puerto Ricans doing it. "I ain't going to dirty my sneaks no more. I ain't going to chump my hands no more." We always wanted to keep the b-boy art going but keep our gear clean. The whole idea was to go out there and hit the floor and walk away with your gear fresh. Once you did that, you knew you got your stuff down. "Look at him! He ripped shit up and his gear's not dirty!"

(© Henry Chalfant)

Ken Swift at Common Ground 1981 (© Martha Cooper)

BOM5: Everyone was dying out with it. They left me. "We ain't doing this. We growing up." I was still a young kid. They said I was motivated 'cause I wanted to get into this. The Nigger Twins was still around. The P.A.L. on Webster was a real famous spot. You'd go in there and do your thing. It was all peace. It was still majority Blacks. I had a lot of Black friends, but I didn't know what these new guys were doing. They were doing their head spins, some kind of backspins. When I started dancing more, you could see everyone would stop and pay attention to the MCs. You start losing your circles. People walking away from you when the MCs rocked.

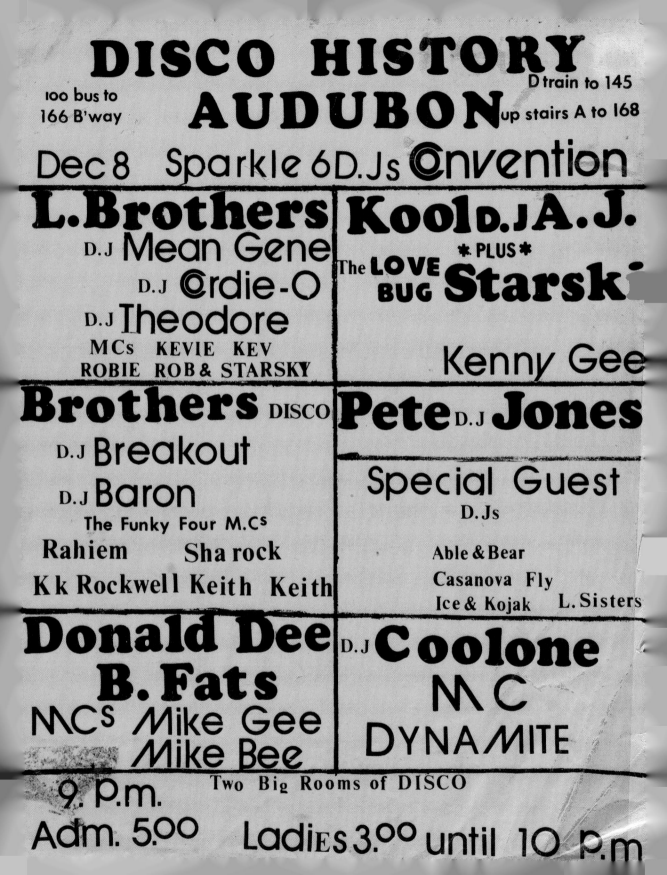

the L brothers

G.L.O.B.E.: There's a schoolyard in my neighborhood that's called 63 Park. It's on Boston Road in the Bronx. DJ Theodore used to play there—the L Brothers, they were called. Theodore was like the son of Flash. You know, Flash was out before Theodore, but Theodore came up behind, and the man is magic on the wheels.

THEODORE: Things didn't work out between Gene and Flash. They had different ideas on how they wanted to see their future, so they up and did they own thing. That's when we started the L Brothers—Mean Gene, Cordie-O, and myself. We started doin' parties ourselves and going around to different projects around the area, going to different parks, and playin' music, lettin' everybody know that we was out there.

CHARLIE CHASE: The first time I saw Flash was in Arthur Park, which was the same day I also saw Theodore for the first time. I had got word that Flash was appearing at the park, which was only four blocks from my house. Sure enough, I go there and they're setting up. He put together his sound system, and he's playing and he's got the crowd, man! He got the crowd and it's building and building, and dusk is coming. It's getting darker. All of a sudden, Theodore is setting up with his people like maybe a hundred yards away, in another section of the park. I already got a dose of what Flash can do, but Theodore was a kid I never even knew existed. He just came out of nowhere, and this kid blew me away, because he's only this big, at the time [holds his hand a few feet off the floor]—he was only this big and he was DJ-ing. And what amazed me about Theodore was that he picks up the needles without having to spin back, and catches the beat, time after time after time after time. Throw a record on, pick up the needle, drop it. Continuously! And he's rocking this thing, he's just ripping this party up. And Flash's crowd left—they went over to check out Theodore. Actually, what helped scare off Flash's crowd was one of the speakers fell off, and people thought it was a fight or a shootout or something; they started running. That was the first time I saw Theodore, and he stayed there until about two, three in the morning.

THEODORE: We was doing a block party one day. Back then all the DJs had to do block parties to let everyone know that they were around, so that when the wintertime comes and it gets real cold and you start handing out flyers for your parties, people would say, "Okay, these guys did block parties, and the music was nice, I had a good time. Let's go check them out." We used to do a lot of parties in the centers. This one particular day, this guy walked up to us and said, "Can I get on the mic?" I was like, "Sure, get on the mic." So he got on the mic, and he started rappin', and the crowd really liked him. His name was MC Kevie Kev. He sounded good. After the party we said, "Why don't you come to the house and you can be our MC." After awhile, we found out that his brother Rob was writing the rhymes. So we put both of them on together.

KEVIE KEV: Everybody was liking me, feeling me. I was doing, "Yes yes y'all. And you don't stop. To the beat y'all and you don't stop, like hot butter on the popcorn." I was the first Kevin to turn Kevie Kev, and I had a brother called Robbie Rob. The only reason we doubled our name is 'cause of Melle Mel with Grandmaster Flash and the 3 MCs.

I was an original L Brother. When I touched the microphone, it was all over. It was over. I was the first rapper to get in the group. We played in parties, like in somebody's house. We had Mean Gene; he played a certain kind of flavor on the mix, old-school joints that made you do "The Hustle." Then we had Cordie-O, a middle brother that would bring the tempo up with "Ain't No Half-Steppin'," and that was mad gangster back then. But then we had the little brother, who created scratchin'.

THEODORE: The first time I ever played was in Davidson projects, where Starski lived at—158 School Community Center. We used to play in there 'cause we knew everybody down there. Busy Bee was always playing with Disco King Mario.

BUSY BEE: I was approached by Mean Gene. He said, "I went over across town, I saw you man, you rockin'. But you don't belong over there. Me and my brothers, we're the L Brothers, and Kev and Rob, they brothers. We put this whole group together. You belong over here."

KEVIE KEV: I knew him as David Parker; he went to school with me. I remember my brother telling me, "Yo Kev, I know this cat he wants to be in our group. What do you think?" I was like, "Naw, I don't like him that much 'cause he don't stay in one group." Rob was like, "Let's give him a chance. We'll tell him not to run around, to stay on our team." That was when sheepskin jackets came out. My mother bought me and my brother sheepskins, and Busy couldn't get no sheepskins until his mother asked my mother how much they cost and would we take care of him and can he get in our group and then we won't let nobody rob him. So he started rapping with us.

120

BUSY BEE: Mean Gene and Theodore and Cordie-O, they was the original L Brothers, because their last name was Livingston. But with Kevie Kev and Rob being brothers, the whole group was all brothers. Everybody's got brothers but me. I was the misfit. I wasn't down with nobody. But they respected me, and they all wanted me to join because "I was the one with the golden voice, the people's choice." They said by me bein' down, I could be a brother to them, so we were a family. So that's why they called us the L Brothers—the "L" was for Love.

Morris High School was my debut. They told me, "Come on, we going to play in the park." I said okay, I went by, I seen 'em settin' up. I waited, let the people start coming around. Kevie Kev and them was fixin' the microphones. So I walked up and they were like, "Hey, Starski!"—because I was Starski then, I wasn't Busy Bee—"You're going to be down with us, man. It's going to be on." So right then I felt a little comfortable. As the night came, we started rockin' beats, and when they gave me the mic, I did my regular thing, and my little regular rhymes, the little shout-outs, and they was impressed.

(Busy Bee sings a rhyme that he wrote for the L Brothers, to the melody of the popular jump rope song "Miss Lucy had a steamboat, the steamboat had a bell ...")

> DJ Cordie-O is incredible, Mean Gene is on the scene,
>
> And Theodore cuts twice as nice, and that's why that boy's so mean.
>
> Kevie Kev has all the ladies, pretty sure you will agree,
>
> He has the golden voice and the people's choice and so does the Busy Bee.
>
> Robbie Rob is slick and bad and cool, you have to know this too,
>
> That Trevor is our manager and we are the L Bros Crew!

There was a rotation of DJs. If Gene wanted to do a spin, Gene can spin. If Theodore wanted to spin, Theodore can spin. Then there was certain records that Theodore could spin better than his brothers. Cordie-O was the electronics man. If anything broke down and needed fixing, that was him. Mean Gene was the general boss, and he could hook up the system. Mean Gene knew what to buy; Theodore knew what to play. So we broke it down technology-wise for all three.

We had females in the group, too—"the L Sisters" with sweatshirts. Their moms would always be out looking for them. Gene had a house with twelve rooms; it was like a hotel. We made our own shirts, ironed on the letters ourself.

THEODORE: There was so much that we needed to learn—like when a needle broke or we needed a record, we would never have the money to buy a new needle or the record. When you make some money, it's wise to reinvest it to build up your system. My average take was $80 from doing a club like the Sparkle. I would take $20 and go buy two copies of that record we needed.

WHIPPER WHIP: The L Brothers was incredible. Mean Gene, Cordie-O, Theodore, and on the mic was Kevie Kev, Busy Bee, and Master Rob. It was the same formula as with Flash, 'cause Busy was the type of guy to rock the party, to rock the crowd. Master Rob was a great rhymer; he had a nice tone in his voice, and he was real smooth. And Kevie Kev rocked the echo, like Creole. They really tore up the Bronx; the L Brothers' parties were big parties. Just like Flash's parties were huge, the L Brother parties were real huge.

BUSY BEE: We was like the Beatles. It was on. I had the golden voice. Kev had all the girls. Rob was slick. We was just some pretty rappers. We wore up-to-date fashions; we looked real good to the ladies. We were celebrities. Wherever we went, they knew who we was.

> L Brothers with the 3 MCs
> that'll rock you to your knees
> Kevie Kev, Robie Rob, Busy Bee Starski.

We was in high school at that time. I was the only guy out of the L Brothers who went to Clinton. Rob went to Evander, I think. Kevie Kev went to Gompers. Kevie Kev and I were on the basketball team. We was popular within our sports. We had good grades; we wasn't dropouts.

We'd play other people's territories all over the Bronx. L Bros spread like a disease! "St. Mary's, isn't that AJ's park?" We'd arrive with station wagons, tie into a lamppost. Gene would show up and ask someone, "We'll be here playing a little music. We can give you $30, if we can plug into your house for three hours." Run the extension cord out their window, we on! They got a little chicken to sell, a little beer. They be in business until about 11 p.m.

The police didn't really know about hip-hop at that time. They knew what time to tell us to stop, they knew that much, but as far as bothering us or harassing us, they didn't do it. Come about 10 o'clock, or close to 11, they would come around. "You want us to turn it off now?" "Yeah." Or, "No, turn it down just a little bit. We'll give you another hour or two." You know? That's how we did it. We cooperated with them. It wasn't like, "Cut that off!" You know what I'm saying? And when you left the party, you went home. You went to school the next day and you heard, "Yo, the L Brothers' party! Everybody was dancin', it was freakin', it was partyin'!"

There was the battle with Grandmaster Flash versus the L Bros at a high school gym. They closed off the girls' side and boys' side. When those doors closed off, the battle begins. Flash went and rented equipment. He comes with a U-Haul truck. [This was cheating; you were supposed to use your own sound system.] Bam didn't like that. He sent someone for his special crate of crazy beats records. He was there, leaning over Theodore. "See that, right there? Play that marked spot right there!" The bat-

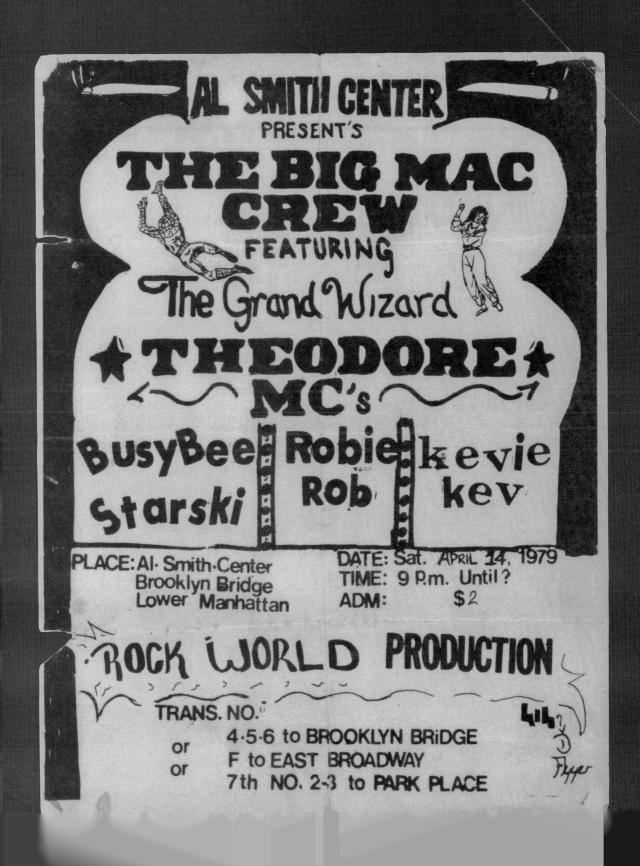

Caz and Wiz versus Bambaataa, at the Webster P.A.L., 1978. Flyer designed by Grandmaster Caz

tle was in Bam's area, and everybody knew Bam's music. When he heard Bam was helping Theodore, Flash just gave up. He came over and shook Theodore's hand and said, "Yo! This here's my son, Grand Wizard Theodore!"

grandmaster caz
& disco wiz

GRANDMASTER CAZ: DJ Casanova Fly and my partner, the Magnificent Disco Wiz. That was the bill—1976—that was the bill.

DJ DISCO WIZ: Yeah. We were friends first. We were b-boys; we used to go to house parties and break-dance and get our clothes dirty basically [laughter].

GRANDMASTER CAZ: I always had a talent for writing—poetry and stuff like that—it was something that I just was good at. It was a gift. It's not anything that I thought would come into play later on, but when hip-hop came along, that just opened up a whole new world of expression for everything. Every talent I had I could apply to hip-hop. The graffiti I had been doin' since I was a kid—I started building it and it got to a point where I thought I got as good as I could get at that. Then I moved on to the next thing: I was a b-boy with the Casanova Crew [not Flash's security crew]. We used to dance together, break against other b-boy crews and stuff, and then I just evolved with the music into the DJ-ing aspect of it.

I had been dabbling. I call it dabbling because I don't consider you a real DJ until you have equipment and you do parties. Prior to that, I had a turntable, and he [Wiz] had a turntable; he would bring his over, and they were both attached to receivers. We didn't even have mixers yet. We would just turn one up and turn one down, and that's how we would blend the records back and forth. But after I saw Kool Herc DJ-ing at the Hevalo in 1974, I saw enough to convince my mom. I said, "Look, Ma, I got some little money in the bank. I wanna be a DJ." And she just seen the conviction [laughs], and she said, "Hey, go ahead." So I bought a DJ set. This was like my starter kit. I bought two turntables, a mixer, an amp, and two speakers. Cost me like 700-some dollars at the time, the whole thing, wires and plugs and all.

I started collecting records. There wasn't much to it. There wasn't any trickery on the turntables yet. Guys were still just playing records. Herc used to just play records at random. When the record would go off or the beat would get ready to go, he'd just slap another one on, not particularly on time.

WIZ: I was basically a graffiti artist, an ex-gang member. I crossed over and got into the b-boy scene with Caz. I used to box at the P.A.L.—I was trying to train to be a boxer.

CAZ: Roberto Duran, yeah, no doubt—he was trainin' in the streets, knockin' niggas out. If I hadn't brought him into the DJ life, it would have been another hoodlum out there...[laughter]. We just was friends. We was like brothers. We used to dress alike, you know what I mean? I mean, we both had our own style of dress, but we used to dress. I mean, we was fly every day, you know?.

At the time, before the microphone came into play as a instrument, you didn't have an MC or somebody to talk for you. It was just me and him, two DJs, and if I'm on the turntables, he would talk. The microphone was only used for announcements—to let people know where the next party was, maybe to shout somebody out in the crowd, or big me up while I'm on the turntable, like "Yeah, my man Casanova Fly is on the wheels of steel. Check him out, check him out." And I would do the same for him when he was up: "My man, the Magnificent Disco Wiz on the turntables. Check him out." Like that.

WIZ: It was funny in the beginnin' because I'm the first Latino ever to make a presence in hip-hop. Before then, Latinos was basically b-boying and graffiti artists. So when we first started as a DJ duo, people were under the impression that Disco Wiz was a brother. When they used to come to the jams and they used to see me on the ones and twos, they used to ask Caz, "Who's that Puerto Rican guy, man [laughter]?

TOGETHER: That's Disco Wiz!

CAZ: His name would precede him—people would come to see him after hearing about him, because he used to cut fast. He was really aggressive on the cut, and he had a little cult following, you know what I'm saying? So people would come to see Disco Wiz, and they'd see him up there on the turntables and be like "Yo?"

WIZ: See, Caz was always an entertainer. He's always been the entertainer. He's probably one of the first DJs to incorporate a lot of special effects in mixing; he used to incorporate effects like Richard Pryor and Raider X during the cuts and get the crowd into it.

I mainly catered to the b-boys. I never really liked to play just straight-out dance records; I was more like a battle-style DJ. My thing was always the beats. I was a beat junkie. I used to just cut the beats back and forth, come with a whole arsenal of just beats. The b-boys used to be fidgeting on the sidelines, sayin', "Wiz, when you gettin' on? Wiz, when you gettin' on?"

CAZ: I used to play music for like an older audience, because I'm just a student of the music, period. And I would play offbeat things that you wouldn't expect to hear. Like, if I find a record with my name in it or somethin', I don't care who made it or what kinda record it is; I'm gonna play it. I found a record by Barrabas called "Casanova," and he used to go "Casanova, Casanova, call me Casanova," you know, so I would use that.

WIZ: He was more of a complete DJ than I was. My thing was just goin' and turnin' the crowd into a frenzy. I limited myself to just break-beats, which was only a few seconds long so I had to cut fast to keep up that frenzy. Caz DJ-ed more like the disco, the hustle, more of a slow melody. He used to throw some Elvis in there. Everything. Because you're talkin' about a long party—eight, maybe ten hours.

CAZ: Yeah. I would play whatever I felt like playin'. I didn't play what you wanted me to play because I'm goin' to play that, my man, goin' to play that in a minute. In between, I'm gonna open your eyes to some stuff, you know what I mean? I'm gonna play some joints that you might not ordinarily listen to. Bambaataa was great like that. He would take music from any kind of different culture or any different kinda music, and if it had a beat in it, he would play it, you know?

But we had what it took. We prepared better. Ain't nobody runnin' over us; we're a notch above. The only thing that kept us in check, so to speak, was that we didn't have the system like a Kool Herc had or a Breakout had or Flash had. We couldn't hang on the same level, equipment-wise. But as far as records, as far as bein' able to cut, and as far as having a following, we had it. We had it all.

At this club called the Blue Lagoon, 184th Street a block from the P.A.L., me and Disco Wiz was together playing one night, and he was on the mic urging me on, "Faster, faster!" I was just a blur. "Oh shit! Go go!" The crowd was getting hyped. "Grand Master! Grand Master!" Flash was the fastest on two turntables. "You reached Flash's level. You cutting as fast or faster than him!" So I kept that title 'cause I felt it was given to me. I felt like I reached the level. I earned it.

RAY CHANDLER: I heard of him because they had a club on Jerome Avenue that used to be run by Art Armstrong, and Casanova Fly used to go there and do shows. He was a great rapper. People on the street was talking about him—he was getting a lot of juice on the street. So eventually he decided to call himself Grandmaster Caz. Flash would compare himself to the chess masters: "How can you have all these Grandmasters coming up trying to get with my title?"

DJ DISCO WIZ: Around 1977...we used to record all our battles. Every party we had we always had a boom box on the side, and we used to record what we did and who we did it to. And those things used to sell—we used to sell them in high school. So one time this guy came up to us, this tech-head in the lunchroom, and said, "You know what? You can take that downtown to this recording place and put that on wax." We looked at each other like this guy was from another planet. We said, "Word?" He said, "Yeah." So we went and checked it out. We did the homework; we confirmed it. Then we went to Caz's house, and we spent about three days cutting back and forth, making tapes, and then narrowing it down to one tape.

GRANDMASTER CAZ: We made a pause tape. Now they got samplers, you know, different machines that can do these things automatically. But we did it manually. We gathered all the break-beats and the special effects records, sound bites and stuff, and we just paused it together. Just played a piece of a record—a fraction of a second—stop it, go back, let it play again. Boom. Maybe five or six times. I had a record that used to go, "Alright now, I want all you freaks to line up against the wall." Then I would play a record scratchin' the break part where it goes "Wheeep," paused it like six times and then let it play. So the plate would go, "Alright now, I want all you freaks to line up against the wall."

TOGETHER: *"Wheeep, Wheeep, Wheeep, Wheeep, Wheeep."*

CAZ: When we were done it was like twenty-somethin' minutes.

WIZ: First of all, I gotta tell you, it was the ugliest lookin' thing you'd ever wanna see. It looked like a old 78. It was a metal plate. It was ten inches, and it only had wax on one side. The other side was metal.

(Those familiar with such things will recognize the "plate" as an acetate—the shellac and metal disc used primarily as a demo or test pressing prior to the late 1960s, when vinyl test pressings became the norm.)

CAZ: I taped a piece of cardboard to the other side [laughs]. But that plate made us famous. DJs used to invite us to their parties and say, "Yo, bring the plate!"

WIZ: Yeah. It was a secret weapon.

CAZ: 'Cause we had a secret—we had something that nobody had and everybody wanted.

WIZ: We combined our routine with our plate. When it was time for our set...you have your two lights over your turntables, and you have me and him behind the set. We would put the plate on, turn off the lights, walk away from the set, leave the whole thing unmanned, and the plate would just play. We would stand over on the side with our arms crossed, in the b-boy stance, and the plate would play for itself.

CAZ: [Imitates turntable scratches] *Screech, screech, screech, screech, screech.*

WIZ: And the opposing DJs would lose their minds when we did that [laughs]. It was like a KO punch.

CAZ: It's like, "Yeah, we don't even gotta stand here and cut. I mean...this is us, you know?" It was great.

* * *

DJ DISCO WIZ: One time in 1977, in the summer, we decided to bring our system out to the park on 183rd Street and Valentine to battle. And we had a pretty big crowd.

GRANDMASTER CAZ: It was the same park where we filmed the basketball scene in Wild Style, years later.

WIZ: We were out there. That was in July of '77. We were in the middle of a frenzied battle. In those days, we used to plug our stuff into a lamppost, and many a time we blew the lampposts out. This particular day, we were in the middle of a battle, and it started getting dark. Caz was on the ones and twos, and we had our stuff roped off like always.

CAZ: While he did his thing, I'm just waitin'. He turns off, it's my turn. I throw on one record over here, boom, the crowd is goin' nuts, 'cause they know I'm gonna get into my thing. I take the other record. I know this is gonna kill 'em. So, boom. Time comes, boom! It was the back of "Indiscreet," by DC la Rue. I bring in the record. "Love, loove, looooovve ..." It just slows to a stop.

WIZ: The light blew out.

CAZ: Went off. The whole set went off.

WIZ: Two lights blew out.

CAZ: And then the streetlights started goin' out one at a time, all the way up the block, like "poof, poof, poof, poof, poof." We looked at each other. I go, "Oh shit," 'cause we're plugged into one of the streetlights, and I thought we blew out the whole street! The whole neighborhood went dark.

WIZ: And you know what it was? It was the blackout of '77.

CAZ: We were in the park with our equipment. The crowd realized it at the same time. Gates started comin' down on the bodegas, the stores started closin' up, but they couldn't close fast enough. Those stores knew what was coming. They knew they getting ready to loot. People are like, "What's happening?" Then one person screams, "Blackout! Hit the stores!" By now the whole city is dark. People are charging right for us. My man Disco Wiz, he's got a 45 pistol, and we jump up on the speakers and yell, "Don't run this way. Run the other way!" We thought they might start grabbing our stuff.

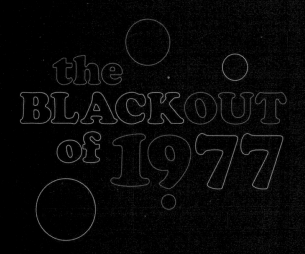

the BLACKOUT of 1977

"It was insane. It was something I'll never forget for as long as I live. You can imagine having a whole system out there, during the blackout, in a crowd." ● **DISCO WIZ**

CAZ: It was panic everywhere in the streets. We're trying to get our stuff home safe. This was a block off of one of the main shoppin' areas in the Bronx, okay? Then I see this store called the Sound Room that was one of the first audio stores. There was like eighteen people on the metal gate. Boom. They pull down the gate and kick in the glass. People are crawling in there and running out with speakers and turntables. I was like, "Yo, people breakin' in there anyway—might as well run in and see about getting us a new mixer and turntables!" People were breaking into check-cashing places and getting food stamps. There were whole families walking down the block all carrying living room sets and bedroom sets. The next day, the streets was filthy, stuff strewn all over. Every store was broken into. It was crazy. People were selling shit left and right. You'd see people with bikes and all kinds of shit they never had. Someone said, "God made Christmas for Black people." Word.

TONY TONE: The blackout? I was sitting in front of the building I lived in. My mother wouldn't let me leave the block. Everybody was looting. A lot of people was stealing mopeds, 'cause they had just came out and that's what everybody wanted. At that time, if I knew where Sam Ash [a popular music store] was, that's where I would've been trying to get to.

WHIPPER WHIP: I was living on 149th and Riverside at my grandmother's house, and as I was on the phone with a little honey, the lights went off. I said, "Man, my lights are goin' out." She said, "My lights went out, too!" She's in the Bronx, and I'm in Manhattan. I'm like, "Hey! What's goin' on?!"

I didn't go out, I didn't loot, I didn't do any of that stuff. I stayed home with grandma; we went downstairs and stayed in the neighborhood. But the next day, it was like all of New York was on sale [laughs]!

BUSY BEE: The blackout? I was where I was supposed to be [laughing]. But I didn't know the lights was going to stay out! I was getting ready to get me some love! And the lights went out right on time to where she said, "Turn them on." "Sorry, but there's nothin' happening, babe, no lights to be turned on! So we have to get down and do it, or that's that!" I was at the perfect place at the right time. The next day I was mad, because I found out I could have got two new pairs of sneakers, two TVs—because the stores was getting looted, and all the places was getting robbed. I had to be layin' down with a broad [laughing]!

WIZ: It's funny, 'cause I have a theory. You know what? Before that blackout, you had about maybe five legitimate crews of DJs. After the blackout, you had a DJ on every block…That blackout made a big spark in the hip-hop revolution.

"Everybody was a DJ. Everybody stole turntables and stuff. Every electronic store imaginable got hit for stuff. Every record store. Everything. That sprung a whole new set of DJs."

● **GRANDMASTER CAZ**

4 AND YOU DONT STOP:

the scene matures

As the '70s draw to a close, what started as a diversion, an excuse to party, is fast becoming a business. Grandmaster Flash provides a good example of the change—he's gone from spinning records in the park with an open mic for neighborhood MCs to an established crew with multiple MCs, security and technical backup, and an established indoor home club with a street promotion team and loyal fan base. A front line of multiple MCs, each with a specific role, becomes the norm, and having grown up on the Jackson 5 and Gladys Knight & the Pips, the MCs begin to develop stage routines to go with their intricate word-play. Slowly but surely, the scene is growing beyond the boundaries of the Bronx. Harlem has been part of the action for a while, but as news of what's happening in the Bronx spreads, kids from other boroughs either make the journey to check out the scene or buy the tapes that are beginning to find wider circulation. At the same time, the major crews, with their increasing promotional savvy, are beginning to perform throughout the tri-state area.

As the scene and the sound change, the Zulu Nation remains strong, but Kool Herc's influence begins to wane; the new styles pass him by, and a violent encounter puts him out of action—he is stabbed at a party and fades from the scene for a while. While some of the pioneers move to the background, newcomers move up to challenge the authority of the established crews, and there is a sense that something big is about to happen.

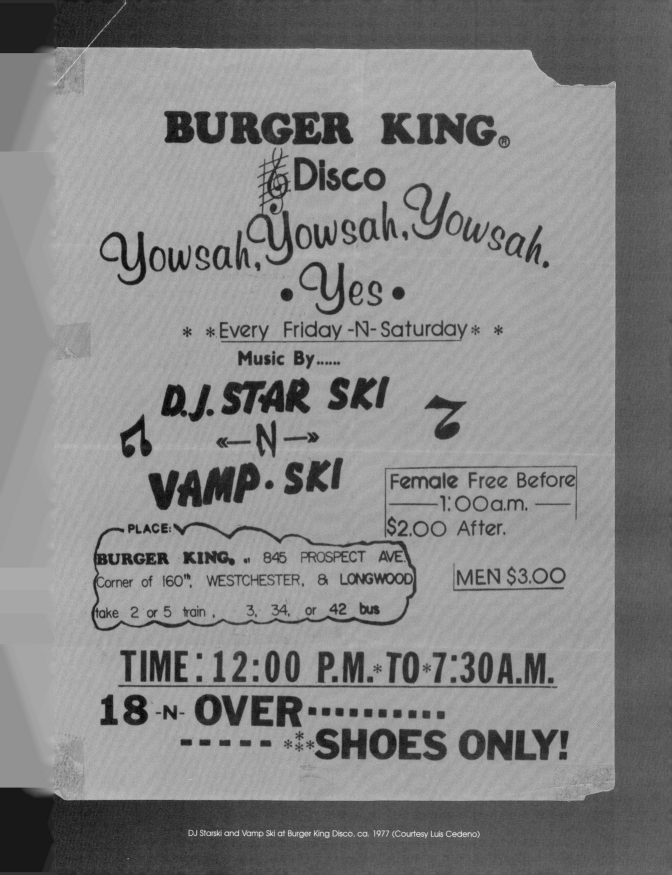

DJ Starski and Vamp Ski at Burger King Disco, ca. 1977 (Courtesy Luis Cedeno)

mcs in the spotlight: changes in the established crews

kool dj aj & love bug starski

KOOL DJ AJ: I first got into the rap game as a promoter in 1978; I tried to do parties with a couple of friends from round my way in the South Bronx. I was like nineteen years old. We started off with Pete DJ Jones. I used to get Social Security checks, and I would use that to promote the parties that I did with Pete. His assistant was Love Bug Starski. Love Bug was like a guy who was really friendly, and as it went along, Love Bug and me got real close, and he started coming round my way in the South Bronx and hanging out with me. He talked me into buying some turntables. He was like, "You should buy some turntables 'cause you can make a lot of money. I'm gonna teach you how to DJ, and I'm gonna be your rapper." He pushed me, kept coming around, coming around, coming around, until he convinced me.

LOVE BUG STARSKI: I put AJ on the map. He wanted to be a DJ. He used to hire me and Pete DJ Jones to play the Morehouse Center. AJ was very determined; he wanted to be a DJ. We sat up for nights—yeah, I showed him how to do the shit.

KOOL DJ AJ: We started off coming to the parks. Love Bug had a little name, because everybody know he was Pete DJ Jones's protégé, so just Love Bug himself drew a crowd. Everybody would say, "Love Bug is in the house." It wasn't about DJ AJ because I was a student—he already had a following. So people would come and see Love Bug, and then as I got greater, by his showing me how to play, then you would hear, "AJ's in more houses. AJ and Love Bug." I was DJ AJ, because...my name is Aaron, and the girl I was dating back then, who I had my baby with, her name was Janine. So, Love Bug said, "We should say, A., J."

Love Bug, he was a great guy. He might be one of the first to have that crowd response. "Look in the sky, look in the tree, who do you see? Star-ski!" And that "Bob didda bob de danga dang diggy diggy diggy, diggy diggy with the bang bang boogie." People used to love that. And he'd make the people shout, "Chant my name. Somebody say AAAAAA-JAAAAAY."

DJ AJ at the Ecstasy Garage, 1980 (© Charlie Ahearn)

LOVE BUG STARSKI: You know the way some people go to church to catch the Holy Ghost? That's how I caught the Holy Ghost—at a party. That was my spiritual thing. When I was about fifteen, between fifteen and seventeen, and I used to stay out way beyond my hours and accepted that ass whipping from my mother, for real. She thought I was on drugs at one time, and all I was doin' was house parties and playing in the parks.

BUSY BEE: Love Bug Starski was the only person I ever heard that played in a Burger King. Imagine that: Coming to a disco in Burger King! The lights is out, and you're playing in Burger King, you know? That's crazy! And he used to pack the house like that, play the music, and it was different, I mean...a party in the Burger King, where you buy your burgers and fries at? That's amazing! And he did it.

KOOL DJ AJ: I dropped out of high school when I was DJ-ing. Everybody knew who I was. In that type of environment there was a lot of haters, and it got real depressing because everybody was coming at me from all type of angles. 'Cause I was the man to see right then if you wanted to try to get into the hip-hop business.

BUSY BEE: Kool DJ AJ was one of the highest paid DJs in New York, him and Grandmaster Flash. Those two was on, playin' together; they went everywhere together 'cause AJ was down with the Black Door Production plus he did shows of his own. AJ had Love Bug Starski and a guy named Kenny Gee as a rapper. And Love Bug was like the DJ, too; sometimes Love Bug would be spinnin' and rappin' at the same time. I was still an L Brother then. But AJ told me that Kenny Gee wasn't always around. "Kenny Gee can't do what you do, Busy Bee. Come on and be with me. You'll be the highest-paid MC in the rap game." And back then, you know, $200? On a Friday? For just talkin' shit? [laughing] You know? And I started getting that, a couple of times. He was right! Even with the L Brothers, with Mario, with Bambaataa, I never went home with $100.

AJ said, "First of all, I do my own parties. I promote my own parties. So when I get the money, it's my money!" And when I found out about that, I stepped up my game! Oh yeah! So me and AJ became partners. We had shirts like we've got right now. We had a following.

flash & the furious

RAHIEM: I would say that the MCs really didn't play the pivotal role in hip-hop until the three MCs that were down with Flash became the Furious 4. That's when it was more of an entertainment thing; it became a spectacle, something to look at as well as something to hear. Prior to that, the atmosphere at the parties was basically a party atmosphere, very much about the DJs.

GRANDMASTER FLASH: Mel got his best friend interested, Scorpio, who was then known as Mr. Ness. Mr. Ness was more like a fly guy. How can I say it? Women used to be just going nuts over him. He was the cool, silky smooth, fly type of guy. Incorporatin' him into the style made more of an impact visually.

KID CREOLE: Shows would normally start like about 10 o'clock, something like that. If it was a high school, that meant that the crowd was built in, because all the high school students would wanna be at the dance at the high school that they attended.

GRANDMASTER FLASH: When I think about it now, it was almost like we had an account with the schools. There were certain schools that whenever they had a function, they would just call us. If it was the last day of school or the end-of-the-year school events, they would hire us. Whether it would be a boat ride or a dance in their gymnasium...whatever the case may be.

KID CREOLE: It was an exciting time. We used to party until like 4:00, 5:00, 6:00 in the morning. We used to have like different levels of shows that we would do. Flash would always play one certain record right before the party started, so once you heard that record, you knew that it was on. From, say, 10 o'clock to about maybe 11:30, we'd get on the mic and just kick stuff around, little old phrases..."On down to the last stop,"..."On to the break of dawn," stuff like that. Then like around 12 o'clock, we would do the first throwdown. We would call it Phase 2. We would get on there and do a routine and let people know, "Yo, it's on right now!"

Then about maybe like 1 o'clock, 1:30, 2 o'clock, Flash would put on some slow stuff to just cool everybody out, to let them know, "Hey, look...we gettin' ready to gear up to something else, but right now we want y'all to get y'all's energy together, go get a drink, whatever." And then around 3 o'clock or 3:30, we would do the final throwdown, and that's when we come with something that we rehearsed. Whatever we was going to do that night, it was going to be something raw. Not no haphazard deal, we're going to try to rock the crowd, rehearsed. That kind of set us apart from everybody else at that time, because we took what we were doing really serious.

Flash and the Furious 4 rock the Renaissance Ballroom, 1979 (Courtesy Luis Cedeno)

WE'VE COME TOGETHER...
RIGHT NOW..
WITH AT THE **P.A.L**
183 ST & WEBSTER AVE

THE **Brothers Disco**

D.J. Breakout D.J. Baron

THE FUNKY 4 M.C.S

Sha·Roch Keith·Keith
Rahiem K.K. Rockwell

THE GRANDMASTER FLASH

AND THE RETURN OF THE ....

Furious 4 M.C.s

·Mele·Mel Kid Creole
Keith·Keith Mr. Ness·
SPECIAL PEOPLE OF THE NITE ....

FRI. MAY 11, 1979
9PM–UNTIL
HE $4.00 SHE $3.00 ..
A JAZZY DEE PRODUCTION...

Sisters Disco

TO MICHELE

Brothers Disco versus Flash and the Furious 4: The battle for Rahiem

GRANDMASTER FLASH: The MCs would come up with these, like, Temptations dance steps, and I would come up with some cuckoo way to mix the records, whether it be with my elbows or my mouth or behind my back, or whatever the case may be. And then we had introduced to the group this manually operated drum machine that was made in England by the VOX Company. The drum machine I used to call a beat box. Once all these elements was in place, we were a real force to reckon with, for sure. There were quite a few great groups out there, but we were a force to reckon with.

furious 4 vs. funky 4: the P.A.L. battle

K.K. ROCKWELL: One time Melle Mel and his crew came to one of our block parties. I'd get butterflies whenever Melle Mel came around 'cause I admired him from going to Flash's parties. But I knew Rahiem was going to get to them. He was our secret weapon.

RAHIEM: We were number two in the Bronx. K.K. had been gassing me up for like a month before we even agreed to do the battle with them, saying that I was better than Melle Mel. I remember listening to Melle Mel, saying to myself, "I'm good, but I'm not that good." You know? Then one day, after weeks of rehearsing routines and writing new rhymes, K.K. comes up to me again: "Yo man, I'm telling you, you could take Melle Mel." And it sounded real good that day, I'm like, "Yeah, I could take Melle Mel."

K.K. ROCKWELL: Flash heard how popular we was getting and thought maybe we should battle. Ray Chandler was against it because he thought we didn't draw. So Flash went behind his back and put the battle on a flyer. Flash liked our sound system—the Mighty Mighty Sasquatch. It was bad. We practiced everyday for a week before the show.

RAHIEM: I was feeling myself; I was looking forward to the battle. We had done all of this rehearsing, practicing singing routines while dancing and doing tricks with the mic stands and all that. I thought that we had a legitimate shot to take these guys. To me, at that time, Mel and Flash and Cowboy carried the group. Cowboy because of the way that he incited the crowd, Mel because of his lyrical ability, and Flash because he was something to see.

They were the more popular group—they had a following pretty much throughout the tri-state area that time, whereas our following was isolated to mostly the North Bronx...and Far Rockaway [laughs]. And nobody goes out there. Still I felt like we could really take them.

TONY TONE: We in the P.A.L. setting up. They battling us on our system. The Casanova Crew was in there. I'm coming out of the gym, and one of the Casanovas was trying to talk to Breakout's girl, and she says something to him, and he hauls off and slaps the shit out of her. God bless the dead. When he slapped her, I grabbed her and said, "Go upstairs." When she went upstairs, she told Breakout. He was like, "That's good for you. I told you not to come anyway." I'm saying, "Breakout. He just slapped your girl." He was like, "Fuck it. We just going to have to take that slap." 'Cause the tension was thick! We just trying to make it through the night 'cause we know at any point something could happen with the Casanovas. I got my crew, the Soundview Crew, and they pull me to the side, and they say, "Yo, we got your back." They had snuck two 45s in.

RAHIEM: The Furious 4 went on stage first. We were surprised by that: "Yo, we were supposed to go on first. They pulled something on us." So we just went out in the audience and watched them. Well, they pulled out all of the stops; they threw it all at us. They sung. They danced. Flash cut and danced and did some new tricks that we had never seen before; then he whipped out the beat-box, and they sang these songs. The future for that battle seemed kind of bleak. If you saw them first, you'd be like, "The battle's over." And I think that other members of my group had the same feeling at the time. They were intimidated by the way that the Furious 4 hit the stage.

TONY TONE: So now we on the stage, and Jazzy Dee, Breakout's brother, is over talking to Ray Chandler and the Casanova Crew. When I turn around, I see him fighting somebody so I run across the stage and I reach down and grab him under the arm and pull him up on the stage. All of a sudden a black bag comes out of nowhere. It was full of guns, and I'm like, "Ray. Come on Ray. What are we gonna do here?" And that's when the Funky 4 was supposed to go on. The fear was so great that they couldn't do nothing. They were stuttering.

RAHIEM: Everyone was leaning against the back of the stage. I was amped, like, "Yo, let's blaze this! We gonna do this, we gonna take these guys." And I saw like this look in K.K.'s eyes, he had this look of doubt, not the same fire that he came with in telling me that I could take Melle Mel. Instead of "Eye of the Tiger," it was like "Eye of the Neckbone." He didn't say verbally that he quit, but his body language suggested that. And that infuriated me. I was there to win. As soon as they saw the Furious 4 doing their thing, the routines that we practiced were thrown out the window; we totally abandoned our game plan. I stood on the same stage with them, but I stood in the back, and let them do whatever they were going to do.

K.K. ROCKWELL: Right before we was supposed to go on, Rahiem said there was something wrong with his voice and that we couldn't do the routines we practiced together. I knew we was going to tear them up with our fresh stuff, but Rahiem didn't really perform, and we just did our regular rhymes.

KID CREOLE: I think we did three sets apiece. We came on, we changed clothes on them, we made up new routines. We did a chair routine off of "Get Up, Get Into It," where we sat down on chairs, crossed our legs all together, stuff like that. After we did the last set, Rahiem was the only one from his group that actually wanted to rhyme still. The rest—I'm not going to mention any names—but they was in the back while he was rhyming. We had totally took their heart from 'em. It was like they just couldn't compete with us. So instead of getting up there and doing their last set, they said, "Naw, we ain't rhymin'."

RAHIEM: I waited until the other MCs were finished, and then I went on after them and did my thing. I was like, "There's no way that I'm going to be slighted because one person doesn't wanna do what we worked so hard to get here for." I remember distinctly scanning the audience, and I saw the Furious 4 in the shadows, and they were like rooting me on. The adrenaline rush that I got from that was incredible, and that just made me keep going. I did fifteen minutes by myself. I was soaking wet. Mel, Creole, and Cowboy were like staring at me. "Yo. You did your thing. You are so fucking bad!" This was supposed to be a battle. They were not supposed to be fans!

After that night, we didn't do too many more parties together as the Funky 4. But each party that we did after that, Melle Mel and Scorpio—if not the whole Furious 4— would be there. They would always wait until I got on, and they would be right there in the front, attentive as any audience member. And that was real cool to me.

MELLE MEL: We talked Rahiem out of the Funky 4 so there wasn't no competition. We battled them at the P.A.L. Crushed them. They were all weak-looking.

DJ BARON: I don't know what happened with Rahiem. I guess he was feeling the Furious 4 MCs, he felt they were a little better. And then it was like a money thing, where we couldn't pay the MCs the way we wanted to pay them—we were still building the system. There were a lot of frustrations here and there, so he jumped ship and went over to Grandmaster Flash. He left us, and then Sha-Rock left us, too.

K.K. ROCKWELL: After that night I could sense something was up with Rahiem. He was always singing "Flash is on the beat box, playing, Flash is on the beat box ..." (part of a Furious 4 routine). I didn't want to hear that shit! I felt betrayed, so I said, "What's up with that? You got to go." Rahiem said that was OK because we wasn't making any money anyway. Sha-Rock got so upset when she heard.

SHA-ROCK: Rahiem was like my brother. After Rahiem left the group I was like, "Well, if he's leaving, I'm gonna leave, too," you know? I didn't leave to go to another group; I just left just 'cause he did. I just took a break.

RAHIEM: One day after we had done a few more parties, someone rang the intercom at my mom's house, and it was Scorpio. I was really shocked; I didn't even know that he knew where I lived. He came upstairs, and he was like, "Yo, man, you should think about getting down with our group, because we feel like you're one of the of the best." So I was like, "That sounds cool," just trying not to get too excited about it.

the funky 4 plus one more

JAZZY JEFF: Me and Lil' Rodney Cee was part of a rap group called the Magnificent 7. It was four rappers and three DJs. Me and Rodney was in Lehman High School; I was on the varsity basketball team in Lehman. After one of our games, they was doing a dance, and our basketball coach inquired whether anybody on the team knew of a DJ they could hire for the dance. The fellows on the team knew that I was MC-ing with a rap group, so they was saying, "Yeah, let Jeff do it! Let Jeff do it with his group!" So we did it.

K.K. Rockwell, who was a part of the Funky 4 at that time, went to Lehman also. K.K. happened to come to the game and then hang out after at the dance. He heard us, and after we finished, he asked us would we be interested in going for an MC try-out with their group.

K.K. ROCKWELL: One night I went to a jam at Lehman High School, and I saw Rodney on the mic. I thought, "This kid can rhyme!" So I told our record boy Pookie D to tell their record boy that we were having tryouts for a new MC. Rodney and Jeff made a pact: if one of them didn't make the cut, the other one wouldn't join.

Before Rodney and Jeff came, we had tried Special K (later of the Treacherous 3). I liked him a lot, but I thought, "We can't have two K's in the same group, can we?" When Rodney and Jeff came over, Baron turned on the tape, and I kicked it off then passed the mic to Keith who then passed it to Rodney and so forth until we just filled up a whole tape of rhymes. Baron had never heard them before, so I yelled back to him, "Yo, Baron, what do ya think?" Baron comes out and says, "Can ya start today?"

DJ BARON: I heard Rodney Cee do his thing, and he was off the hook, just what I was looking for. He had flow. Jeff was a little weak to me; he was still an amateur compared to Keith and K.K., but he came along with the package. So that's where we said, "OK, y'all both can get down." So we became Funky 4 again.

JAZZY JEFF: About an hour or two after me and Rodney left the house, Breakout called us up.... He wanted to just bring us right out.

So as they were setting up outside in the park, the four of us got together—me, Rodney, Keith, and K.K.—and spent two hours putting the routine together to come outside with. We knew Sha-Rock and Rahiem and everybody was doubtin' this move that Breakout was makin' by adding me and Rodney; they all felt it was like his doomsday.

K.K. Rockwell, Jazzy Jeff (on the mike), Rodney Cee, and Busy Bee rock outdoors at the Valley, Summer, 1980 (© Charlie Ahearn)

JAZZY JEFF: It was July 11, 1979—that was the first day that me and Lil' Rodney Cee touched the microphone with the Funky 4. It was DJ Breakout's birthday, and that was the day that we got down; we came out in the park. So we did that, we came outside, and we just like rip shit. And then before we know it, Sha-Rock wanted to be down with us. Sha liked what she saw in me, Rodney, Keith, and K, and then she came with us.

SHA-ROCK: I went to see the Funky 4 one time after about a month. They was all upset at me because I had left. Jazzy Dee says, "Sha-Rock, I want you to get on the mic. The crowd wants to see ya." So I got on there, and the crowd started just going crazy. So they said, "OK, Sha, this is good for us. Just go ahead and come back."

DJ BARON: I think Jazzy Dee talked to Sha-Rock, and Sha came back into the picture. That's how we became the Funky 4 + 1.

152

SHA-ROCK: We were all young, going through these phases, whatever...but I went back for the love of hip-hop, for the love of the whole scenario.

JAZZY JEFF: We had Sha-Rock, the first female MC. And it wasn't that she was just a girl and she was with the group, but she was good. If you heard her, you loved her. With the whole realm of this MC-in' and hip-hop being dominated by males, she held her own. There was no way you could take anything from her. You had to totally respect her.

She's Sha-Rock an' she can't be stopped. At the Valley, June 1980 (© Charlie Ahearn)

We could tell if we was gonna have a good show or bad show by how they treated the flyer—a person folds up a flyer and puts it in their pocket, if you don't see no flyers on the floor, you're gonna have a good show. ● **VAN SILK**

BUDDY ESQUIRE: I made my first flyer back in November of '78. My first client was the Brothers Disco—Breakout and Baron, and the Funky 4. I met Tony Tone back when I was going to Stevenson High School. He figured I was a pretty decent writer, so he introduced me to Breakout and Darnell.

It was sort of on-the-job training: the more I made flyers, the better I got at it. I made flyers for various DJs, from roughly from '78 to '83. I was kind of a shy and withdrawn person. I used to go to parties, but a lot of times I just stayed home and made the flyer.

VAN SILK: As a promoter you never had a say in how the letters and stuff were done. What we would do is write out what we wanted on the flyer, and like Phase 2—a graffiti artist—did the graphics. You had Buddy Esquire who did flyers; he and Phase were the best flyer makers. We was paying $40 for the master, another $60 for a thousand flyers.

BUDDY ESQUIRE: One of the first flyers that I noticed—this was before I was even making flyers—was a flyer by Phase 2. I've always had a lot of respect for his skill and talent. I thought it looked alright, and soon after that I was making flyers. There were people that told me that my style was very similar to Phase. I'll admit it to an extent, but if you really look and you're into art, you can tell how my flyers differ from his.

VAN SILK: Basically, we gave Phase the pictures. "This is who is on the show," and we wrote out what we wanted on the flyer, and then he would correct anything I misspelled. We would go to his house and take it to him and come back a couple hours later on. Phase actually sat in his mother's living room and did the flyers. We'd be so glad to get that master cardboard flyer; I wish I still had those masters, but we'd give them back to Phase. I lived right up the block from him, so I always used to walk to his house, get my work done, and get on the train—the number 2 train up to the Bronx. Take the train to Gun Hill Road and walk to Larry Schwartz, the printer, and sometimes wait for him to make the flyers right there. 'Cause we were so happy to have a brand new flyer. We'd come with an empty bag and come back with a bag filled with flyers; as we're gettin' on the train, we're hittin' people with flyers.

Guys 3$ B/4 10 Gals 2$ B/4 10
4$ after
3$ after
K.P.R. Productions Presents:
Grand Wizard
THEODORE
FANTASTIC 5 M.C.s
Kevie-Kev Master Rob Ruby Dee
Dota-Rock Whipper-Whip
I.S. 167
1970 W. Farms Sq.
9pm-until
167
Cold Crush 4 M.C.s
Grandmaster Caz Jerry D. Lewis
Easy A.D. Kay-Gee
Special Guest:
LIL RODNEY-C
Sat, Jan. 17, 81
2&5 train, 20, 40 & 36 buses to E. Tremont
1st 25 GALS FREE!
Buddy Esq.

Flyer by Buddy Esquire

Phase 2 (center) and friends at the Ecstasy Garage, 1980 (© Charlie Ahearn)

Ecstasy 1508 Macombs Road
Garage
"Disco-jam"
With Master of Records D.J.
Afrika Bambaataa' and
D.J.'s Jazzy Jay & Red Alert
Also Soulsonic & Cosmic Force M.C.'s
Mr. Biggs-Pow Wow-Lisa Lee-Ice Ice-Globe-Chubby Chub-& Ikey C and it's...
Grand Master "Caz" & Jerry D Lewi$
"Amazing"
Mean Gene
M.C.'s Tricky Vic & Tipski
Its all going down
Friday, Dec. 12, 1980
Doors open 9:30 pm
Damage 2$ Before 10:30
This is a sure nuff smoker so bring your body n' party!
Checkout BAMS NEW HIT: Throwdown!
Directions 4 train to 170th walk 2 blocks
50 GALS & GUYS FREE!!!

Flyer by Phase 2

Buddy Esquire advertisement.

DJ Breakout wearing a stage outfit painted by Buddy Esquire (Courtesy Angelo King)

You will enter another dimension with the sights and sounds of two djs...

The return of the incredible dj: **BREAKOUT BARON**

FRI. FEB 23

The Amazing DJ

The Original Funky 4 MCs that are guaranteed to rock you on down to your knees....

M.C. Sha Rock · M.C. Keith Keith · M.C. Rahiem · M.C. K.K. Rockwell

~ Introducing the ~

BROTHERS DISCO

FRI FEB 23 · FRI FEB 23

AT...

Bronx H.S. of Science (75 West 205 Street)

(D Train to Bedford Pk / 4 Train to Bedford Pk / #28 Bus to School / #1, #2 Bus)

7pm-until $3.00

Buddy Esq.

Buddy Esquire's first Breakout logo flyer, 1979

BUDDY ESQUIRE: I was going to the Ecstasy Garage, and I used to run into Phase a lot there, 'cause he was also making flyers for Arthur Armstrong, who ran Ecstasy Garage back then. It was a nice little place. I went there almost every weekend back then, '80 to '82.

I never had to pay. I knew the people that were giving the party, and I got in for free. It felt good to know that people recognized you, respected your skills. The thing was, a lotta times they didn't give me the money for the flyer when I finished it. It's like, "Oh, come to the party and get paid."

Breakout showed me a video game that had "Breakout" down the side with letters and bricks. He told me he wanted that on his pants. It was a little difficult, but I painted it, and then after I painted the pants, he wanted it on a flyer. I remember doing it twice on a flyer, one Bronx High School of Science, and the second for Stevenson High School.

The problem with Bambaataa's flyers was he liked to put a lot of stuff in them; he wanted a lot of information on the flyers. I made a few for him, but after a while I didn't really want to make any more because they took more time than the other flyers. So I got my brother to take that job, 'cause he was helping me paint the pants back then. He eventually went on to make a lot of Bambaataa's flyers. His name is Eddie Ed.

Nubian & Jazzy Dee Productions presents Funkin for the funk Disco

dj afrika **Bambaataa** **Brothers Disco**

THE ORIGINAL DJ · Jazzy Jay · "Baron" "Breakout
Soul Sonic Force MCs · Funky 4 plus one
Mr Biggs Pow-Wow · Keith Keith KK Rockwell
Hutch-Hutch Lisa Lee · Jazzy Jeff Lil Rodney-C
Sundance Ice-Ice · Sha Rock
Master Ice Master B

Bronx River Center

SUN. FEB. 10 1980 9:00 until

Donation 2 with flyer #11 $4 all night

The Message

Do Not Forget the knowledge That The Honorable Elijah Muhammad Has gave our people

Come in Peace

A Bambaataa flyer by Eddie Ed

While Phase and Buddy Esquire dominated the Bronx scene and set the style for most of the other flyer artists, different looks sprouted up as hip-hop spread to other boroughs. Here are a few flyers from the Harlem scene done by Aton E.

the L brothers & the galaxy 2000

ARTHUR ARMSTRONG: I used to promote R&B acts locally. In 1979 I went to a spot in the Bronx to rent it, and I ran into Kool Herc. Herc had been giving shows there, and he was there to try to rent it from the guy also. He started explaining to me about rap. I had never heard of rap music. Herc explained to me that it was a new music, and there was a large clientele. The kids loved it, it was their music, and he was the primary mover behind it, the inventor. I think his exact words were that he was the Mohammed Ali of rap [laughing] at the time.

So we met a few times, we talked, and I decided to give it a try, to turn the club into a rap club. I rented it every Friday and Saturday. It was like a catering hall but I named it the Galaxy. The Galaxy 2000 really, but Galaxy for short.

I started promoting shows there. Herc introduced me to the business; he introduced me to everybody. That went on for a year or so. After that we had an incident there, and I decided it was time to close it down.

BUSY BEE: The Galaxy was on University, on the West Side. We were from the East Side. It was the L Brothers' first show out of our area.

KEVIE KEV: We went over there to play, and I'll never forget that night, I cross my heart. I called all my cousins; they called all their girls to come to this party. It's over on the West Side. West Side was always considered more down and dirty than the South Side. So going over there was going to be chance anyway.

We went there, took our system, and something was wrong. We didn't have power. Herc let us down, or he didn't call. Things were kind of ugly, but we got our system up, got it pumping.

BUSY BEE: Place was jam-packed. People paying $5 a head to get in! We counting paper (money) now! And happy as a motherfuck! Music was rocking! We're doing routines. Mean Gene and some females were at the door collecting the money. Everyone came up the stairs, got searched, paid, then came inside.

KEVIE KEV: While we on the West Side, we lettin' Kool Herc be rockin' the East Side. Now the East Side where we let them play is our side. The West Side where we playing is their side. So it's like a change of territories. But we didn't send nobody to go stick them up over on our side. They sent niggers to stick us up.

Trevor, he was Jamaican, was supposed to be our manager. He says, "Yo! They getting ready to stick it up!" He must have seen them getting out of a van or something. So they come in with their arms strapped up and their faces strapped up. They smacking people. They yelling, "Where's the DJ? Where's the DJ?"

BUSY BEE: I heard a POW! "Don't nobody move! Everybody freeze!" Girls started hollering and screaming and falling down. I heard, "Where's the DJ? Where's the DJ?" They probably figured the DJ's got the money.

GRANDMASTER CAZ: I was standing right next to Theodore, and the nigger told him, "Turn off the music." Mean Gene must have been collecting the money. I was diving over shit upstairs. Me and Kevie Kev.

KEVIE KEV: That night Busy Bee jumped in a box of pickles. Rob jumped over the bar. The bar came down on my brother's leg. I was punching people in the face, trying to get them off the bar, 'cause I thought it was going to break his leg.

BUSY BEE: There was a drop of one floor to the ground, and people was jumping out the windows and diving under tables! Guys had on ski masks, with just eyes showing. There were three of them. Security hadn't stopped them from coming in. They came straight up with their guns out. They were there for the money.

KEVIE KEV: We never did nothing to them. They knew who we were. Most people have a lot of guns at these parties for security purposes, but we didn't have a lot. We usually had sawed offs and all that. That night, only one of our friends had a gun, and they [the robbers] had guns and shotguns.

ARTHUR ARMSTRONG: They tried to rob the money on the door, and they went upstairs trying to rob the bar. They ran into security when they went upstairs, and that's when the shooting took place. The robbers started shooting in the air to make all the kids hit the floor. They wasn't aware they were being shot back at.

BUSY BEE: Then I heard gun shots. One of the crooks never made it; he got it. That was a message to his two pals. When people was trying to leave, they couldn't 'cause his body was blocking the bottom of the stairs. His legs was shaking.

KEVIE KEV: He died down on the steps, and that song, "And the Beat Goes On," by the Whispers, was playing.

GRANDMASTER CAZ: Afterwards it was, "Galaxy got stuck up." Nobody said nothing. No names about who did it. Nothing. But it was something that everybody knew.

KEVIE KEV: We don't know for sure who sent them over there. The guy that died, we knew his name after they took his mask off. As far as pursuing who did it, we didn't pursue it. It wasn't our job. Our job was being artists. Whoever was behind murdering and guns, that was their business. As an MC you rock the mic, you a pleaser, you don't got problems like that.

ARTHUR ARMSTRONG: It was a situation with the police after that, so I closed the Galaxy down. Once there's a shooting, you know there was going to be a problem with the police.

GRANDMASTER CAZ: Nobody can talk about that but so much. I think the people who was involved in it is dead right now. Both of them. One was shot that night, that was his brother. If they knew it was Crazy Eddie, they wouldn't have shot his brother. He was a local gangster, drug dealer, that everybody knew. There wasn't going to be no repercussions. Nobody was going to go back to Eddie and do nothing. He could have walked in there without a fucking mask, and the same thing would have happened. They would just hand over the money. That was just some overzealous motherfucker. After that party, that was the end of the L Bros.

BUSY BEE: That killed the L Bros for a while.

new players
new voices

CHARLIE CHASE: I come from a family of musicians; there was always music in my house. I was a bass player before I was a DJ. In high school I got into a Spanish rock band—we'd play Santana cover songs. As I got better with my bass playing, I got into a funk band that was forming in the projects. It took off from there.

I got into a salsa band, and I became friends with these guys named Ruben and Tony. They had just started learning how to DJ. Everyone knows them now as Tom and Jerry. I went to their house one day, and I saw them DJ-ing, and I was amazed. I'm like, "Oh...so this is how this works." Seeing the mechanics, watching everything happening, I was like, "Oh, I wanna do this." Because I knew a lot about music and timing, it was easy for me.

I was playing disco music. It was cool, but I wasn't feeling it. Then one day these guys called the Monterey Crew threw a little party in a community center down the block from me in the same projects. This had to be in '77. I was in the other end of the center playing ping-pong, and I'm hearing this music. I go over there and this place is just packed. It's dark; all you see is the light from the turntables and these shadows off the ceiling, moving around quickly. I get a closer look, and I see these guys DJ-ing, but they're playing beats. They have two copies of the same record, and they're just concentrating on this one section of record, going back and forth. Then this one guy, every now and then he'll say a little one-line rhyme. The crowd was totally into the vibe, people are dancing, they're just enjoying it like it's a thing that's supposed to happen, it's the norm. They weren't amazed like I was. That just blew me away.

I threw myself headfirst into it. I started increasing my collection of records and perfecting my style. The first record I got was Karen Young's "Hot Shot." It had that little break in the middle, where it goes, "Hot Shot, Hot Shot, HOT!" and I'd cut that into the little break, and I'd practice with that. I broke a couple of turntables [laughs], practicing with that one record until I was able to perfect the "Hot Shot" back to back continuously, without stopping. That's when I said, "You're getting this, man."

So I'm still with Tom and Jerry, I'm DJ-ing at clubs, but now I'm armed with my hip-hop records. They're playing the disco music. They were good, but they sometimes dragged things out, and the crowd would die. They'd go, "OK, it's dead. Stick Charlie in there." I play my hip-hop records—the beats—everybody likes it! The floor gets packed, and I get bumped off the turntables [laughs]. "OK, Chase, sit down man. We're takin' over from here." 'Cause now the party's back.

CAZ: Charlie was the hip-hop bastard of the group; he was like the little Puerto Rican guy playing the Black music. Tom and Jerry would let him get on for a half-hour, play a little hip-hop or whatever, get him off. So I would come across some of these parties sometimes, and I would catch Charlie during his half-hour, I would get on with him and rhyme and stuff while he DJ-ed, so we got a camaraderie going.

CHARLIE CHASE: I put up with that for about a year, and then I said, "It's time to go out on my own. I see that I can do this." I started playing in the streets, because that was where you got your notoriety. I was making the tapes, I was playing in the street jams, and I'm getting popular, and everybody's listening.

CISCO: Charlie started DJ-ing, and being hip to the Black thing, he started playing these records that Kool Herc was playing. That was around '77, '78, when it really started getting pumped. There was a jam over at the Monterey Community Center on Thursday nights. We used to rock it with live DJs—Dizzy Diz, Mighty Mike, DJ Ray, Kool DJ Ron, and a few of the other kids. With Charlie Chase, we said "Yo! We gotta follow him. He's the man to watch."

CHARLIE CHASE: The first MC that I ever had was Cisco Kid, who also did flyers. I always heard him around the community center rhyming, and I said, "Look, I don't know any other MCs. You wanna be my MC?" He said, "Sure," and we started doing parties together in the little social clubs and little local bars. That's when I met Tony Tone. I had acquired another MC called RC who used to go to school with Tony Tone.

TONY TONE: I was telling RC—a young kid who lived in my building—that I was thinking about putting my own group together, and he says "There's this Puerto Rican guy named Charlie Chase and he's good. I'll introduce you to him." I told Charlie who I was, but Charlie didn't seem like he was impressed. I went to his house, and I wound up liking him.

CHARLIE CHASE: That was the beginning of our little thing. We were together for about a year before we even started the Cold Crush. Tony was part of the Brothers Disco at the time, and one of the first parties he took me to was a Breakout party. That was the first time I was ever taken to a real, honest-to-goodness hip-hop party.

TONY: The first time I took Charlie to a Brothers Disco party, I put him behind the ropes, and I went back out to take care of something. When I came back, security had him, shaking him and pushing him outta the room. So I walked up, I go, "Yo! What y'all doing?" and security's like, "Oh, you know him?" I was like, "Yeah, he with me!" They was like, "Oh, I'm sorry, I'm sorry." It was like bringing a young bird into the nest with the bald eagles, and they ready to attack.

CHARLIE CHASE: That was when I got the real look, feel, and intensity of a sound system, 'cause Breakout had a sound system that could punch a hole in the wall, man. The bass was incredible. When I saw Breakout's set, I said, "I gotta have a set like this, man....I gotta have a set like this." And God knows we blew more speakers than anybody I've ever known, trying to get to that set, man. We made a lot of mistakes because we were learning on our own—we didn't have any teachers. Like everything else in this business of hip-hop, we learned on our own, nobody taught us.

Tony and I joined forces, and since he knew all the promoters and all the people, we were getting booked with these other bigger acts. I think the thing that really made people take notice of me was one day, I'm playing at the P.A.L., and Flash appeared [laughs]. And if you know Flash, he has this certain air about him. He walks around like he's the man! He's Flash, you know what I'm saying?

He walks in. We got the sound system cranking. The place is packed. The party's going, and Flash just walks up on stage. He's like Don Corleone, you know? It's funny. But somebody convinced him to get on the turntables. The record that was playing was "Let's Dance." He was on my turntables—back then everybody had a different type of turntable, and it needed a little getting used to, you had to have the right touch to make it work. He's trying to get on my turntables to rock this record, to make it go, "Let's Dance, Let's Dance ..." over and over again. He's trying to do it—he couldn't do it! He couldn't do it for the life of him. It kept skipping on him, and he got up and he walked away. So, something just compelled me—I walked over, I picked up the headphones, and I did it, continuously back and forth. I wasn't trying to show him up or anything. I was just doing it because I could do it. The crowd is losing it! So you know how the rumor machine goes...by the end of that summer I had taken on Flash in a battle [laughs]. And it wasn't really all that. But that was when people started taking notice of me.

TONY: When I started, the Bronx was the world. I saw hip-hop no place else at the start, but I wanted it to be everywhere. Graffiti was the world—I used to wake up dreamin' about writin' on the wall. One night I was dreamin' of something, and then I woke up and I was thinking "Cold Crush." Cold Crush, when I thought up the name, meant anybody steps in our way, they get crushed, cold crushed, no remorse. Once we get on the stage, it's no friendship, we got to walk off the stage victorious.

168

Tony Tone during a Cold Crush party at the T-Connection, circa 1980 (Courtesy Angelo King)

EASY AD: Me and a gentleman named Donald D was together MC-in' and our group was called the As-Salaam Brothers, which means "peace." We broke up...I met DJ Tony Tone, and he said, "You an MC?" He said he was starting a group called Cold Crush Brothers. He said, "I know this Latino brother named Charlie Chase, and I'm gonna put him in the forefront and make him a star."

TONY: My idea was to have Charlie out front. I thought, "Let the Puerto Rican DJ have the front seat this time, and see how that helps us." And it helped us, 'cause we had a big Latino following. It worked to our advantage.

CHARLIE CHASE: Caz had this crew, the Mighty Force, and Whipper Whip and Dota Rock were with him. At that time Caz was having a lot of problems with MCs—a lot of MCs are intimidated by him because he's just such a gifted guy. Wherever Caz goes, he shines, and you either have to accept it or walk away from it. Don't get me wrong— Whipper Whip and Dota Rock are excellent MCs. But Whip and Dot needed somewhere to go. I needed MCs, and I said, "Come aboard."

WHIPPER WHIP: I had hooked up with Caz, who at that time was DJ Casanova Fly. I started writing and Caz helped me. Dot was a rhymer from the project near the P.A.L. where we used to hang out. We started writing together; we'd write little routines. I think it was Mean Gene or Cordie-O from the L Brothers who said, "Y'all like Salt and Pepper. Every time I see one, I see the other." So that's when we came up with the Salt and Pepper name, and we started writing Salt and Pepper routines, where we go back and forth and go in between each other's rhymes.

GRANDMASTER CAZ: Whipper Whip and Dota Rock were younger cats around my block, maybe a year or two younger than me. They were like a team—Salt N Pepper they were called, they were that close. I taught them the basics, and after a while they just wanted to get out on their own. They were ambitious. They learned what they needed to learn from me.

WHIPPER WHIP: I really don't know how we hooked up with Charlie. I think Dota Rock was friends with Charlie, and he was like, "We need to hook up." We was with this guy named Mister T (aka T-Bone) and Easy AD, myself and Dota Rock. We got together and it was a cool thing. We were Cold Crush; we did a lot of shows. We did all the parks, the usual circuit: 118 Park, 82 Park, 129—these are all school numbers— 63 park, they're all in the Bronx. Then as me and Dot kept doin' our writing, we told Charlie, "Yo, man, we just want us on the mic, we don't want no other MCs." He was like, "I got my boys. I know it's business, but they're friends, too." I was like, "You can't mix friends and business—this is business." Charlie was like, "I can't get rid of my boys."

CHARLIE CHASE: We're talking about a few months after I had Cisco Kid and RC. Now I got Whipper Whip, Dota Rock, Easy AD, T-Bone. But Whipper Whip and Dota Rock, they wanted to leave.

CAZ: Kevie Kev and the guys from the L Brothers were lookin' at Whip and Dot to be down with them. Charlie and I, we were like down here, and the guys with the big systems and stuff, they was like up there. The larger your system was, the more powerful your crew was. As far as records and skills and people knowing you, we was right there, but that sound system really put you over the top. Everybody wanted to perform on a big system, so everybody was looking for greener pastures, that kind of thing. So they went with Kev and them, and they turned into the Fantastic 5. They went from the L Brothers to the Fantastic 5 when they added Whip and Dot.

it's a business now: up against the black door

RAY CHANDLER: Flash was always the Grandmaster. As far as he was concerned, this was his group. Then Melle Mel and them started stepping up to the forefront, and that started a lot of dissension. Melle Mel would rock the crowd so hard that the girls used to come back to see the Furious 5. It got to the point where Melle Mel, I think it was in the Black Door, he said, "You know I'm a Grandmaster, too! I'm the Grandmaster of the MCs!" Flash took offense with that. "There's only one Grandmaster!" Melle Mel was extremely defiant, and he stuck to his guns. He started calling himself Grandmaster Melle Mel.

DJ BARON: I heard stories that Flash parties always made more money than we did, but the MCs didn't get paid that kind of money. I heard they'd get paid like $50, $75 per person, and they'd have like 2,000 people at their party. Ray Chandler took all that money. Whatever money we made we tried to break down fairly. So even though Rahiem left the Funky 4, he went to a dictatorship.

CHARLIE CHASE: Apparently the Furious 5 had gotten into a fight with Black Door Productions, which was Ray Chandler and Flash, and they left Flash and became my MCs for a while. Rahiem had just left Funky 4 and got down with them, and they were so pissed off at Flash and them that they came to me. They needed a DJ, I was available, and I was the only DJ that could match what Flash was doing.

TONY: I think it was Scorpio who came to Charlie and said, "Listen, Charlie, we want you to be our DJ. We left Flash, and we want you to be our DJ." When Charlie came to me with it, of course I agreed—the Furious was the hottest thing at that time. We cut our MCs off, we took the Furious 5, and Chase was their DJ for three parties.

MELLE MEL: We broke up with Flash, 'cause he'd been taking too much of the money. We did a show with Charlie Chase at the P.A.L. Ray Chandler shows up and takes some of the money and has the Casanovas rough us up. Ray was like, "What the fuck? You let these niggers in here without me?" He put the fear of god in your moth-erfuckin' heart. We took our P.A.L. share and gave it to him.

TONY TONE: The Casanova Crew was sent to "convince" them to come back to Flash. They came to the P.A.L.; we was having a party there, and we told the MCs, "Don't leave the stage. We can't protect you." I was like, "Are you going back to Flash, or are you staying with us?" So I would know how far to go. "'Cause if y'all are going to go back to Flash, go ahead back. Don't get me into no beef with them."

RAHIEM: This was my first impression of the Casanovas: We did a show at the Webster Avenue P.A.L. and we took a break. I had to go to the bathroom. I'm walking down the stairs, I go to the men's room. The door of the men's room is cracked open a few inches, I'm standing outside looking at the mirror. Through the mirror in the men's room I could see two members of the Casanovas—Cletus and Football—robbing Scorpio and Kid Creole for their jewelry. And these guys were our security!

TONY TONE: They caught Creole and Ness off the stage, and they beat them up. They made them go back to Flash. "Enough of this bullshit. Y'all are going back to Flash." Ray Chandler sent them. Ray Chandler paid the Casanova Crew—they worked for him as security, enforcers, as whatever. That was his money.

RAY CHANDLER: During this temporary separation, Tiny [Casanova], he had a close relationship with Melle Mel. Keep in mind, it was still family, so he would go out of his way to convince him to come back. Other members of the Casanovas would sort of intimidate them, tell them, "Look you ain't going to be doing any parties here or there." They had some confrontations. It started getting rough because they were scared of the Casanovas. The Casanovas was not a joke to be playing around with. But the effect was like the breaking up of the family. Eventually we talked about it, and we got back together again.

Grandmaster Caz and Grand Wizard Theodore at the Ecstasy Garage, 1980 (Courtesy Luis Cedeno)

CHARLIE CHASE: They wanted the MCs back, and the MCs didn't really want to go back, but they went back. They were coerced into going back, because Black Door wasn't making money anymore. Flash was still doing parties, but he was missing what he needed, and I guess there was collaboration between Flash and Black Door Productions. The Casanovas could be very persuasive, man. They were pretty rough when they wanted to be. They were notorious for that, and a lot of people respected them for that. They didn't play with them. And Ray Chandler—Black Door Productions—had 'em in his corner.

ART ARMSTRONG: When you booked Flash, Ray controlled things. Like when the guys decided to leave Flash: it was a matter of going back to Ray or you don't do no shows at all. The word went around—it was a small family back then, so word went around that you didn't book them. It may have been a loose-developing type of business, but there were unwritten rules. If you went against the grain, you had problems, you know? That's the way rap was in that period.

MELLE MEL: He was the Don King of rap. He could talk a motherfucker out of the grave. "How much you think you're worth?" You'd be scared and say anything. "I'm worth $75!"

RAHIEM: Ray Chandler was a very big man. Not big like husky big, but he was really tall, and he had some bulk to him. He was a really imposing figure, like if you saw him standing in a crowd of people and he raised his voice, it was like, "Whoa! Paul Bunyan!" Most people were really afraid of Ray.

TONY TONE: Ray was 6'4". To kids, he was a giant.

ART ARMSTRONG: Basically, I got along with him, but some things went down that wasn't correct when we did business. I guess I had my detractors, too. You always have your detractors. But Ray is the type of person...say, he got killed, say there's twenty rappers there. All of them would be suspects, you know what I mean [chuckling]? That's the kind of a guy Ray was.

Original b-boy style: Tony Tone at the T-Connection in the late '70s (Courtesy Angelo King)

5
RAPPER'S
DELIGHT:

hip-hop goes commercial

Hip-hop's pioneers in the '70s either hadn't had the connections or the wherewithal to make records. More importantly, it seems that they hadn't even considered the possibility. So when "Rapper's Delight" was recorded by the Sugar Hill Gang and became a smash hit in late 1979, the fact that the group recording it came from outside the Bronx hip-hop scene perhaps shouldn't have been a surprise. Mainstream music journalists had begun to take note of the new trend, and funk veterans the Fatback Band had put a rap by a local radio DJ, "King Tim III," on the b-side of their single "(You're My) Candy Sweet" a few months earlier. But the advent of rapping on vinyl sent shock waves through the older street-based hip-hop scene.

Sylvia Robinson gets the credit for having the foresight to put the Sugar Hill Gang together, rush them into the studio, and push the record onto the airwaves. Ms. Robinson was a longtime veteran of the recording business. In fact, she was a recording star, with several hits to her name, beginning with Mickey & Sylvia's "Love Is Strange" in 1956, and with her husband, Joe, she ran All-Platinum Records out of New Jersey. They didn't set out to start a controversy by recording "Rapper's Delight." They just heard a new sound and decided to put it on record. But the decision to bypass the established crews in favor of newcomers caused a controversy within the close-knit hip-hop community. Not only did it change the rules of the game, but it changed the goals as well. Within weeks of the release of "Rapper's Delight," Bobby Robinson (no relation to Sylvia) of Enjoy Records recorded Grandmaster Flash and the Funky 4 + 1. More great records that were actually quite representative of the Bronx scene followed, and then, just in time for the holidays, Kurtis Blow's "Christmas Rappin'"—a novelty record with ties to the DJ Hollywood-flavored Harlem scene—hit big. Before the end of 1980, Blow's "The Breaks" would be the first rap single to go gold.

Hip-hop had become a business; now it was on its way to becoming national.

DJ Hollywood, Kurtis Blow,
Bam Bam, and Sal Abbatiello
celebrate Kurtis's Gold
Record award for "The Breaks"
at Disco Fever, 1980
(Courtesy Sal Abbatiello)

the rules change

GRANDMASTER FLASH: Prior to the year 1979, we had DJ crews like DJ Breakout and the Funky 4 with a sound system, Kool Herc with a sound system, the L Brothers with a sound system, Kool DJ AJ with a sound system, Grandmaster Flash and the Furious 5 with a sound system, Afrika Bambaataa, with a sound system.... But right around that time, DJ Hollywood changed the whole game of how DJs played a party. Hollywood would book himself in five spots in one night, and you would wonder how in the hell he could be in five places at one time. He would be at this party for a certain amount of time, but he would jump over to the next party at a certain time, and then jump over to the next party and the next party and the next party...

That became the way promoters hired DJs. This made the sound system a dinosaur. Everybody started putting their stuff away because you could be at two or three parties in one night and make triple the money, you know?

disco fever

SAL ABBATIELLO: My father opened his first bar in 1969 in the Bronx. As time went on, he partnered with a Black bar owner, and they branched out, opened other spots. 1976 rolled around, disco's starting to explode, and my father decides to open up an adult, classy R&B nightclub. John Travolta had just come out with the movie *Saturday Night Fever*, and we're watching the commercial, and my mom goes, "Hey, why don't we call it Disco Fever?" So that's how it became Disco Fever.

My father put in a white Spanish trendy DJ from uptown in the North Bronx. He used to play at one of our other clubs, but he just wasn't cutting it for the South Bronx. At about 4 o'clock he would leave, and this Black DJ would come on. His name was Sweet G. Four o'clock in the morning was the legal hour to close, but in the South Bronx it was kind of lenient—if you weren't having trouble you could get away with staying open. When Sweet G comes on he's playing all these hot R&B records, and he's talking over the music. He would be saying nursery rhymes and asking the crowd to repeat things, "Throw your hands in the air...." The energy of the crowd would change.

I'm leaning on the wall, observing the crowd, how the people who weren't dancing were involved with the music as much as the people who were dancing. It was bringing people together: people were talking to strangers, smiling across the bar at somebody, all doing the same thing. And I said, "Wow, this is some gimmick to maybe do a night with."

Sweet G starts telling me about hip-hop music and bringing me places to hear the music. I keep hearing this name Grandmaster Flash coming up, so I tell my father I want to get one of these street DJs to do a night, and I go meet Grandmaster Flash. I say to Flash, "I wanna do a Tuesday night, and I want you to DJ. What do you take?" He gives me these crazy prices. I say, "Look, this is a nightclub that's gonna be open every week. You can't charge me a one-nighter price. It's only a little club. I'm trying it out. I'll start you out with $50." He's laughing. He says, "I'll call you back."

Two or three weeks later he calls me back and says, "Look, I'm interested in doing it." I say, "I think you'll get discovered here, maybe you'll get on the radio. You know, DJ for the radio or something." We didn't think about records or anything. So he comes in. I handed out flyers for like three, four days, and 600 people show up the first night. We're overwhelmed. When the night finally ended, I knew this was something big. And we did it the next week. And the next week...

After about three weeks Flash started bringing in the Furious 5. They were rapping, and now the night's kicking—now it's spreading all over the high schools and the colleges, about this one night at the Fever. So instead of having this one night, I went and found another rapper, Love Bug Starski, put him on Monday. I found Eddie Cheba, put him on Sunday. Reggie Wells—Thursday. And then finally June Bug left 371, came over to our club, and I gave him Thursday, Friday, Saturday, with Sweet G as the MC. So every night you came to the Fever, every night was a different MC, a different style of DJ.

Now the club's starting to blow up. We added another floor, we're adding rooms in the back. The older crowd started drifting out, and the younger crowd started coming in. Now every kid knows that they could come and hear their sound, their school sound, their street sound, in this club, and it's a major club with a great sound system, being run properly. A major operation, right in the middle of the South Bronx.

By now it's 1979. Things are really going good in the Fever. I'm in my office one morning, and it's only like 11 o'clock, 11:30, and I hear somebody rap. I'm like, "Who the hell's here so early rapping on the mic?" I go out to see who it is, and I don't see nobody there. I'm like, "What the hell? What is this?" Somebody said, "Somebody made a record."

rapper's delight: the beginning and the end

LOVE BUG STARSKI: Sylvia Robinson will tell you: I was "Rapper's Delight." She got the idea off of me. I did her birthday party at Harlem World, and that's where she got the idea. She said, "I've got to have him." She'll tell you that. But I wasn't interested in doing no record back in them days, 'cause I was getting so much money for just DJ-ing.

JOEY ROBINSON: I said, "Mom, I've got somebody really great that I know, that can really, really rap, and he has a great sound." So she said, "Go find that guy." I went and found him; his name was Casper, and he used to rap with Sound on Sound, the same group where Wonder Mike used to rap.

I let my mom hear a tape of what he did, and she loved it! So my mother said, "Give us a couple of days." They were going to go in the studio and record a useful track, because back then we'd never heard of sampling. Our company at the time was called All-Platinum Records. It was a big R&B/soul company, and we were known for putting violins, strings, trumpets, bass, the whole nine yards on our tracks. She wanted to cut a track that was like "Good Times"—that one little part of "Good Times" that was really great, the bass line. And then we came up with another part, and we put them both together, and she went into the studio and cut the songs with her musicians.

The next day I went looking for Casper, the rapper, and all of a sudden I didn't hear from him for like two or three days. I finally found him, and I said, "Casper, we cut the track. We're ready to go," and he was like, "Listen, my father advised me not to do it." His father was a DJ, and at that time my parents' company was in a big litigation with Polygram Records overseas. That was public knowledge. They were trying to take over our company. And Casper's father told him not to do the record with us.

Later I was with a friend named Warren Moore, and he said, "We know some other people that rap, don't worry about that.... Get in the car, and we'll take you somewhere to let you hear somebody."

So we left our studio in my Oldsmobile 98 and went to Palisades Avenue, which was about five minutes away. My friend Warren knew of Henry Jackson—I didn't know Hank, didn't know he could rap. Warren went in the pizza parlor, and said, "Listen, Mrs. Robinson is auditioning rappers ...."

BIG BANK HANK: I grew up with people like Kool Herc; he lived two buildings down from me. We're going back to like '74, '73. Coke La Rock, Kool DJ Herc, we all went to high school together. We all lived within one minute of each other, and every party we was always together. We always hung out at night. Then I hooked up with a person by the name of Caz.

GRANDMASTER CAZ: I met Big Bank Hank at the Sparkle. He worked the door, and I'd kick it with him. He had a genuine interest in hip-hop and seemed to have his head on straight. He was a little older than most of the guys I was around, and I felt like he could help us. I thought he'd be good as our manager. We had the records but lacked a good sound system—a set. Hip-hop was still at a time where it was about the DJ and your sound system. You had to have a big sound system to be competitive with the Kool Hercs and the Bambaataas and the Flashes, the Breakouts, so that's what we went about doing.

Hank went to his parents—his father was a superintendent of a building behind University Avenue where he lived. They gave him a loan so he could buy us some equipment. He had this Jamaican guy build us four speakers the size of refrigerators. This was before the Cold Crush—the group was the Mighty Force. We got a big power amp. We thought we was ready! Four Dynaco 700 power amps, four big double-15" speakers!

But money was coming in too slow. We was only charging $2 to get into our parties back then. In order to pay back the loan, Hank got a job at a pizza shop in Jersey. I used to make practice tapes at my house, saying my rhymes and DJ-ing my beats. Hank took the tapes to work with him. One day Sylvia Robinson's son came into the pizza shop. They heard Hank rhyming along to the tape, and they asked him if he wanted to become part of this group they was forming called the Sugar Hill Gang.

HANK: My friend owned a pizza shop, and I was on summer break. I'm making pizza, and Joey and his mother walk in. I don't know these people at all, right? It's like somebody walking up to you and saying, "I want you to make a record for me." I'm looking around going, "Did I miss something here? It's a joke, right?" No, no, no—they were serious! Picture this: I'm full of pizza dough, and I'm like, "Okay, they want me to come outside and audition in the car?" I'm like, "Ooookkkkaaaayy..."

JOEY: So people was eating at the pizza parlor, and all of a sudden he's kicking everybody out the pizza parlor. "Take your food and leave, you gotta go!" Then he's got all this dough on him, and an apron. He gets in the back of my Oldsmobile car, and my car goes like [makes car groaning noise].

HANK: Okay, I am a big guy. That's where the Big Hank came from. I'm a football player.

JOEY ROBINSON:
In 1979 my mother—Sylvia Robinson—had a birthday party in New York City at a famous place called Harlem World. That's when she first saw a rapper, like spinning records and talking on the mic, and seeing the people respond to it. That's where she got the idea to do a rap record.

The Sugarhill Gang at Disco Fever, c. 1980 (Courtesy Sal Abbatiello)

JOEY: So he gets in the car, and I play the musical track on the tape deck, and he starts rappin'. And all this commotion starts going on around my car, people started singin'...I was like, "Wow! He's rockin'!" Then, with all the commotion going on, another friend of mine happened to be walking by with someone else, and he heard all this stuff going on. I rolled my window down, and he says, "Joey. Hank...he's nice, but listen to my man. He's even nicer than him!" And that was Guy O'Brien, Master Gee. So then Guy gets in the car, and he starts rappin', so now the two of them are battlin'.

HANK: I did my thing, not thinking of the immensity of what could happen. I mean who could have even dreamed of something like that? When Guy came and we started battling, it gave me a little bit more enthusiasm, you know?

JOEY: So then Wonder Mike happened to be playing a guitar across the street, and he says, "I can rap, too." So I have all this commotion going on, all these people hearin' this stuff, the crowd's getting bigger and bigger.... He jumps in my car, and we go to my mom's house. That night my mother's listening to Guy—Master Gee—and Hank, and she says, "That's it! That's it! I just came up with a new record company called Sugarhill Records, and you all are the first group on Sugarhill Records. We'll name you the Sugar Hill Gang." Then Wonder Mike, who has asthma, says, "Mrs. Robinson you didn't hear me..."

WONDER MIKE: I was sittin' there, and Guy and Hank were going back and forth— this is in Ms. Robinson's living room, it's about midnight—and they're, "Yeah, yeah, that sounds good!" I'm thinking to myself, "Look, speak up. This could be your chance." So I said, "Mrs. Robinson, you know, I can rhyme, too."

JOEY: She wasn't really interested in hearing Mike because she already heard these two guys here really rap. But she says, "Okay, let me hear you rap."

MIKE: So I start, "The hip...hop...the hibbit, the hibby dibby hibby hibba ...," and I kept going, incorporating everything I saw in the room, from the dog to the statue to the library books...That was how it started. Our voices and styles blended so well that she said, "We're going to use all three of you guys."

CAZ: Hank came over to my house and said, "Yo. These people want me to make a record." "You? You ain't no MC! You tell them about me?" Hank said, "Yeah, but they wanted me." Personally, I was shocked because Hank is not an MC, you know? He was the manager, so I would figure that he would say, "Well, I'm not an MC, but I manage these guys that are on this tape." But whatever.... So he came to me, and he told me about it, and I figured if somethin' comes out of it I guess we're next. I guess if you get anything from it, it can only help us.

MIKE: The audition was on a Friday night. She said, "Come in Monday, and we'll cut a record." It took one day to make "Rapper's Delight." A few hours to do the music, and the raps were done in one take, except we stopped one time; the rest of it just went straight through.

We gleaned the lyrics from our own repertoire and just improvised from there what we were going to use. But I didn't want to just open "Rapper's Delight" by going into rhymes. I thought, "There has to be a little phrase where I'm explaining what's going on, because this is like new to the world." So I said: "Now what you hear is not a test, I'm rappin' to the beat...." And I kinda explained it right then, and it went on from there. In fact the only thing written for "Rapper's Delight" was the intro; all those other rhymes throughout the whole fifteen-minute song was already in our repertoire. But I said, "We have to start this thing out right."

rapper's delight hits the airwaves

HANK: I'm in the pizza shop making pizza. The shop is jam-packed with people. There's a radio station by the name of KTU that's on, and I hear, "We have a new record by the Sugar Hill Gang." I'm like, "Whoa man! Turn this up! This is me!" They play the record. Now you have to understand, this record is almost sixteen minutes long, right? They played it in its entirety. When they got maybe three minutes into the record, the DJ got on and said, "Our phone lines are locked. Please do not call this station anymore. We will play the record again." They had to play the record twice, back-to-back. That's thirty-two minutes!

JOEY: When we released the record, it was massive. I mean, people were waiting in the stores for weeks upon weeks. We couldn't sell the record fast enough; we couldn't press it fast enough. People were calling the radio station...the radio would go on the air and say, "Stop calling, we're not going to play the record any more. We're going to play it at 7 o'clock, we're going to play it at 10 o'clock, we're going to play it at 12 o'clock." Just so that the phone lines would be free, because so many calls were coming in on this record.

BILL ADLER: I was working as the pop music critic at the Boston Herald in 1979 when "Rapper's Delight" became this phenomenon on radio there. I used to listen to the Black music radio station in Boston, and they played "Rapper's Delight." What was remarkable about it to me wasn't so much the fact that these guys were rapping, but that that particular song lasted fifteen minutes. It was fifteen minutes long. There was an edited version of it, but I never heard the edit because it was such a smash that people wanted to hear it at its full length. I mean this was a Black radio station, but it was a pop format—most of the songs were three minutes long—yet this song would play for five times that length every time you heard it. So that was remarkable to me. More remarkable than the fact that these guys weren't singing, because in terms of the music, the Sugar Hill Gang just sounded like the R&B of the day.

MIKE: We did our first show in a place called Club Paradisio in Newark. We did two shows there, and ohhh it was crazy! The first show was on a Friday night; the second show was a Saturday matinee show with younger kids. During that matinee show on Saturday, there were girls fainting, and they were passing them over the crowd. We didn't even get to finish the show. We had these big burly bodyguards standing in the front of the stage, and the crowd just pushed them aside, rushed the stage. We had to run off the stage through the crowd, through the back door, down the alley, and there were like 100, 150 kids chasing us. And we ran into the van and just got out of there. It was crazy.

HANK: I mean one minute you're walking down the street. The next minute you've got bodyguards and being chased down the street.

MIKE: I originally thought hip-hop was going to be big in the tri-state area—New York, New Jersey, and Connecticut. And when we got calls to do shows in South Carolina and Virginia, I said, "Wow this is really spreading fast!" And we'd get the Billboard magazine and see that we'd been added to play lists in San Diego, L.A., Texas. And then London and Italy, and I said, "Well, this is here to stay! This is not a fad."

Spoonie Gee staring down the heat on 125th Street, August, 1980 (© Charlie Ahearn)

Phillip Edwards
Record Report

Singles   WE ARE NUMBER ONE......   **Albums**

49th Week, 1979   Dec. 2-8

1	SECOND TIME AROUND	SHALAMAR	BIG FUN
2	I WANNA BE YOUR LOVER	PRINCE	PRINCE
3	DO YOU LIKE WHAT YOU FEEL	RUFUS/CHAKA	MASTERJAM
4	SPOONIN RAP	SPOONIN GEE	12"
5	STILL	THE COMMODORES	COMMODORES
6	ROCK WITH YOU	MICHAEL JACKSON	OFF THE WALL
7	KNEE DEEP	FUNKADELICS	7"
8	RAPPERS DELIGHT	SUGARHILL GANG	12"
9	CRUSIN	SMOKEY ROBINSON	WHERE THERE'S SMOKE
10	FOREVER MINE	O'JAYS	IDENTIFY YOURSELF
11	LADIES NIGHT	KOOL AND GANG	LADIES NIGHT
12	NO MORE TEARS	D. SUMMER/B. STREISAND	GREATEST HITS
13	DEPUTY OF LOVE	DON ARMANDO	12"
14	SEND ONE YOUR LOVE	STEVIE WONDER	SECRET LIFE OF PLANTS
15	DO THAT TO ME ONE MORE TIME	CAPT/TENILLE	MAKE YOUR MOVE
16	DON'T LET GO (LP cut)	ISAAC HAYES	DON'T LET GO
17	SHOW ME HOW TO DANCE	ARCHIE BELL/DRELL	STRATEGY
18	SPECIAL LADY	RAY, GOODMAN & BROWN	RAY, GOODMAN & BROWN
19	ROTATION	HERB ALPERT	RISE
20	DIM ALL THE LIGHTS	DONNA SUMMER	BAD GIRLS
21	RAPPIN AND ROCKING THE HOUSE	FUNKY FOUR	12"
22	SO GOOD SO RIGHT	BRENDA RUSSEL	12"
23	ROLLER SKATIN MATE	PEACHES AND HERB	TWICE THE FIRE
24	MOVE YOUR BOOGIE BODY	BARKAYS	INJOY
25	MUSIC (LP cut)	AL HUTSON	ONE WAY
26	COME TO ME	FRANCE JOLI	FRANCE JOLI
27	STREET LIFE	CRUSADERS	STREET LIFE
28	GANG BUSTERS	GARY'S GANG	12"
29	HARMONY	SUZI LANE	FIREDUP
30	LOVE GUN	RICK JAMES	FIREDUP

NEW RELEASES

DO YOU WANNA MAKE LOVE	MILLIE J. & ISAAC HAYES	
DON'T STOP THIS FEELING	ROY AYERS	
LATE NIGHT SURRENDER	JEREE PALMER	
DANCING TO KEEP FROM CRYING	BARBARA JEAN ENGLISH	
DON'T EVER WANNA LOVE NOBODY BUT YOU	CREME D' COCOA	

Dynamite Pick

BOUNCE, ROCK, SKATE, ROLL   Vaughan Mason & Crew D211

HIT TOWN

611 WEST 125th STREET, NEW YORK, NY.
Tele. (212) 662-2230

SOUND OF NEW YORK
2 great disco 45's

SPOONIN RAP
I DON'T DRINK SMOKE OR GAMBLE NEITHER
I'M THE COLD CRUSHING LOVER
(Spoonin Gee)
SPOONIN GEE
QC 708 B

WILLIE RAP
(Kevin Johnson & Willie Wood)
Willie Wood & Willie Wood Crew
QC 709 A

This *Record Report* from December, 1979, charts the moment rap singles landed with "Spoonin Rap" leading the pack at #4. "Rapper's Delight" has dropped (from November) to #8 and "Rappin' and Rockin' the House" has come in at #22. Not charted yet are Kurtis Blow's "Christmas Rappin'" and "Superrappin'" by Grandmaster Flash.

GRANDMASTER FLASH: I knew all the crews, what they were doing, when they were doing it, and where they were doing it. But strangely enough, in '79, there was this record that came on the radio: "to the hip hop the hibby dibby...." I'm like, hold off. This is not AJ. It's not L Brothers. It's not Herc. It's not Bam. It's not Breakout. Who are these people? Turned out it was some crew from Jersey. I'm wondering why don't I know about them because I was real particular about who was doing what, at least the ones that was rocking, you know what I mean? This group consisted of three people. One person I knew to be a bouncer at the Godfather's Club, Kool Herc's place. And some of the rhymes that he was saying I knew from Grandmaster Caz. I'm saying, "Well, damn, I heard these rhymes said by Caz." But this guy, who was a bouncer at the club is saying these rhymes on the record. These other two guys, I didn't have a clue who they were.

CAZ: Hank was like, "Yo. I want to use some of your rhymes." I said, "Here..." It wasn't like, "How much you gonna pay me?" or none of that. I just threw the book on the table and said, "Use whichever one you want." That turned out to be "I'm the C-A-S and the O-V-A and the rest is F-L-Y"—that's Casanova Fly, that's my name. He never changed it. He just took the rhymes like they were, and he didn't change it up. "I'm the Grandmaster with the three MCs," and all that. That's my stuff. The Superman rhyme about Lois Lane, flying through the air, panty hose? That was one of my earliest rhymes before I really developed as a writer, in 1977 or '78. It was one of the most popular rhymes on the street—everybody that knew hip-hop knew that rhyme.

WHIPPER WHIP: When you'd go around town you'd hear people say Caz's rhymes, 'cause Caz was a story writer. His first thing was this Superman rhyme, what Big Bank Hank did on the Sugarhill. He had the whole city saying his Superman rhyme. I mean we'd go places and hear other rappers saying his rhymes as if it was theirs, you know?

CAZ: I didn't see Hank for another month. When I saw him again, he came to my house with the acetate of "Rapper's Delight," and he played it for me. I fell asleep listening to it 'cause it was garbage. "That's not MC-ing. None o' you niggas is MCs. That ain't what we doing. That's some cornball shit."

At the time hip-hop was limited to a small group of people. Whatever you did, everybody knew what it was and who was doing it. Boom...every car that went by was playing "Rapper's Delight." People would be coming up to me, "Yo! I heard your record! Yo! I heard you on the radio! I heard your rhyme!" I was, "Nah, that ain't me. That's just my rhyme." "Yo! I know you're getting paid!"

RAHIEM: Big Bank Hank bit a portion of my rhyme in "Rapper's Delight"—the first rhyme that I had ever gotten any kind of notoriety for: "I said I'm hip, the dip, the women's pimp, the women fight for my delight...." I don't remember how the rest of his rhyme went, but I do know that Hank was a bouncer, and he had access to all of the tapes of everybody who was doing shows at the time. So that's how he knew everybody's rhymes.

DISCO WIZ: Hank used to take Caz's practice tapes and sing along a little...but that's it! Like if you were to sing a Britney Spears joint, you know what I mean? There's no connection—you're just singing along to somebody else's stuff. Hank's not an MC! He was just hangin' on. Caz, being the way he was, trusted the guy, because Caz was looking for a shot, too. Hank used his rhyme, word for word, and Caz never saw a dime from that. It's funny, because "Rapper's Delight" skyrocketed hip-hop onto the map, but it's a farce. It's a total farce. You know what I mean?

MIKE: Yeah, people say they wrote our stuff. I remember everything I wrote and where I wrote it. That food rap, where I went over to a friend's house to eat, I wrote that in an alley next to a record store and a ladies dress shop. It just came to me, and I just stopped and I wrote it right there. But I think there's no denying there's a lot of shout-outs and phrases that were just like the common vocabulary at the time.

JOEY: I see different interviews where some of the rappers have a lot of animosity for the Gang because they say they wasn't from the streets, they wasn't from this, and they wasn't from that. But Hank was from the Bronx. He was from the streets. Master Gee was in the group called Phase 2. Wonder Mike was in a group called Sound on Sound. So these guys were all in rap groups at the time that my mother had the idea to do this. She happened to come up with it first. And whenever you come up with something first, people knock you for something, where truthfully it should be praised.

MIKE: You cannot deny the fact that Sugar Hill Gang was the first big rap group! And if we don't get respect from someone, screw 'em! We opened the doors for a lot of people. Ninety-nine percent of the hip-hop world respects us, and they show us mad love. But this pocket of people...instead of concentrating on their own careers and getting a record deal, their life consists of trying to belittle the Sugar Hill Gang. It's unfortunate.

CAZ: Hank never got back in touch with me. Not only did he not compensate me for my rhymes, we didn't even get to keep the equipment! Hank is still on the road, touring with that shit. By the time I caught up with him, Hank had two Cadillacs. He had rings on every finger. He was living!

WHIPPER WHIP: When "Rapper's Delight" first came out, I was really proud. I had no idea what the money was like, but just the fact that you got a record that's being played on every radio station everywhere you go, and you know it was written by your people, said by your people—this was a great thing. I had no idea what publishing meant, I had no idea what writers meant...'cause a few of my lines are in there, too, you know? So it was good in a way, but then it turned out to be a nightmare for Caz, 'cause when you think about it, he'd be a millionaire right now. Literally, because that is the classic, and he never saw 10 cents from it. The record went and sold I don't know how many million copies, and to this day it's still getting played, and it'll be getting played forever because it was the first of its kind. So Sylvia Robinson knew what she was doing. Joey Robinson knew what they were doing. It's just that that's what happens when you don't know.

christmas rappin'

J. B. MOORE: Robert Ford and I got to know each other at *Billboard* magazine [the primary music trade journal]; Robert was there for eight years, and I was there for five. I started in '75. He was a Black guy from the middle of Hollis, Queens, and I was a white guy from the north shore of Long Island. As we got to know each other, we realized that our record collections were virtually identical—we had much of the same taste in music, especially jazz.

I was at Downstairs Records [in midtown Manhattan] one day, asking John—one of the owners—what's new, and he said, "B-boys and b-beats." Kids from the Bronx had been coming down and requesting some record that had the lyrics "sex machine" but was not James Brown. They were desperate for this record, and John finally tracked it down. He had ten guys come in, and they asked him the same question. I thought... there must be something going on here.

I came back to the office and talked to Robert, who then had the Rhythm and Blues column, and said, "Robert, this is interesting. You should go talk to him. There's something happening here." Because it had the aroma, to me, of doo-wop, which was something that came from the street up rather than from the top down.

ROBERT FORD: Thanks to J.B., I went up to Taft High School in the Bronx with Nelson George, and we met DJ Kool Herc, who was really sort of the father of a lot of the rapping and cutting DJs up in the Bronx. That was the start for me; I did stories on DJ Kool Herc, DJ Hollywood, Eddie Cheba, DJ Starski. My early stories ran as far back as '77.

At one point I was on the bus, and I saw a kid putting up these stickers for Rush Productions. The kid turned out to be Russell Simmons's brother; he went on to become Run [of Run-D.M.C.]. I became friends with Russell. He was always at my house, at my office, and he was, to a certain degree, my ambassador to rap music. Russell introduced me to a lot of people and was directly responsible for the series of interviews I did with Starski, Hollywood, Cheba.

Russell had this bright idea to make a record with this guy called Kurtis Blow. Now ...for me, Russell was more important than Kurt was himself, only because Russell understood the business end that I couldn't understand. I was already thirty years old, and I felt that I was a little long in the tooth for this art form.

Around that time, Nelson and I went to Harlem to the Apollo to see the Ohio Players, Kool and the Gang, and DJ Hollywood. At that point in the history of the world, the Ohio Players and Kool and the Gang were the two biggest acts in Black music, and yet, by the end of the Ohio Players set, people were yelling to bring back Hollywood, 'cause Hollywood was so talented—he had so much charisma. He wasn't the matinee idol–looking type of person, but he could do everything. He talked, he rapped, he sang ...he did almost everything you could want anybody to do. He, to me, may have been the most talented rapper I ever saw. If DJ Hollywood was available, there's no question, I would have made records with Hollywood. Or for that matter, Eddie Cheba who is also very talented and had a lot going for him. But they weren't available. Hollywood was apparently well connected with some very well connected people in Harlem, and they were the sort of people who were not necessarily conducive to a long, healthy, happy career.

I discovered I was gonna become a father in 1979, so I needed money. So Russell's idea about making a record with Kurtis Blow suddenly made a lot more sense to me. One of my mentors at *Billboard* was Mickey Addy. He was the person who taught me about music publishing. Mickey always had nice little checks from writing old Christmas songs for Perry Como, so I said, "I'm gonna write a Christmas record." I had this idea to write a record and use Kurtis. Russell just, basically, wanted to get over....He wanted to be a part of it and obviously wanted Kurtis to be a part of it. I had no idea how to write it or anything like that. Then one day, J. B., who I talked about everything with, called me up with 90 percent of the "Christmas Rap."

SUGARHILL'S 1st ANNUAL RAPPER'S CONVENTION

Starring:

SUGARHILL GANG   **GRAND MASTER FLASH and the FURIOUS FIVE**   **FUNKY FOUR Plus 1**

Special Guests:

★ **CRASH CREW**

★ **SPOONIE GEE**

★ **TREACHEROUS 3**

SEQUENCE with BLONDY

TO BE HELD AT

T. S. MONK

369th REGIMENT ARMORY

2366 FIFTH AVENUE, NEW YORK CITY

SATURDAY EVENING, MAY 9, 1981

Invited Guests:

★ JUNE BUG & THE CREW DISCO FEVER   ★ BAMBAATAA with THE ZULU NATION   ★ D.J. STARSKY from HARLEM WORLD
★ GRAND WIZARD THEODORE with THE FANTASTIC ROMANTIC FIVE
★ MR. MAGIC - RADIO STATION WHBI THE MEAN MACHINE
CHARLIE & WAYNE - THE RAPPER DUMMY

TICKETS ON SALE— IN NEW YORK: RECORD SHACK, TICKETRON, BERDELL'S RECORDS. Brooklyn.
IN NEW JERSEY: BAMBERGERS — Newark, BAND WAGON — East Orange,
BIG SOUNDS and RECORDS ARE US — Plainfield

TICKETS: $10.00 Advance — $12.00 At Door

J. B.: We both had quit Billboard in September of '79 for different reasons, but we were still both writing. We ran into each other in the office in September, and Robert said he had the idea for a "Christmas Rap." I went home that night and did a parody, basically, of "The Night Before Christmas," done in rap. Robert and I got together the next day. I had a studio that I liked in New York, which was called Big Apple, and an engineer that I liked, Roddy Hui, who's since done quite a few rap records. I knew a couple of musicians, and Robert knew some musicians, and we all got together and wrote that song—Robert and I, Kurtis, Denzil Miller, who's a well-known keyboard player, and Larry Smith. We assembled everyone down at the studio and made this record in a big fat hurry.

I had been saving money for five years to leave *Billboard* to write a book. I had about $10,000 saved, and that got invested in making "Christmas Rappin'." The record went to twenty-two or twenty-three different labels—all of whom turned it down.

ROBERT: This is before any other rap record, with the exception of the Fatback Band's "King Tim," which really was the first charted rap record. Nothing else had been out at the time we started doing it, so I kind of expected all of the majors to just turn us down. You have to remember the fact that rock 'n' roll, in its very early days, was rejected by a lot of labels. But I also knew that it was a record that was going to sell, if it ever got to the light of day. Rap was something that any idiot had to know was at some point going to be big, so I fully expected other people were working on it. Then "Rapper's Delight" came out in October. All of a sudden, it was the biggest-selling record ever, you know. I mean...it was selling 100,000 copies a week in New York City alone. So we knew that this was going to sell. Unfortunately, corporations generally are fairly slow to understand.

J. B.: When we finally got the deal at Mercury, it was because it was releasable in England. The record was discovered by a newly arrived English A&R man in Los Angeles as a tape on his desk. His name was John Stains, and he called up Chicago, which was where Mercury headquarters was then, and said, "I can recoup this out of London." So they picked it up for $6,000 and did, in fact, recoup it out of England. The record broke the Top 30 over there.

Our idea was to make an acceptable-to-major-label record on the first four minutes of it and make a rap record on the back four minutes, which was exactly what we did. And it was the back-end lyrics that made the difference on the record. The record was basically a great funk record with a rap on top of it.

ROBERT: The record sold about 100,000 records before Christmas and about 300,000 after Christmas. Russell was still somewhat green, and I was enlisted as Kurtis's road manager. We were on the road, working in markets like North Carolina, South Carolina, Detroit...Cleveland was very big for us, Baltimore was very big for us. Mercury ended up releasing the flip side as something called, "Rappin' Blow." That was Kurtis's free-form rap, his contribution to the record; he did a lot of the stuff that he was doing live.

One of the great advantages with Kurtis Blow was that he could travel light. It was me, Davy D—who was his original DJ, Kurtis, and a garment bag, which they carried turntables in. So we were able to do shows at the drop of a hat, things that other acts couldn't do. If somebody called us on Thursday and said, "We got a date for you on Saturday," we could be there. We could fly, which is something that very few live acts could do, so we could go anywhere.

One of the interesting things about the early days of rap was that nobody involved knew what they were doing. I knew most of the old standard record-business clichés: go to the town, meet the promotion man, go do the radio station interviews, that sort of thing. I learned from working at Billboard that I had to do that. That was another reason I became Kurtis's road manager, 'cause I could maximize things early on, which Russell took a while to pick up on. Mercury stayed out of our way, which kind of was nice.

J. B.: Our deal with Mercury was a so-called "step deal." You make the first 12", we give you "x" number of dollars; if we feel like maybe you could make another one, we give you the next 12", and thereafter you finally give an album. They asked us for "The Breaks" in March or April 1980. "Christmas Rappin'" had been the winter of 1979. And we began in late April, early May of 1980 to make "The Breaks," which was the biggest dance record of the summer of 1980.

post—rapper's delight: the fallout

MIKE: It's a strange feeling. When "Rapper's Delight" came out, the world heard my voice first. Sometimes when I'm alone, I think, "Wow! Out of all the people that have done hip-hop records and gone to the concerts and bought the clothes, and practiced and wished and dreamed and failed and succeeded in this world, no matter what anybody says, they heard the Sugar Hill Gang first, heard my voice first!"

JOEY: You can't take away the history. You can't take away the reality that it was Sugarhill that had the idea to take this kind of music, take a chance, and put it out on wax—record it. But if people say, "Did you invent rap?" No, we never said we invented rap. But we made it mainstream, took it to another level. So many people try to knock what we came with, but the reality is, if we didn't come with "Rapper's Delight" and it wasn't as big a record as it was...you never know...

RICHARD SISCO: Not takin' anything away from Sugar Hill Gang or nothin', but Caz's style was one of the best in rap. He really had the stories down pat, with his rhymes, the story line....He was a master, not just some guy who could do it or a wanna-be. If he was the one recording, it would've been a different thing. You would've had a leader, and everybody would've followed him, but the way it happened, there wasn't a real leader out there. If the leaders of the street thing that we was doin' had got to do the record first, it would definitely have been something different. But, you know...that's neither here nor there.

ART ARMSTRONG: The beginning of the end really started when rap started being recorded. A lot of artists from the first period didn't understand a change was coming, so I don't think they took recording seriously enough. Rap was becoming more sophisticated, and I don't think that a lot of the old-school rappers really understood that.

It was like when Jackie Robinson made the major leagues. They had the Negro League during that period, so what happened was, Black people started going to the majors, and that signaled the end of the Negro League. That was what happened when rap started being recorded. Of the rap artists who were very popular before recorded music, only a few started recording, and everything started focusing on who was putting out records.

GRANDMASTER FLASH: The game of hip-hop changed. "Rapper's Delight" just set the goal to whole 'nother level. It wasn't rule the Bronx or rule Manhattan, or rule whatever. It was now how soon can you make a record.

REGGIE REG: Guys was going crazy over this "Rapper's Delight" thing. It was a very good record, and seeing how good that record was doing, the attention that record got, we knew we had to make a record.

SAL ABBATIELLO: When "Rapper's Delight" came out all the kids started becoming recording artists. Each week we had a new kid becoming a recording artist, so it was a very fun time and exciting, except we were still in a very poor neighborhood. The people making records was still poor 'cause they weren't getting advances or anything. They was just like, "Oh god, I got a record out." This went on for a few years before they even started thinking about money, you know? This was just so exciting, coming back to their neighborhood with a record.

AFRIKA BAMBAATAA: When we started seeing the recordings, a lot of us in the Zulu Nation stayed away from that at first because people thought once it got into vinyl it was going to kill the culture. We waited on the line just to see where everybody was going because we started hearing that a lot of people was getting robbed; they wasn't getting paid for this and that, and certain record companies would keep you away from knowing about how many records you were selling. They didn't teach you about your mechanical rights or your royalties or your publishing. The same thing that happened with a lot of the groups in the '50s and the '60s, they was doing it again to the groups in the '70s and the early '80s.

DJ BARON: We pioneered the rappin' in the street. We had our stint between 1977 and 1980, but it really never happened for us. You have to do your homework before you get into this game, 'cause if you don't do your homework, you'll be lost in the sauce. And that's a fact. People just sign on the dotted line; that first check, oh... they're all happy with that. And then, as time goes by, they say, "Well, where's the money at?" Record company's got all the money.

SHA-ROCK: Putting it on vinyl did change things a lot, and I think it changed it for the best. What recording did was open it up. A lot of people that didn't have the opportunities to listen to it in New York when it first started could now see that it was something good. This is a part of history. So I think that it was for the best.

The Sugarhill Gang and Sugar Hill records emerged simultaneously. When Sylvia Robinson rushed "Rapper's Delight" to market in 1979 the company had not yet developed the distinctive logo that appeared on subsequent releases.

FRESH, WILD, FLY AND BOLD:

the scene: 1980-1981

"Rapper's Delight" hit in October 1979. By November, Bobby Robinson, a music industry veteran who had been putting out doo-wop and R&B records since 1951, had released "Superrappin'," by Grandmaster Flash and the Furious 5, and "Rappin' and Rockin' the House," by the Funky 4 + 1, followed by singles by Spoonie Gee and the Treacherous 3. Fans will tell you that these records were superior to the fare being released by Sugarhill at the time, but Sugarhill remained the more successful label, and over the next couple of years they lured Bobby's most successful acts to their stable with promises of fame and fortune. Sugarhill delivered on the fame part: Flash and the Furious had their first gold record on Sugarhill with "Freedom," and the Funky 4's "That's the Joint," also on Sugarhill, was their biggest hit. On the strength of this success, the Sugarhill acts hit the road in 1981, providing a heady experience for these kids from the Bronx, many of whom were not yet out of high school.

But the fortune never came about for most of these groups. Flash and the Furious 5 had a huge hit with "The Message"—a song that rivaled "Rapper's Delight" in impact—but as had happened with pioneering artists in other genres, the contracts they signed in their youthful exuberance didn't serve their interests. Seeing that their more successful peers weren't being treated fairly reinforced the skepticism of the groups who were watching and waiting rather than signing with a label. While the new recording stars were on the road and in the studio, the newly formed Fantastic 5 and Cold Crush Brothers took over performing on the Bronx scene. In Manhattan, the Treacherous 3 signed with Sugarhill along with the Crash Crew and other newcomers. A new label and a new group seemed to spring up every week.

ENJOY
RECORDS

Sweet Soul Music
BMI
EN 1003
Time: 12:03

#6001
℗© 1979

SUPERAPPIN'
(E. Morris, R. Wiggins, N. Glover, M. Glover, T. Williams, B. Robinson)

GRANDMASTER FLASH
and the FURIOUS FIVE

Produced by Bobby Robinson

33⅓ RPM

superrappin'
flash & the furious 5

RAHIEM: There were a handful of record company people that hung out at the parties around that time, and on a few occasions they had approached us about making a record. We had flatly turned them down. We was like, "No! Nobody wants to hear this stuff on a record." Then the first record that we all heard was "King Tim III." It was rap, but it wasn't anyone who was known to us. As far as we knew, we were the best doing it at that time, and we felt like this "King Tim III" guy, he's kinda wack. He's not a real MC. Then when we heard "Rapper's Delight" for the first time, I remember discussing it as a group, and we were saying how we were gonna approach the record label that they were signed to and see if we could make a record.

FLASH: There was this wrinkled old guy who used to just come in and watch us perform. Now my audience ages range between sixteen to maybe thirty, so he could only be one of two people: he could either be the police or he was somebody's father looking for his daughter. Either one I definitely did not want to get entangled with.

He eventually stepped to me at a party, after I was breaking down my sound system, and asked if I would like to make a record. His name was Bobby Robinson, of Enjoy Records. We agreed, then, that this was a new goal. Doing the street thing, it's okay...let's make records now. And the record was called "Superrappin'"—that was our first record on Enjoy Records.

RAY CHANDLER: Bobby [Robinson] started recording them without me knowing. One night I went up; they was playing in the studio and I seen Bobby up there. I said, "What are you doing? This is my group." "Oh I'm just making this little thing with the fellas." All along he was making deals with them. He was perpetrating that he was my friend, but he was a snake.

KID CREOLE: When Sugar Hill Gang came out with "Rapper's Delight," every jerk with a producer or promoter was trying to get a record out. We had released two records before we got down with Sugarhill Records. One was on the Brazilia label, and the kid who put it together wanted us to change our name. I guess the Furious 5 wasn't good enough for him; he wanted us to change our name to the Younger Generation, and we recorded a joint called "We Rap More Mellow." Then we did a joint on Enjoy called "Superrappin'." That was the joint that we played like a fifteen-minute version of "Bra" (by Cymande).

RAHIEM: I don't remember exactly how we met Bobby Robinson, the president of Enjoy Records. All I remember about that meeting was that one day we were talking to him, and less than a week later, we were in the studio recording "Superrappin'." Melle Mel and I made up most of the words to "Superrappin'" just walking through Crotona Park one day.

We recorded a few songs with Enjoy. I guess the reason why we left Enjoy Records was because we felt like we didn't get an accurate accounting of our record sales. I remember us getting paid $1,200 apiece for "Superrappin'", and that was it. We each bought motorcycles—except Flash. The five of us bought these little Yamaha GT-80s.

We met with Bobby Robinson on this one day, and we were discussing our royalties with him. There was something that we thought was kinda shady about him, so we were more confrontational, not just laid back and willing to listen to him give us an explanation as to when we were gonna get the money. Well, one thing led to another, and it turned into a really big blown-out argument, on 125th Street and 8th Avenue. I remember it was like 95 degrees in the shade, and at that time, if I had to guess, I would say Bobby Robinson was in his late fifties. He fell out. He fell out backwards, like he fainted, and hit his head on the sidewalk. I remember his daughter running from his record shop across the street, and we helped him up and carried him inside of a clinic or something like that. And we sat there and waited for him to come to. When he came to, we said "Bobby, where's our money?!" [laughs] But nevertheless, we never got any more money from Bobby.

KID CREOLE: When we started hearing rumblings that Sugarhill Records wanted to sign us, we was real excited. Even though we considered the Sugar Hill Gang a bunch of frauds and our archenemy—at that point, Sugarhill was the only game in town. We went out to the house; they showed us the big house and the whole thing. It was real exciting.

RAHIEM: We met Joey Robinson from Sugarhill Records. His cousin knew Flash, so he introduced Flash to Joey Robinson, and then Flash and Joey brought the group to Sylvia. Sylvia Robinson bought us out of the contract with Bobby Robinson. She paid him $10,000. I remember us getting a contract from them, and I think it was about $1,000 apiece. When we were issued Sugarhill recording contracts, we signed them on a car, like on the trunk of a car. Now I was a minor, so my signature didn't mean diddly. I took it to an attorney, and he advised us not to sign it, and my mother was totally down with the attorney, the advice the attorney gave us. So I really didn't sign with Sugarhill until I turned eighteen.

Bounce, rock, skate, and roll at the Ecstasy Garage, 1980

CHECK IT OUT... More Exciting! More Luxurious!

The New **Ecstasy Garage Disco**

1508 Macombs Rd.
Bet. 172 st. & Gobel Pl.
Near Jerome Skating Rink

Presents Our

GRAND RE-OPENING PARTY!

FRI, JUNE 6, 80

GRAND MASTER **FLASH**
Disco Bee
E-Z Mike
Furious 5 M.C.s
MELE-MEL MR. NESS RAHIEM
COWBOY KID CREOLE

ROCKWELL CREW
Kevie-Kev
& THE 4 M.C.s

LADIES FREE 8-4 10:30
GENTS $4 ALL NITE
9:30 until

SAT, JUNE 7:
THEODORE
Fantastic 5 M.C.s
Kool Dee Crew

4, D Train to 170 or 173 st.

Ladies $1b/4 11
Gents $3 all nite

Martin Williams/Buddy-Esq.

Man Dip Lite
Presents
PART 2 OF

"THE Grand Master
FLASH SHOW"

Starring
Grand Master **FLASH**

Furious 5 M.C.s
Mele·Mel Mr.Ness Rahiem Cowboy Kid Creole

N.J.'s No.1 Crew

T.FLARE & THE
**ACT II KAOS
CREW** CREW

**FRI,
JUNE 13,80**

American Legion
Forest Ave.

9pm-until

SPECIAL GUEST
THEODORE
THE GRAND WIZARD

$4 BEFORE **10PM $5**AFTER

Buddy·Esq.

MAN DIP LITE
PRESENTS:
"THE GRAND MASTER FLASH SHOW"

STARRING GRAND MASTER **FLASH**

E·Z Mike Disco Bee
Furious 5 M.C.s
Mele·Mel Mr.Ness Rahiem Cowboy Kid Creole

ALSO STARRING **ALLAH SOUNDS**
DJs **Divine & Kendo**

SPECIAL GUEST:
THE GRAND WIZARD
THEODORE

SPECIAL ADDED ATTRACTION:
RECORDING STAR
KOOL KYLE

Master Scott & R.G. Kid

SAT, JULY 12, 80

Rochdale Village
Community Center
BET FIDEL & 137 AVE
9pm-until

Guys **$4** ALL NITE Dolls **$3**

Buddy·Esq.

FLASH: We got sort of...bought by Sugarhill, where we made songs like "Freedom," which was pretty big for us. "It's Nasty," was pretty big for us. "The Message"—later on—was probably the biggest one of all. With those songs, along with the help of Sylvia Robinson, as a group we were pretty successful making records.

KID CREOLE: We toured with everybody who was somebody—The Commodores, Rick James, Cameo. The only person that we didn't tour with was Earth, Wind, and Fire. But the first time that we went on the road, everybody thought that we was a band. We'd go into the arena, and we'd pull our stuff out, and they'd say, "Um, where's your instruments at?" They thought the turntables were for the intermission. And we used to routinely get jerked for time and space on the stage. They used to put our stuff like all the way to the front of the stage, and we'd have like a few feet to perform in. Routinely, night after night, we used to bust they ass. It wasn't like we was that much better than anybody else; it was just the way our show was—it was geared to havin' a crowd get loose. That's how rap is. So night after night we busted they ass. And then after awhile, they started givin' respect. We got more stage space and better times.

SHA-ROCK: The true performers that really, really stand out—and you have to give it to them—was the Furious 5. The Furious 5 just made the crowd, the girls go crazy.

GRANDMASTER FLASH: We were all showmen, and within a show the MCs had their show, and the DJs had their show. That played a big part in our audience, you know?

KID CREOLE: It wasn't just the average, ordinary, microphone in the hand, walking up and down the stage thing. It was a coordinated five guys. As far as our roles and how they were defined, Flash was always the guy that would come up with all the music. Flash might say, "I feel this song, and we need to try to make up something for this," but he wasn't saying to us, "Yo, you need to do this."

Most of the time, our ideas came from Mel as far as our routines and stuff like that. He was really talented when it came to that kind of thing. You could basically call Mel the heart and soul of our group, because he was the guy that everybody looked to if something went wrong.

Grandmaster Flash and the Furious 5 at the Ritz, 1981 (© Charlie Ahearn)

GRAND MASTER FLASH

Management— Mort Berger

(212) 514-8747
(914) 425-6484

Cowboy—God rest his soul—he was a person who was basically no nonsense. He didn't know how to be a diplomat when it came to certain things. So if he got into a situation where you made him feel uncomfortable about a certain thing, he would fight you. And he was really, really good at that.

He was also real good at crowd response. He was really good at judging the crowd and what he needed to do in order to bring them higher. Cowboy wasn't a person who wrote a lot of rhymes, but he was able to get a microphone in his hand and just say something to get a crowd motivated.

Scorpio—who was Mr. Ness back in the day—he was the one who actually was instrumental in comin' up with the ideas for some of the costumes.

Rahiem wrote rhymes that was slightly different than the way my brother and myself wrote rhymes; he had more of like a swing to his rhymes. And he was the best singer in the group.

And me, I was just a guy who tried to plug all the holes, you know what I'm sayin'? Wherever they needed me, I was there. Like that. I had no real special purpose.

RAY CHANDLER: The Furious would have the crowd jump up and scream. Kid Creole was the first one with the phrase, "Yes yes y'all!" I was witness to that. Cowboy created, "Throw your hands in the air and wave 'em like you just don't care!" Melle Mel would rip off Cowboy's rhymes. Flash would be cutting and spinning. Rahiem was very mellow with his riffs, very smooth like Luther Vandross. The ladies liked that smooth sweet silky voice. My favorite rapper of all time was Melle Mel. He would literally tear the house down. He put his heart and soul into it. When he left that stage, that man would be sweatin'! He was fiery.

the message

RAHIEM: We were at an awards ceremony—an award that really never got off the ground called the Urban Contemporary Award—and it was held at this club in Manhattan called the Savoy. "The Message" was new at that time. I'm standing alone, the rest of the group are off doing whatever—it's a party. Quincy Jones and Lionel Ritchie come up to me like, "Hey, I love your new song. What a breath of fresh air. You guys are like Shakespeare, the way you depict urban life. You're painting a picture for the entire world, so that they can understand some of what it's like to live in urban America." They were talking about "The Message." That was a very memorable moment.

KID CREOLE: When it came to "The Message," we were like, "What in the hell is this? What are we doin' with this?" It's slow, it's plodding...the hook...what is it? We was used to all of the break records, but Sylvia had a concept of us doing that song, and she felt that we would be perfect for it because we came from the inner city. We was afraid of the song because we didn't think that it would work. We were surprised like hell; it worked like a charm. Matter of fact, it worked so good that the next 50 million songs that we did after that all tried to be like that, because that formula worked [laughing].

Original flyer art for the Furious 5 by flyer master Buddy Esquire.

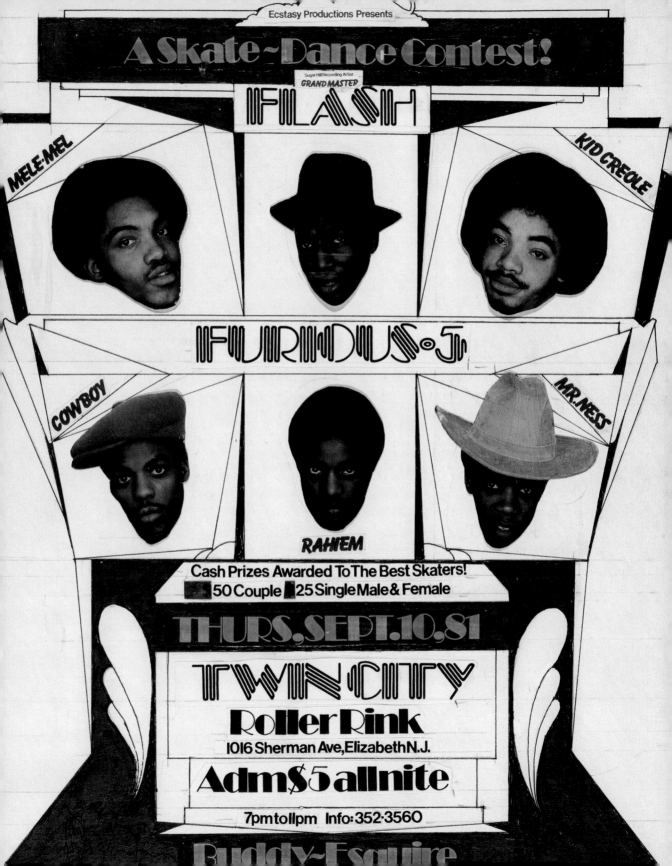

rappin' & rockin' the house the funky 4+1

JAZZY JEFF: Before records, we had a salary of like $75 a party. That was for the MCs. It was about your sound system then. You couldn't do it without the system, so Baron and Breakout and Jazzy Dee made most of the money.

DJ BARON: We did parties and we was trying to invest the money back into the system. We used to play at the Galaxy, Executive Playhouse, and all these other places, and the MCs went along with us in investing money back in the system.

K.K. ROCKWELL: I took Breakout and them to a project on 129th and St. Nicholas. We played there outside, and people were all up in their windows enjoying the music. Not many people came, but a record producer showed up—Bobby Robinson of Enjoy Records.

JAZZY JEFF: Bobby Robinson talked to our manager Jazzy Dee. He wanted to know if we was to do a record, what would we do? So we invited him to one of our practices, and we did a routine, and that was it. He just took us right inside the studio.

K.K. ROCKWELL: We practiced with Pumpkin [drummer/producer who recorded many of the tracks for the early hip-hop records, now deceased] who played drums in his garage to the Cheryl Lynn record. Bobby laid the track down for us, and we came in and did it in one take. No rehearsal. Nobody said how long it was supposed to be, and we just kept rapping. Fourteen minutes of nonstop rapping.

SHA-ROCK: At that time, to think about records wasn't even an issue. We never even really believed that it would go that far.

DJ BARON: That was our downfall, when we met Bobby Robinson and made "Rappin' and Rockin' the House." When we went into the studio, and they got their first payment of $600 it was, "Ha ha...we don't need Breakout and Baron no more. We got our own money. We let our records play for us. That's how that went. That's how we faded away.

SHA-ROCK: When we'd perform live, our DJs was a part of our show, doing the mixes, the introductions, the records. But when we went into the studio with "Rappin' and Rocking the House," we used a live band; we didn't use a DJ. Then when we went on from Enjoy Records to Sugarhill, we still didn't use a DJ. We never really used the DJs in the studio; we always used live bands.

The Funky 4 + 1 (Lil' Rodney Cee, Keith Keith, Sha-Rock, Jazzy Jeff, and K.K. Rockwell) at Bruckner Roller Rink, 1980 (© Charlie Ahearn)

JAZZY JEFF: Before records, it was about having a sound system, so Jazzy Dee always held that over our heads. Then overnight we was making records, and we didn't need the sound system to make our records. By him not being able to deal with that transaction, that just was a headache we didn't want. We took a couple of aspirins and got rid of him. We just dropped him. We wasn't signed to him or anything like that.

SHA-ROCK: Jazzy Dee wasn't a part of the Sugarhill thing. What happened was Sylvia Robinson sent someone to scout us out and see whether or not we were willing to leave Enjoy Records. We felt, as a group, that we weren't getting the money that we was supposed to be getting, and we said, "OK, she's doing good by the Sugar Hill Gang, so we're gonna switch over." We didn't know anything about the money or the music business. We were thinking about the fame, just being able to get people to know how great we were. That's what it was all about. So we said, "If the Sugar Hill Gang is being recognized worldwide, maybe they can do the same thing for us, because we know that we're as good as the Sugar Hill Gang. We started this, so we need to get out there to let people know that we started it."

JAZZY JEFF: It was a business move: Sylvia offered us more money, paid us, and then bought out our contract. I think we got $50,000. $10,000 went to buying out our contract from Bobby, and then the other $40,000 we split amongst the group. For doing what we was doing at that time, it was good money. I mean, I was in the tenth grade, and I had $5,000. Yeah! For all of us, that was money! We were satisfied, because first of all it was a hobby; now the hobby was turning into a good job. We took the money and we went. But we was jumping into something that we really knew nothing about.

DJ BARON: Me and Darnell took it hard and didn't do too many more parties. Eventually they rehired Breakout to do tours when they got down with Sugarhill, but that was when the parties really just stopped.

SHA-ROCK: Even though these were my high school years, I was spending more time out on the road because we had the Sugarhill tour where we toured with the Sugar Hill Gang and Sequence and other different groups on the Sugarhill label. We toured like fifty-two cities. The promoters promoted it very well. We never went into a place where they didn't know we were coming, where they said, "No, we're not liking this type of music" or whatever. Because they knew "Rapper's Delight." That opened up the doors for everybody else. Even if they hadn't heard your song, they gave you the opportunity to just go off, to show them what you were about.

crossing over

SHA-ROCK: Once "Rappin' and Rocking the House" came out, we pushed that record, but we was pushing ourselves to a different audience. We used to perform in places like the Mudd Club, with the punk rockers. We brought a different type of feeling to a different type of people; we geared ourselves toward making them accept hip-hop music. We figured if we can do that, then we can go different places. We used to get write-ups in different newspapers and be on different cable TV shows, and that's how we wind up being approached by Blondie.

JAZZY JEFF: We were booked in this place called the Kitchen in 1980, which was in the Village. It was the first time we ever played in front of a Caucasian crowd, and Deborah Harry was in the audience, hangin' out. Then when she went to Saturday Night Live, she remembered us and put us on with her. She had her choice between the Sugar Hill Gang and Flash and the Furious 5, and a few other Sugarhill groups. But she pulled us because she actually saw us live, and she liked what she saw.

CHRIS STEIN: We were on Saturday Night Live and for some reason or other we got to pick a musical guest act to come on with us. So we got the Funky 4, who were on Sugarhill at the time. It was really a struggle trying to get the people on Saturday Night to understand what these guys were doing, 'cause they just didn't have a clue about what scratching was, for example. "You have these two turntables and then by switching back and forth...blah, blah, blah"...I really, really wanted them to be able to do a live scratch to their thing, but they just couldn't do it. They wound up going on with a tape.

But I'm pretty sure that that appearance of the Funky 4—who they saved for the last goddamned moment of the show, and who went on over the credits—was probably the first time there was a rap group on national TV in the country.

SHA-ROCK: The spot that really sticks out in my mind is the Ritz, because the Ritz Club had their certain type of people, high society, whatever. Rap music was from the streets. Our thing was "OK, we're playing down here in the Ritz. This is like a rich club, and we can pull it off, make the people just go crazy over us." And we did it. We had them going crazy, shouting, repeating "ho!" screaming, hollering, and that's when we knew that we crossed over. When we was able to get a different type of listener to listen to our street music, to me that was the ultimate.

We had just gone to a different level. We basically had left the street scene and started recording. We did go back to performing the streets, but we wasn't out there like we were in the beginning. So you had the other groups to come up and represent for New York, a lot of different groups emerging that may not have made a record yet were out in the streets. That gave a lot of other groups the opportunity to spruce up and get to the point where they needed to be, for people to hear them.

216

The First All-star Disco Concert for 1980

Featuring

Four Super Recording Artists Performing Live and In Person

SATURDAY, FEBRUARY 16th - 10 p.m. until 3 a.m.

at the

JAMAICA ARMORY

93-05 168th Street (one block south of Jamaica Ave.)

"The Living Legend Himself"

GRANDMASTER FLASH
And
"The Furious Five M.C.'s"
Mele Mel, Rahiem, Kid Creo, Cowboy, Mr. Ness
Plus Disco Bee & E-Z Mike

Vs.   ## The Incredible Brothers' Disco

The Funky Four plus One (New York's No. 1 Lady SHA-ROCK!)
Rodney C, Jazzy Jeff, Keith Keith, K. K. Rockwell & Sha-Rock
Plus D. J. Breakout and D. J. Baron

His First Appearance In Queens
SPOONIN GEE Doing His Spooning RAP

Mr. Woody Wood and His Woody Wood Crew doing his Woody's Rap
★ SPECIAL GUEST STARS ★

Grand Wizard Theodore with Master Robby Rob, Kevy Kev, & Ruby D

"New York's No. 1 Female Crew" **Mercedes Ladies**

Jazzy-B, Eve Of Death, Sheri-Sher, R.D. Smiley And Vina Zee
"Queens Newest Crew"

DISCO PLEASURE with BREAK MASTER FUN and DISCO HUB
Plus ROYAL SOUNDS
"AND TO CHILL-OUT THE SHOW"
The Immortal DISCO TWINS
(Featuring NASTY T)

$5.00 With This Flyer And $7.00 Without   Do Dress   Note: Heavy Security

For Information Call: (212) 946-0489
Produced By LIFE STYLE PRODUCTIONS
Who Provides The Best In Entertainment, And Security!

DIRECTIONS: FROM MANHATTAN, BROOKLYN AND BRONX
Ride the back of the E or F train to 169 st., walk to Archer Ave. & 168th st.; four blocks
from subway 1 block south of Jamaica Ave. "J" Train to Queens Blvd., transfer to the Q49
bus. Ride bus to last stop. Armory is one block away (Archer Ave. & 168th St.)
FROM NASSAU AND SUFFOLK COUNTY: Take bus to Jamaica Bus Terminal walk down 165th St. to
Archer Ave. make a left to 168th St. L.I.R.R.: Take train to Jamaica Station walk up to
Jamaica Ave. and catch the Q53 or Q56 bus to Jamaica Ave. & 168th one block south of
Jamaica Ave.

CEY ADAMS: There was a place called the Jamaica Armory in Jamaica, Queens, where I lived, and they would throw these hip-hop jams in the building. They would charge five to seven bucks, and I couldn't even afford that. They had this little gate that had about a seven-inch space, so me and my brothers would just slide under the gate and you were in the club. Grandmaster Flash, the Funky Four, just everybody would play these gigs.

SHA-ROCK: I was like seven-and-a-half-months pregnant at the Armory, but that show was the ultimate. We had been out on tour, the Sugar Hill Gang, Sequence, the Funky 4 + 1, Grandmaster Flash and the Furious 5, Wayne and Charlie—which was like a ventriloquist, it was crazy. This was the first time that we brought that show home. This was like the ultimate for everybody, 'cause we can show everybody what we was doing out there on tour. It was huge.

RAPPER'S CONVENTION
Featuring In Person
★ ★ ★ SUGAR HILL GANG ★ ★ ★

SUGAR HILL GANG

ALSO:
✶ **GRAND MASTER FLASH and the FURIOUS FIVE**
✶ **SEQUENCE**
✶ **SPOONIE GEE**
✶ **FUNKY FOUR Plus 1**

FRIDAY, FEBRUARY 13, 1981 8 P.M. UNTII.

TO BE HELD AT
369th REGIMENT ARMORY
2366 FIFTH AVENUE, NEW YORK CITY
TICKETS: $10.00 Advance --$12.00 At Door

TICKETS ON SALE— IN NEW YORK: RECORD SHACK, TICKETRON, BERDELL'S RECORDS, Brooklyn.

IN NEW JERSEY: BAMBERGERS — Newark, BAND WAGON — East Orange,

BIG SOUNDS and RECORDS ARE US — Plainfield

The Funky 4 + 1 performing at the Armory, February, 1981 (© Charlie Ahearn)

Keith Keith and Sha-Rock during a Funky 4 + 1 jam at the Ritz, 1981 (© Charlie Ahearn)

The Funky 4, 1981 (© Charlie Ahearn)

the ♥ WOMEN

Sha-Rock wasn't the only woman on the hip-hop scene. The all-female MC crew Sequence were labelmates on Sugarhill Records, and the group featured Angie B, later to find greater fame as Angie Stone. Afrika Bambaataa's Cosmic Force featured Lisa Lee, who would join Sha-Rock in the Us Girls along with Debbie D, a popular MC who performed with DJ Wanda D. Master Don and the Death Committee featured female MC Pebblee Poo, and the Mercedes Ladies had been performing for a couple years by this time.

Sha-Rock and Angie B (Angie Stone) pose at Disco Fever in the early '80s (Courtesy Sharon Jackson)

GRANDMASTER CAZ: Lisa Lee, Little Lee, Sweet and Sour, Pebblee Poo...I mean, they was bringing it! They were bringing it! Okay? And I had the first female DJ—her name was Pambaataa. We went to school together. She was cool, she hung around my crew. I was like, "I'm going to teach you how to play. You're gonna play!" Wiz and I taught her how to DJ and debuted her playing out in public. We introduced her to Bambaataa and named her after Bambaataa because her name was Pam. This was like '76.

There were the Mercedes Ladies; that was the first all-female crew. There were some other girls back in the day. Nobody really stood out. You had a certain amount of girl MCs everybody knew: Lisa Lee was down with Bambaataa; Little Lee was down with AJ; Sha was with Breakout.

SISCO: Debbie D had a voice that dominated. Sha-Rock had a voice that dominated the mic. Girl rappers I hear nowadays don't have that power and that presence, the determination of what they do. They're good and everything, but it's like they're testing the waters, you know? They're not commanding the waters.

SHA-ROCK: The first time that I became aware of Lisa Lee was when we performed at Stevenson High School back in like '78, '79. Lisa was a part of the Cosmic Force. I didn't know that they had gotten a girl, and my group was saying, "I think they have a girl now. Why don't you just go ahead and show her what you can do. No other girl is gonna take you out, you just go on." Lisa would come on, then I would go on, and then Lisa would come on. A lot of people thought that we were battling, but for me, I wanted a rapport with any female rapper that was out there, because we were all out there doing the same thing. When people realized that there were somebody else out there now besides Sha-Rock, a lot of people used to say, "You have the Funky 4, and then you have the Cosmic Force....There's another girl out there now, y'all could battle each other." But it didn't happen like that. I knew that I was Sha-Rock, and I was there first, but that didn't take away from me trying to be able to get along with the others who had came behind me. Even though we were a part of different groups, it was never that competitive, because we formed a friendship before anybody could really put that into our heads.

Sha-Rock and Lisa Lee shared a friendly rivalry between their groups the Funky 4 + 1 and the Soulsonic/Cosmic Force as the premier female MCs of the day.

"Later on came the Mercedes Ladies; they were hanging around the L Brothers. There were other females out there, but the solo female that I do remember being right after me was Lisa Lee, and then Debbie D was also a soloist...Debbie D and Wanda D—she was real, real good. A good writer. She was an excellent writer." ● SHA-ROCK

WANDA D: It was very hard. I was a girl in the business, and the guys laughed at me everywhere I went. I had heard about MCs like Sha-Rock and Lisa Lee. I looked up to them. Someone had to break the door in and make it easier for women to enter rap, whether they wanted to be MCs or DJs. It shouldn't be that difficult for a woman to do something like that, but they figure that it's a man's world and you just gotta know your place. That was what I was up against—it was a double standard all the way. I knew what I wanted to accomplish, I knew I wanted to make it easier for the next females comin' up to just go right in there and do what they love to do without havin' to be stressed out about it, or laughed at, or disrespected.

Cheryl the Pearl on the Sugarhill Rapper's Convention Tour, 1981 (Courtesy Sharon Jackson)

WANDA D: I had to work my way up, but pretty soon my reputation started preceding me. But I had to sorta go through Bambaataa—Afrika Bambaataa took me underneath his wing. He would tell the guys, "Get outta her way, let her on, she's good." And once I got on the turntables I proved myself. Bam really looked out for me. He really really protected me in a lot of situations, because it wasn't always safe, many places that I went.

I hit the clubs. I did some shows at the Stardust Ballroom, Harlem World, and all that. Then promoters started hearing about me, so they would call me and ask me to do shows. Somehow I met Debbie D, and we did a lot of shows together. We were pretty well known. We eventually parted ways, but we both went on to do *Beat Street*.

I remember going to the first showing of *Beat Street* in my neighborhood. The theater was packed, and I just sat in the back of the theater. When my part came up, the people just roared to their feet; they were screamin' and rootin' me on. "Go Wanda!" It was like, "Oh my God!" I never knew it would grow to be so big. I was the first female DJ to be inducted into the Zulu Nation, and that really made me proud. It was an honor to be a part of the organization, because it was about rappers and DJs coming together for a common goal.

Funky 4 + 1 with Wanda D and Debbie D, 1982

Sha Rock, DJ Breakout and Lisa Lee in Breakout's dune-buggy, 1980 (Courtesy Sharon Jackson)

stepping up:
the cold crush brothers

CHARLIE CHASE: The Cold Crush Brothers—me, AD, Tony Tone, plus a few other guys were in the group at that time. Other guys are stepping up their game, and Tony and I felt we needed to move to the next level. I knew Grandmaster Caz; I always liked the way he MC-ed, and for years I was after him. He wouldn't do it, he was always out doing his own thing. Finally, I kind of finagled him into coming to a party. I said, "Look, I'm having an MC audition. Why don't you just come by and help me choose some MCs?" He says, "Sure, no problem." And I knew I was gonna get him that day.

GRANDMASTER CAZ: I was duped into joining the group. My group, the Force 5, was dissolving at that time. It was down to just me and JDL. Whip and Dot went from Charlie and them to the Fantastic 5, so that left a two-man deficit in Charlie's group.

They auditioned two guys, a guy named Dynamite T, and KG. Both of them were okay, but KG had potential. I said to Charlie, "Keep the dark-skinned guy,"—which was KG—"he can be brought up." AD had already been a member, so he was down with them already.

I didn't know that Charlie was trying to get me to join the group at the time, but he finally came and asked me. I gave him the condition: "If you put JDL down, then I'll get down with you." He wrestled with that for awhile, because JDL was kinda out here back then, but I said, "If I get down, you've gotta put him down." And that's how we ended up together.

CHARLIE CHASE: I said, "Listen, we can take this and put it in another place nobody has ever seen before." I felt that we were gonna be large. And sure enough, we just started knocking everybody out of the park.

The thing about us was that we weren't MCs in the schoolyard; we were MCs on a stage. That was our mentality. At the time, most of the MCs weren't looking at it like that. Their thing was just rocking the local party to get the girls on them. Not us.

Caz was the captain. He spoke well, he rhymed excellent. KG had the big voice. Then you had JDL. I don't think I ever remember seeing JDL write a line in my life, ever saw him put pen to paper. But he ad-libbed this stuff, and it was rhyming, just off the top of his head! Then he'd remember the rhyme for the next week. Incredible. And then you had AD. He was the cool, suave one; he had the look. The women loved him. The way he came across, he was the Grade A kind of guy, the "I drink milk and nothing else"-type of guy. These four...there hasn't been a match since, man. You could only invent the form once. What can I tell you?

The Cold Crush Brothers (minus Charlie Chase) in the Wild Style offices, 1981 (© Charlie Ahearn)

An Ecstasy Garage jam during the last days of the Force 5 MCs

Ecstasy Garage presents

the FUNKY 4 plus 1 more!

KEITH·KEITH K·K ROCKWELL

SHA·ROCK

JAZZY·JEFF LIL RODNEY·C

Also CASANOVA FLY

Force 5 M.C.s

Lil Gee Jerry D Louie Lew Butch Kid

Ecstasy Garage Disco

1476 JEROME AVE
9:30PM·UNTIL

4 Train to 170 st.

Fri, Mar. 14, 80

Ladies $2   Gents $3

B/4 12

"Happy Birthday Gwen"

Buddy Esquire... The King of the Flyer!

A Cold Crush Brothers party
at the Hoe Avenue Boys Club,
circa 1980. Caz, Easy AD,
Tony Tone, and Almighty KG
(Courtesy Angelo King)

TONY: I was the man in the shadow as a DJ in the Cold Crush. I didn't push the fact that I was one of the DJs in the Cold Crush, because I wanted Charlie to be the focal point. I had been in hip-hop, running amongst the top players for a while, so everybody knew me and respected my position.

CHARLIE CHASE: The thing with Caz is that he had the ability to put a picture in your mind like you wouldn't believe. He's a storyteller. His stories were always very tricky, but they always had meaning to them.

CAZ: The content is really important to me. When I got into the Cold Crush, my thing was to do something that nobody's doin'. I take all my musical influences and experience and run them through the hip-hop mind-set. We reached back, and we did routines off of Gilbert O'Sullivan, Barry Manilow, Simon and Garfunkel. That's what made our routines famous: they came from somewhere that people knew of, but they wasn't really following that road. Let's say "Copacabana." We fused Barry Manilow's melodies into raps, into rhymes:

CAZ, AD, TONY break into a rhyme (to the tune of "Copacabana"):

> Park your Mercedes, fly guys and ladies,
> Come in and say hi ho and cheer, 'cause the Cold Crush Four is here.
> Come hear the beats play, and bust our DJ
> 'cause there's no one in any place who got the cuts like Charlie Chase,
> but he's not on his own, there's DJ Tony Tone
> and the six of us together, we are all well known
> as the Cold Crush, the Cold Crush Brothers.
> Don't try to compare us with others.
> We are the Cold Crush, the Cold Crush Brothers.
> Chase, Tone, and KG,
> Caz, JDL, and AD are the Cold Crush.

BUSY BEE: Grandmaster Caz is phenomenal with putting together acts and routines. He can take a Rolling Stones song, or like...I don't know who sings the song (sings "Alone Again Naturally," by Gilbert O'Sullivan). You know what I'm saying? Some white group sung that song. But Grandmaster Caz made a chorus to that same verse! And that's what the Cold Crush and Fantastics did. The Fantastics had routines, too. If they didn't have the baddest one, then the Cold Crush did. Treacherous 3 couldn't do those things. Master Don and the Death Committee couldn't do those things. You could have your favorite record translated over rap-style with the rappers, and you wouldn't be mad.

At that time, the scene started getting big, and we was givin' rap contests. It would always be Cold Crush and Fantastic at the end—the last two standing.

TONY: We had a whole bunch of different routines. If you want to get down and dirty, we can get down and dirty. If you want us to put on tuxedoes…I mean, we used to wear pin-stripe gangster suits in '80, '81. Then you turned around and Puffy and Biggie and them start wearin' pin-stripes, and everybody think that's new. Come on, that was our show. We were using smoke machines in '80, and we was kids. We sittin' down and brainstormin' and thinking of these things. No coaching, no manager, no "You all should do this." This is us. When we get on that stage, it's us. We're pure, from the heart, straight up. Hip-hop. There ain't no sugar coating.

Grandmaster Caz outside of the Sparkle, 1981 (© Charlie Ahearn)

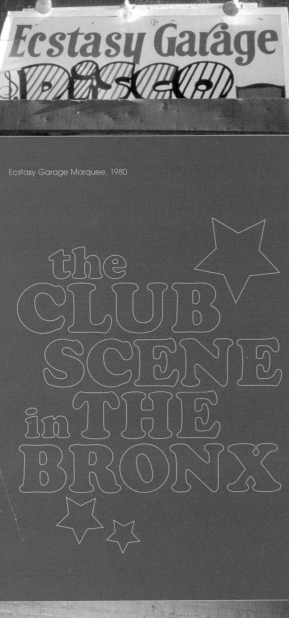

Ecstasy Garage Marquee, 1980.

the CLUB SCENE in THE BRONX

ecstasy garage

CHARLIE CHASE: Arthur Armstrong . . . "Army," we called him. He ran the Ecstasy. [Imitating Art Armstrong] "Well, Charlie, I gotta tell ya. It's all about capturing the crowd, Charlie." That was the way he spoke to me. "Ya gotta go out there and grab the crowd." Army was a good guy. He was all about business.

There were two Ecstasy Garages. The first one was actually a garage converted into a club. He gutted it out, and it was nothing but these benches made out of wood on the side, just a big empty space. It was a pretty long place, and it was dark. Because it was so dark, you couldn't see a lot of the shit that was going on. There were a lot of fights in there, stuff like that.

ART ARMSTRONG: I opened the first Ecstasy on Jerome Avenue. I had financial problems not long after I opened—there was a train strike, a bus strike along with it, and the kids couldn't get there. So I closed it down for a few months to regroup and started giving shows at the community centers, roller rinks in New York City. After that I opened a second Ecstasy, which was a much better club. There was a bar area where there was tables, and then I had a large room they could dance in. The second Ecstasy was safer. I had a crack security force called the 9 Crew. They were well known and feared, so we had fewer incidents there. No shootings took place there; no cuttings took place. It was a thing where kids could really enjoy themselves and feel safe. It was a big hit. We had lines. It was open every Friday and Saturday night and occasionally on Sundays. I kept that open for about two years until '82, '83.

Kids rocking the Ecstasy Garage, 1980 (© Charlie Ahearn)

Tony Tone with T-Connection sign, ca. 1979 (Courtesy Angelo King)

the t-connection

SHA-ROCK: We had the whole uptown on lock-down. The T-Connection was one of our main spots. The T-Connection was this huge place; you had to go up the stairs from the Number 2 train station. You walk up these big stairs and there's somebody standing by the door to take your money. They had this huge stage and this big DJ booth, and then the bar was in the back, but you had this huge dance floor made of wood, and you had this light-ball that went around.

DJ BARON: The hard thing about it, the place had steps that went straight up, and I used to have to carry them big bass cabinets upstairs—it took like four people just to carry one box. It was crazy. And after the party, everybody disappeared. Had to take it home by myself.

> *"Your name had to be rockin' for you to get into the Fever free. If you didn't, you was gonna pay $10. That was embarrassing, to be a DJ and come to the Fever with your girl, and Sal'll make you pay $10. That mean you really wasn't nobody."* ● **KOOL DJ AJ**

Cold Crush Brothers at Disco Fever photo booth (Courtesy Angelo King)

disco Fever

KOOL DJ AJ: The Fever was number one. There was a lot of women; you could go there and hear the best DJs in New York. It was air-conditioned. You'd go into the back room and you could gamble, had the casino games, you'd get your drink on, you could just have a good time. It was also one of the first places that specialized in hip-hop. They mixed it with a little bit of disco; they played the little slow tunes and stuff like that, but they really specialized in rap and hip-hop music.

SHA-ROCK: Disco Fever was the club where you could always find anybody who was a part of the hip-hop scene, whether it was Kurtis Blow or Grandmaster Flash and the Furious 5…that was the club where everybody went on a Friday or a Saturday.

SHA-ROCK: Sal was a character. He always ran the club smooth, always took care of his people. Artists, if they come in and they wanted drinks or whatever, he'd be like, "Go ahead, it's OK." The music was good, everybody was always on the dance floor dancing, and I always felt like he was just a straight-up businessman. It was always, "Go talk to Sal. Sal this, Sal that." He was just running things.

CHARLIE CHASE: The way I saw Harlem World [another popular club] and the Fever, Harlem World was junior high school, the Fever was high school. You understand? It was like you had to graduate to hang with that crowd. It was an older crowd, and they always dressed up. You used to go to Harlem World in jeans and sneakers, and the Fever crowd would be more styled out. They had the chains, everything was in place. The guys went there to impress. So did the ladies. It was more of a disco feel. A lot of celebrities used to stop by, too, because it was the place to be in the Bronx.

RAY CHANDLER: The Disco Fever was where everybody used to meet after the parties. It was the time to cool out, do whatever you wanted to do. This guy Sal used to run it; he was the owner, but the guy who kept it down was Dingo. Mandingo—he WAS the Fever. He was a big muscle-bound guy. He used to take guns away from guys.

WHIPPER WHIP: After we do our shows and we get paid, we go to the Fever and sniff coke and drink champagne 'til 5:00, 6:00 in the morning, and when the Fever closed down, we'd go up to the Hilltop and continue on until about 12 noon. I mean, you coming out like vampires—the the sun's out, you're like, "ugggh," 'cause in these places they keep it dark, so you don't know what it's like outside. You open the doors and whoa.

MELLE MEL: We used to go up to the Fever. Seventy-five percent of the Fever was coked the fuck out. Used to be 8–9 coke dealers up there by the end of the night. And Cowboy would get up on the mic, and he would have motherfuckas going out of their minds! "How many people got ten in their pockets? How many people just seen that Tyson fight?"

"The Fever was beautiful, man. We had two floors. I was the main house jock, along with June Bug, and we had several different varieties of music. The staff was beautiful, everything was beautiful. The only thing I regret from them days is that I was getting high; I guess that was part of the scene." ● **LOVE BUG STARSKI**

DJ AJ cuts it up at the Celebrity Club, 1980 (© Charlie Ahearn)

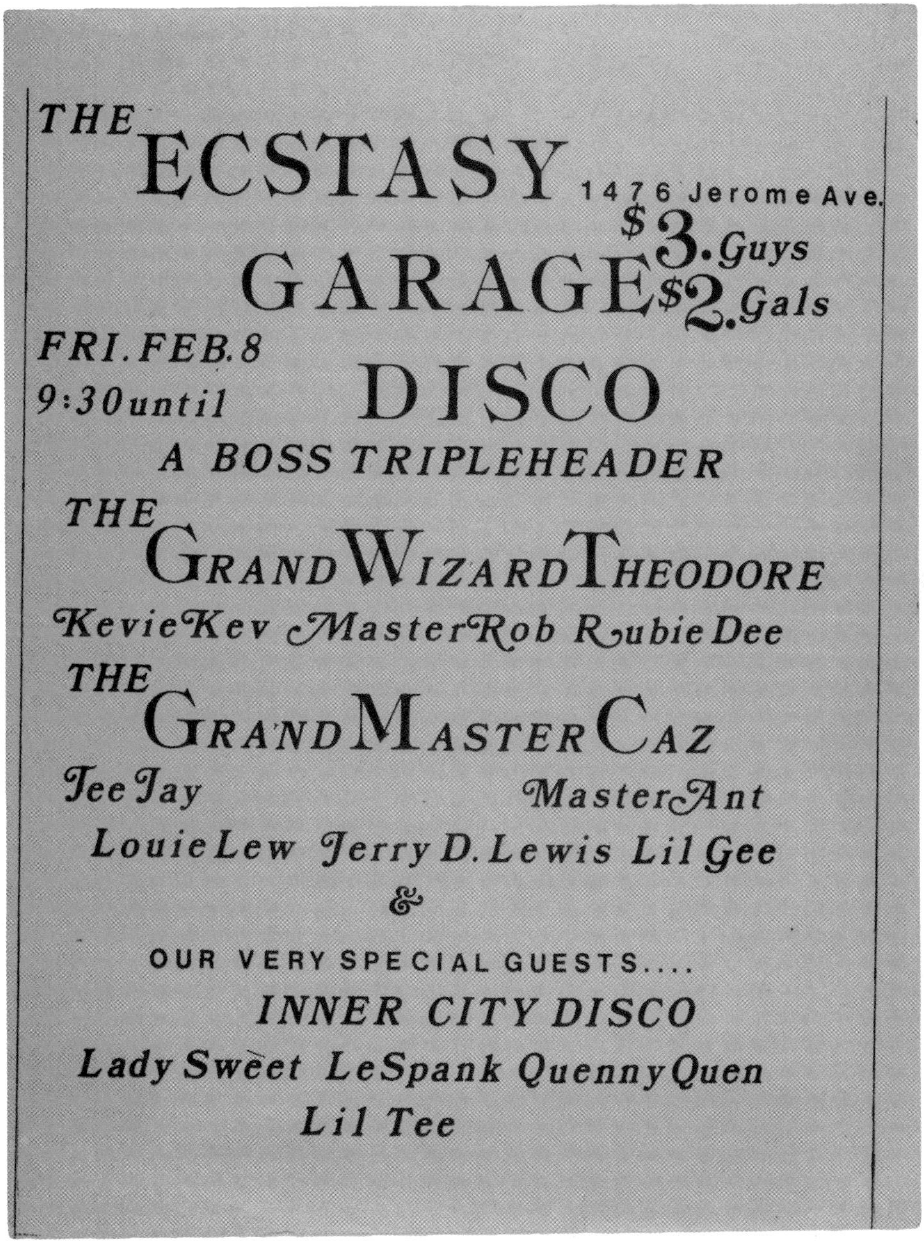

THE **ECSTASY** 1476 Jerome Ave.

$3. Guys

GARAGE $2. Gals

FRI. FEB. 8

9:30 until **DISCO**

A BOSS TRIPLEHEADER

THE

GRAND WIZARD THEODORE

Kevie Kev Master Rob Rubie Dee

THE

GRAND MASTER CAZ

Tee Jay Master Ant

Louie Lew Jerry D. Lewis Lil Gee

&

OUR VERY SPECIAL GUESTS....

INNER CITY DISCO

Lady Sweet LeSpank Quenny Quen

Lil Tee

Theodore with Kevie Kev, Master Rob, and Rubie Dee, 1980 (Courtesy Luis Cedeno).

grand wizard theodore & the fantastic 5

KEVIE KEV: It came time for the L Bros to be over because times was changing. Groups started to transpire from twos, threes to like fours and fives. Furious 4. Funky 4. Then Funky 4 + 1. Furious 5. We added two new cats, so we wanted to change our name to the Fantastic 5.

GRANDMASTER CAZ: It was like baseball, like getting traded, or quitting and going to another team. But after crews were solidified, like after Whip and Dot got down with the Fantastic? Boom! That was their unit, and that was it. After we got down with the Cold Crush? Boom! That was our unit, and that was it.

WHIPPER WHIP: We always went head-up from that point on; it was always like a battle. That was the beginning of that Fantastic/Cold Crush stuff.

GRANDMASTER CAZ: The different crews didn't hang out together. None of that! It was competition. Even though we had allies here and there, we stood our ground; we did what we had to do first. Then when the dust clears, whoever's still around...if you didn't want to be friends that's okay, but we coming at everybody.

DOTA ROCK: Fantastic was formed first out of the L Brothers, Grand Wizard Theodore, Master Rob, Waterbed Kev, and Busy Bee Starski.

KEVIE KEV: Busy messed around and started rapping on somebody else's system, and I got mad. When we threw Busy out, we got Ruby Dee.

THEODORE: Busy Bee wanted to go solo because him and Kev didn't get along too good. His Moms was always giving him curfews. He had to leave the party early, so he had to wait until the next day to get paid. His Moms was very strict. Busy didn't want anyone to really know about it.

BUSY BEE: I didn't want everyone to know my bizness 'cause we supposed to be men! They'd say, "Now you talking 'bout your mama—get the fuck out of here!" No way I could be there at pay time—4 a.m. My moms did come after me one time. We were at Gene's place, and he's counting the money, and my moms comes in with my two sisters. I was busted! Next day I got it: "Bee had his moms come pick him up." It takes years to build yourself a rep, and then your mom wrecks it in one second! Crushes your shit up!

The Fantastic 5 practicing routines at home. 1980 © Charlie Ahearn)

THEODORE: Ruby Dee lived in the projects that we played in all the time. He was a Puerto Rican guy, and we figured it'd be good to have a Puerto Rican MC down with us so that we can get all cultures together to party. Then we met these other two MCs called Salt and Pepper, which was Dota Rock and Whipper Whip, and got them down with us. That's when it became the Fantastic 5.

WHIPPER WHIP: One day we went to a party at a place called Rock City, which we used to call Duck City 'cause it had a low ceiling—you had to duck to get from one room to another. The L Brothers are there playing and we're like, "Yo, we wanna rock with y'all." They let us get on, we did our Salt and Pepper routine, and it just took a matter of minutes before they were like, "Y'all down."

KEVIE KEV: So then it was five of us. The Fantastic 5. Prince Whipper Whip, he was really Puerto Rican, but a lot of people thought Whip was Black. He asked us not to tell the world he was Puerto Rican, 'cause he felt they would accept him in a different way. So Ruby Dee was considered the first Puerto Rican rapper.

WHIPPER WHIP: As Fantastic, we'd do our routines and then the group would break off and let me and Dot do our Salt and Pepper routines. "We are Salt and Pepper MCs..." We'd do our stuff, and then we'd go back into the routines with the rest of the group.

KEVIE KEV: We had this thing called the "Terry Cloth Party" that was up at the T-Connection. Everybody got to wear terry cloth or they don't get in. I had on a white cloth top with sky blue pants, and the fellas had on the same. We would make different kinds of parties. Fantastic was really creative, man. I don't have to tell you how dope we was, 'cause people still remember to this day.

THEODORE: What made these guys unique was they wanted to be different. We started wearing tuxedos and white gloves and stuff like that and putting more into our routines and everything. It just became more serious to us. We practiced sometimes like seven days a week. And our girlfriends used to get mad: "You guys are spending too much time together!"

DOTA ROCK: We were known as sex symbols, you know. We had sexy raps (Dota Rock raps a Fantastic routine):

> Sex is the thing everybody needs,
>
> sometime you do it slow, sometime to speed.
>
> To some people it have them on cloud nine,
>
> to work up a sweat, to have a good time.
>
> ...It's nice to show each other affection,
>
> but it ain't no fun when you ain't got protection.
>
> That's one thing that's really crazy,
>
> you had fun one day, now you got a baby.
>
> A father with a son, look what you have done.
>
> Then you claimin' you ain't due and then you're on the run.
>
> Can't see Kool Herc, you gotta go to work,
>
> can't hang with the fellas because you got a sad smirk.
>
> Eatin' raw cabbage, pushin' on the carriage,
>
> eighteen years old and you're ready for marriage...

WHIPPER WHIP: Usually at a party there'd be two or three different groups performing. A collage of MCs and DJs—Kool Herc, Bambaataa, Fantastic, Cold Crush—all these names would be on the flyer so it would draw. Now you gotta rock. Your thing is, "I gotta go in there and I gotta win these people over."

At that time people were signing record deals. We signed one; we got jerked on that one—"Rappin' Fresh Out the Pack," on Soul On Wax Records, a small label in Harlem. They had a band come in and play, and we heard it, and we were like, "Man, we can't play this." We refused to perform that song at our shows; we never did. We didn't want a record deal. Everybody's puttin' out your stuff, then you get nothing from it. So we didn't want to do records. We just were like, "Man, the crowd loves us. We can do whatever we want. No record, but everybody wants us everywhere." We didn't do any interviews; we allowed no one to take pictures. I guess we were just souped up at that time; our heads were swelled, and we felt like the world was ours.

The Fantastic 5 (Kevie Kev, Whipper Whip, and Master Rob shown) rock the crowd at the T-Connection, 1980 (© Charlie Ahearn)

Fantastic Five pose by the Major Degan Express in the Bronx, 1980 (© Charlie Ahearn)

RAY CHANDLER: One of the biggest battles we put together was with the Cold Crush and the Fantastic 5 at Harlem World. Harlem World was one of the premiere places. It had a huge dance floor, upstairs and downstairs. The total prize was $500, winner take all. They came out there clean—I mean well dressed, they had on suits. They came nice and sharp to impress the girls. Water Bed Kevie Kev was burning up, and Grandmaster Caz...it was so intense.

WHIPPER WHIP: There was a rivalry amongst all groups, but it just happens that we're two unsigned groups and we're two of the biggest. There was only a handful of real large groups coming outta the Bronx anyway. Flash and them had the number one spot...Fantastic, Cold Crush, Funky 4, Treacherous 3, we were battling for the second place.

Cold Crush had a completely different style than we did. They had a style where they would take old records and twist 'em and turn 'em. They were great, but our thing was we're still sticking to the old school.

Sometimes we'd throw separate parties and see whose club would be packed the most. Then it came to a point where it turned out to be nice propaganda, 'cause we'd be in clubs arguing and it'd look like we were gonna break out into a fight, yet backstage we're smoking weed and drinking champagne together. We're like, "Yeah, this is working," you know? But it was a rivalry.

CHARLIE CHASE: There was a lot of hype behind it; a lot of hype was created in the street. We're feeding on this thing, and the intensity is growing, and it got to the point where whenever we bumped into them, we'd tell 'em what was going to happen to them at the battle. We were letting 'em have it. At one point, we actually came close to getting into a fistfight with them in front of Caz's house. It was crazy [laughs]. But the intensity just grew and grew and grew for it, and it was a measly $500 prize, you know?

We get up there, we do our thing, right? We're rocking it! We ripped that party in such a way it was talked about for a long time, man. The crowd was the one who was choosing the winners, and to hear the way they reacted when they voted for us, it was exhilarating. That was when we first realized how big we were. I gotta admit, boy, we were souped for a while [laughs].

WHIPPER WHIP: If you hear the original tape, it was "What we're gonna do is we're gonna hold a hand over each group and find out who won, and y'all are gonna be the judge. Let's hear it for the Cold Crush! Yeah, come on, let's hear it for the Cold Crush!" And all they did was say, "Fantastic," and the crowd just went berserk! You couldn't even hear him no more. As far as they were concerned, they won. I was like, "OK, but the money went home with me [laughs]!"

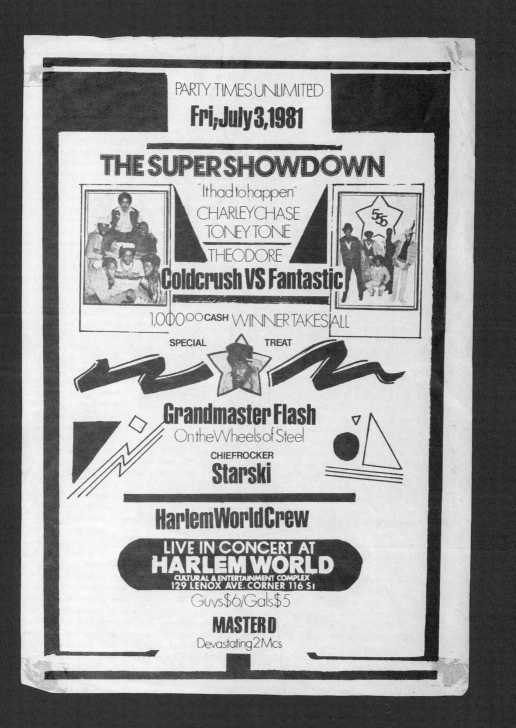

Fantastic versus Cold Crush at Harlem World, 1981

KEVIE KEV: People underrated us for so long. You hear Cold Crush this and Cold Crush that, but who waxed their ass but the Fantastic 5.

DMC: I was going to Rice High School, 124th Street in Harlem, and all through my school, tapes was flowing the way albums would flow and records sell today. Tape of Zulu Nation live at the Bronx, tape of this guy at the Audubon Ballroom, tape of Hollywood...One day this guy's playing these MCs on the box and...they're not just rapping; they're singing the melodies of hits, over Aerosmith, over all my favorite records, the most incredible thing I ever heard—better than everybody. I had to save up $9 so I could buy that tape from the guy who was selling it in school. I had to wait in line for almost a month and a half before I got mine, but I paid my $9 for that tape. And I took it home, and it was a tape of the Cold Crush 4 versus the Fantastic 5 at Harlem World. I heard Kurtis Blow live and Grandmaster Flash live at the Rush parties. I heard all those tapes of Love Bug Starski and all that. But I never heard MCs, crews of MCs, not just one and two, but four and five with two DJs battling each other for supremacy. I was like "Oh my god, what's going on here?"

Cold Crush was the baddest—I don't know what it was about them, the energy, the determination to rock the house—just the things that they would say:

> The All-Mighty KG, the Heartbreaker
> JDL, Grandmaster Caz,
> Easy-AD the Girl Taker.

They were taking melodies from the '60s and '70s and putting their own words to it— just crazy stuff that I never heard. They harmonized; there was a unison, and they was determined to do something that other MCs and DJs would never do. It was the most incredible...I can't even describe what happened. It changed my life.

> You know we're rockin',
> Shock the block, give it all we got,
> 'Cause the force is gonna rock this spot.
> We're Cold Crushin'...

The Cold Crush was the only group to me that took the whole feeling of what hip-hop was and was able to put it on a tape. Their tapes was the roughest stuff—it was the most incredible display of what a DJ and an MC could mean. It was a personification, a manifestation of what hip-hop from the MC and the DJ's standpoint was about.

The Rhythm Den was Richie T's (center) store on East Tremont where you could buy hip hop party tapes. Richie T was not only one of the original Bronx DJs, but also the owner of the T-Connection, the North Bronx home for the Brothers Disco (© Charlie Ahearn)

From SugarHill Records*Ninth Wonder Presents
THE CRASH CREW
First Anniversary Thriller
Video Taped PRESS PARTY Gauranteed
Come hear thier newiest release "SCRATCHIN'"
JUNE 5th. '82 NINE P.M.
•ADM.$6. BEFORE 12P.M. $8.AFTER•
•D.S.T. KeyBoard Sythesizer King•
•Debbie Dee and Wanda Dee•
•Cold Crush Bros.•HarlemWorld Crew•
All SUGARHILL Recording Artists invited! Appearances By:
Spoonie Gee•Sequence•Mean Machine
These ENJOY RECORDS groups are also invited to Rock !!!!
Disco Four(Country Rap)•Treacherous Three
All Mike and Dave Recording Artists '77-'82
HARLEM WORLD
129 LENOX AVE. 116 ST. 866-1150

other voices

REGGIE REG: We all started at the same time; every project had their own MC group. St. Nicholas Terrace was like the Treacherous 3 and the Fearless 4; Lincoln was Crash Crew; Drew Hamilton was the Disco 4; the Eastside was the Magnificent 7. We all clicked before we made records. And then after we made records, we was always right there, neck and neck with each other.

VAN SILK: Manhattan was definitely different from the Bronx. You had Treacherous 3—even though Special K was from the Bronx, L.A. and Kool Moe Dee was from Manhattan; you had Fearless 4, Disco 4, Master Don, Crash Crew—all Manhattan crews. Then you had the East Side of Harlem that didn't associate with the West Side. So you had the Johnny Wa and Ray Von, and the Tantalizing 4 MCs who couldn't get on in Harlem World. Those groups never became big. It was a clique; you had to fight to be who you wanted to be. If you couldn't take out Grandmaster Flash and the Furious 5, then you'd better try to find a way to get on the show with them.

crash crew

REGGIE REG: Mike C, Shubee, G-man, Barry Bistro, and Mike and Dave: Crash Crew was like a Manhattan version of Flash and them. They was the hottest in the Bronx. We was the hottest in Manhattan. There was five of them. There was five of us. They had a production. We had a production. Our production was Mike and Dave; our security was called the Poison Clan. Their production was Black Door and Casanova. It was just two different versions. You had Flash and you had Crash.

We had our own style. We was younger, and we wasn't as wild as them. Flash and them was a little older. They had to be like eighteen, nineteen. But we was only like fifteen and sixteen.

We was known for promoting in Manhattan—we was promoting a lot of parties with Treacherous 3, Fearless 4, Jekyll & Hyde, Magnificent 7. Then we came out with "High Power Rap," and that's when we went tri-borough.

"High Power Rap" was already a routine that we did with our DJ. We was the only ones with this beat, "Freedom." When records started coming out, we told Mike, "Yo, Mike, we got to put this on record." We was lucky because Mike worked in a commercial studio, and we went down there one Saturday and we spliced the "Freedom" break 300 something times 'cause the record is like seven minutes long, and the break is only like twenty seconds. So we spliced it over and over. We didn't know none of the legalities of taking this record, and we didn't think it was gonna be that big. We literally sampled it. This must have been like the first record ever sampled 'cause we got sued over it.

DR. DRE: One of the greatest breaks ever done was by a group that was named Freedom. Everybody called the record "Freedom," but the name of the record was actually called "Get Up and Dance." Disco Dave and the Amazing Crash Crew took the exact break—this was the first time it was ever done for a record—and pressed it on wax. So when you got their record, "High Power Rap," you were like, "Wow." That was one of the most famous breaks ever taken from a record. Grandmaster Flash and the Furious 5 were the second ones to use it, for their song, "Freedom."

REGGIE REG: The Bronx, that was our first stop, 'cause we have to be accepted by the ones that started this. There's this Zulu Nation party so we go up there, and Bambaataa greets us. And so does the Zulu Nation, but they don't know who we are 'cause this is our first time being up there. We get surrounded by a bunch of them on the 2 train. They looking at us. We feeling them out. They feeling us out. We get in the front of T-Connection, and there's Bambaataa and another brother by the name of Trouble, and they's like, "Yo, that's the Crash Crew. We don't have no beef with them." That was like the closest we got to beef up in the Bronx.

After the first couple of shows we did up there, after they know we wasn't gonna back down, they accepted us. I don't know if it was 'cause we had a hot record at that time, because they still was packing parties without us. But they was getting a little more packed, having another variety of MC up in there. Everybody knew the Bronx MCs; they knew what they was gonna do, they knew their routines back and forth. But when Manhattan groups came up there and went to play their records, it was something new for them. Just like with the Bronx MCs coming down to Manhattan. You know what I'm saying? It was like that. So hip-hop just couldn't be stopped. You couldn't stop the growth of it.

DJ Easy Lee and the Treacherous 3—Special K, Kool Moe Dee, and L.A. Sunshine, Easy Lee kneeling—photo cut-out used for paste-up flyers.

264

the treacherous 3

SPECIAL K: My mother was a schoolteacher. She taught Kool Moe Dee. She taught L.A. Sunshine, Easy Lee, DLB from Fearless 4; they was all in our school. So when I got to Norman Thomas High School, we all hooked up; we started hanging out. They had turntables in the lunchroom. I had the tapes, and I had my rhymes together, now I'm getting on the mic in the lunchroom.

So I started working it in the lunchroom. They couldn't touch me up in that school. I was hitting 'em hard. Then Moe Dee seen me in the lunchroom. I have the halls like West Side Story: I'm walking down the hallway, twenty dudes behind me, and I'm rhyming, and they all clapping behind. So Moe Dee got hip. Next thing I know, during his lunch period, he got on the mic, and he blew Norman Thomas lunchroom up. I said, "Oh, oh. Brother trying to take over my spot." So it started buzzing through the school, "Oh, man, they gonna battle. They gonna battle."

One day it just came to a head. I said, "All right, now we gonna go all out. We gonna go in the lunchroom, and we gonna do it." And that was funny, 'cause I had him. See, one day Moe had said this fast rhyme. He invented that, I got to give him credit for that. But what he didn't know is that once I heard it, that was it—I went home and I had me one. I remember being on the train going home; that's when I wrote the fast rhyme that we use on our "New Rap Language" [rhymes in a continuous staccato flow]: "Undefeated, never beat it, never cheat it, bust exceed it. If I need it, to delete it, rhymes all guaranteed...Wheelin' dealin', women stealin', Casanova, booty feelin'. Understanding, reprimanding..." I was on that. I adapted it. He was shocked that I came out with it. He was laughing. After that we was inseparable.

L.A. SUNSHINE: The Treacherous 3 originally consisted of Spoonie Gee, L.A. Sunshine, and Kool Moe Dee. We were just doing gigs for local promoters, and not no promoters like Mike and Dave and guys like that. It was just like the guy that owned a bagel shop on 125th called Randy's Place. We used to do gigs for him, and he used to just pay us pizza money. We were more proud to be affiliated with it than the fools who were getting paid. We wasn't looking at it from a get-paid aspect at that time. We was just trying to get off, and eventually it evolved into making dough.

Then Spoonie had a chance to go cut a track, and he did that. He tried to hook us up with a deal with his uncle Bobby Robinson. At the time, we was putting K down with the crew. Spoonie had his name value out already, so we couldn't have him and be Spoonie Gee and Moe and L.A.. So that's when we took K and put K in and made the Treacherous 3 out of me, K, and Moe. We became Spoonie Gee and the Treacherous 3. Spoonie took off again, and we just stuck with the Treacherous 3.

: The Treacherous 3's Second Anniversary Celebration at Harlem World, 1982 (Courtesy Luis Cedeno)

SPECIAL K: Moe invited me to Randy's Place; they was playing, and they asked me to get on. I got on the mike and ripped it. Spoonie was leaving the fold, so Moe Dee was like, "Yo, we just put Special K down."

We started doing gigs. We would go to clubs and we would tear it up. Mind you, we had the fast rhyming. Whenever we did that, that was it. We went from making a tape to actually putting routines together and really rehearsing. I used to walk all the way from the Bronx down to 125th Street, 127th Street and St. Nick. We'd go behind the schoolyard. We had things going, me and Moe Dee and L.A. Sunshine. All the elements combined.

L.A. SUNSHINE: We was kids. Once we started making records, getting a coupla dollars, we was alright. We was content with making $200 a gig, and then $800 a gig, and then $1,500 a gig; we go on up the scale. That was money to us. Plus we took a lot of pride in what we was doing, and we were getting paid for it. It was gratifying, but I didn't get headstrong about it or nothing. But I will say, the very first time I heard myself on the radio, I blew up. I was buggin', I was like, "I'm on the radio, yo! This is crazy, this is crazy!" Calling my family up and all that. It was fun, but it rolled off my back real quick, you know?

SPECIAL K: Now things is popping: now we got a record deal. We did "New Rap Language," that was how we broke it with Enjoy. That was the gravy. I remember I was a cornball in a sense, I was so proud of myself. I remember there was no cover on the record so I went and got me a magic marker, put my name on there, and I was carrying that record with me everywhere. I would go take my record and have them play it. "You gotta play it, you gotta hear this." 'Cause I couldn't rely on Bobby getting it played. Until one day I heard it—somebody was playing it out their window. Oh. It's on now. Handsome. Smart. Likeable. Loveable. And with a record out. Oh, come on. This was it. Oh, yeah.

MIKE C: My friend Peso used to write a lot of rhymes. I got him together with these guys from my junior high named Tito and DLB, and they got a thing going on. I had won a talent contest for rapping, and I was in a group called the Family, so I couldn't join at that time. They got with another rapper called Mike Ski and became the Fearless 4. One thing led to another...I joined the group. For a while it was the Fearless 5; then Mike Ski left. OC was always one of the DJs. We had another DJ called Bone D, a little light-skinned guy with an afro. Then Bone left, and Krazy Eddie joined—he lived right across the street—and that's how it became OC, Krazy Eddie, and the Fearless 4.

We were introduced through Mike and Dave and the Treacherous 3, because we all grew up together. We was always trying to get the Treach to get us down with Enjoy Records, but Moe Dee always said, "Nah, I can't really do it." So what happened was, me and Tito used to always hang at Bobby Robinson's office. We got to be cool with his secretary, a guy named Spanky, and we'd just be in his office everyday. So every time Bobby came, he always seen us. Finally he's like, "What're you guys doing here?" And we said, "Yo, we trying to get a record deal." He said, "Alright, well if you think you can rap, prove it to me." And me and Tito sat down and did our Fearless 4 routine between the two of us, and after that Bobby said, "I don't believe this. All this time you guys were here, I didn't even know you had talent." And he signed us right then.

We were so, so, so hyped to be on Enjoy. We're like, "Yo, this man Bobby Robinson's a history maker!" Because everybody that signed with him became such big stars, you know what I'm saying? He had Gladys Knight and Grandmaster Flash and the Furious 5, and Treacherous 3, and the Funky 4 + 1. He even had Kool Kyle on the label, you know? It's like, "Yo, this is our chance! We finally got a chance."

DLB: Enjoy felt like we would be joining a family situation, with all of these people who we looked up to. I was happy, I was enthused, and by the time we got ready to sign the contracts, I was sixteen, and to me, I didn't care about what was on the contracts or nothing. I went and got my father to sign it for me, because I was still a minor. All I knew was, "I'm gonna be down with Flash and them, and the Treacherous, the Funky 4! And here it is, this company that sprouts right from my own neighborhood in Harlem!" So, I was just enthusiastic about the entire thing.

MIKE C: We used to go to Harlem World, and a lot of times, believe it or not, we couldn't get in. They'd say, "Fearless 4? Who the hell are you?" Then after we leave, we'd see a flyer that says, "Invited Guests: Fearless 4." But when we came out with our first release, "It's Magic," once we did that, once we performed, it was like we could get in anyplace.

Then we did "Rockin' It," and it was so big that we'd get on stage, and no matter how the rest of the show sucked—'cause there's been times that like, "Man, we ain't working. Ain't nothing happening right," you know?—but "Rockin' It" would come on, and we would get such a big response, you'd be like, "Wow! This is like Michael Jackson just walked on stage." People would go crazy when "Rockin' It" would come on.

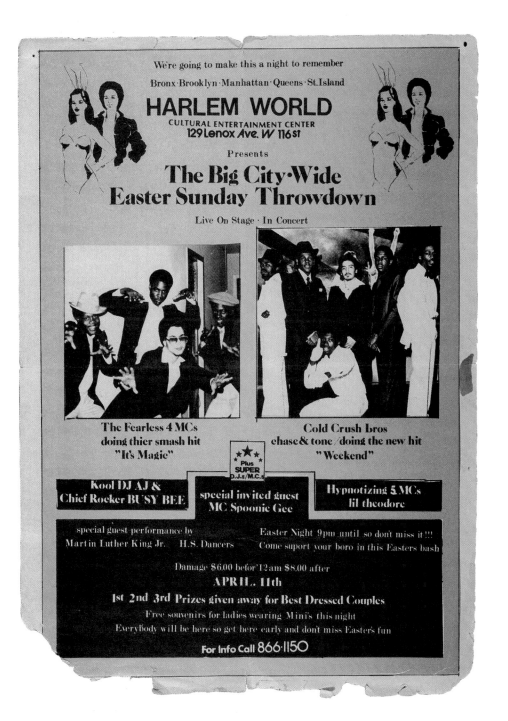

on the road and on to sugarhill

SPECIAL K: After a while we're playing with all these cats. Furious 5! You get respected by the inner circle of people; then you're venturing out. And that was the advantage of the records, 'cause you already got New York. Now you get to go travel. Travel and all expenses paid. Girls jumping all over the place...

L.A. SUNSHINE: We were on the road. There wasn't no tour buses back then. Remember: we was dealing with Bobby Robinson. Bobby rented us a station wagon and put me, Moe, and Special K, Easy Lee, and a driver in a station wagon, packed our clothes up and the music and the turntables and sent us down South. We was following tour buses around. We was doing a little mini-tour with the Bar-Kays, and One Way, and the Double Dutch guy. That was a tour. We was playing sold-out arenas, and we was the only group on stage that didn't have a van. It was an experience.

Then Bobby sold the group's contract to Sugarhill. We didn't want to go. That's like going from the frying pan and into the fire. And that's something I'd really rather not speak about...

REGGIE REG: Sugarhill had wanted Crash Crew to come up there and do "High Power Rap" over the version of "Freedom" they did with a band, but we wouldn't do it. We wouldn't leave Mike and Dave, so they got Flash to do it—Flash did the "Freedom" beat over, and now it was a beef. So what Sugarhill did was sign us to their label so that they could kill our version, and then their "Freedom" with Flash could still go on. By then, we was having problems with Mike and Dave, so we left them and we went to Sugarhill. But their strategy didn't work. We still did our "Freedom."

When we went up to Sugarhill to talk to them we met Master Gee. He come out of the office with a suitcase of money. "Oh, you're the Crash Crew!" They gassed us totally. We see all these nice cars in the lot—BMWs, Rolls Royces. Master Gee with a suitcase of money. We like, "Yo, this is it, right here. We Jacksons now. We gonna be rich." I mean, I was seventeen years old. The rest of them must have been like eighteen. I'm like the second to the youngest. Darryl C was younger than me; he was sixteen. So we got our moms and them to come up there. Our moms advised us, "Get a lawyer. I don't know about these people. Blah-blah-blah." We didn't want to hear that. You know what I'm saying? "Ma, listen, I'm at a age where I can leave you right now. I'm gonna run away if you don't let me. This is my dream right here. This is me out of the ghetto." So she didn't want to do it but she did it.

When we went on the road with Sugar Hill Gang, we was performing "High Power Rap," but we was told not to perform it, because Flash and them was doing "Freedom" also. We got into a little beef with that, and we settled that with a football game with Flash and them. And they won. They had Big Bank Hank from the Sugar Hill Gang with them. You know what I'm saying? They beat us. But it was a good game, and we settled it like that.

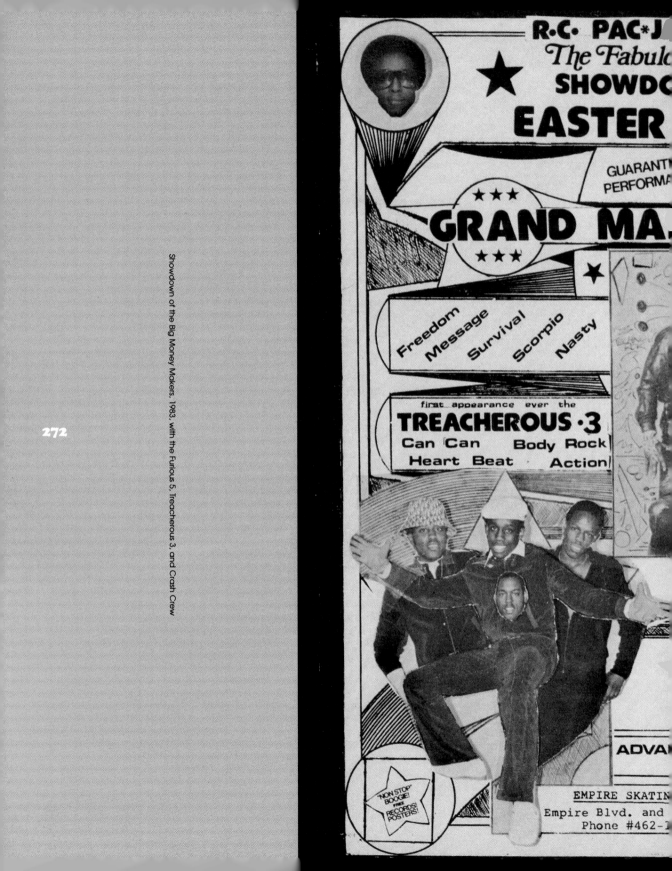

Showdown of the Big Money Makers, 1983, with the Furious 5, Treacherous 3, and Crash Crew

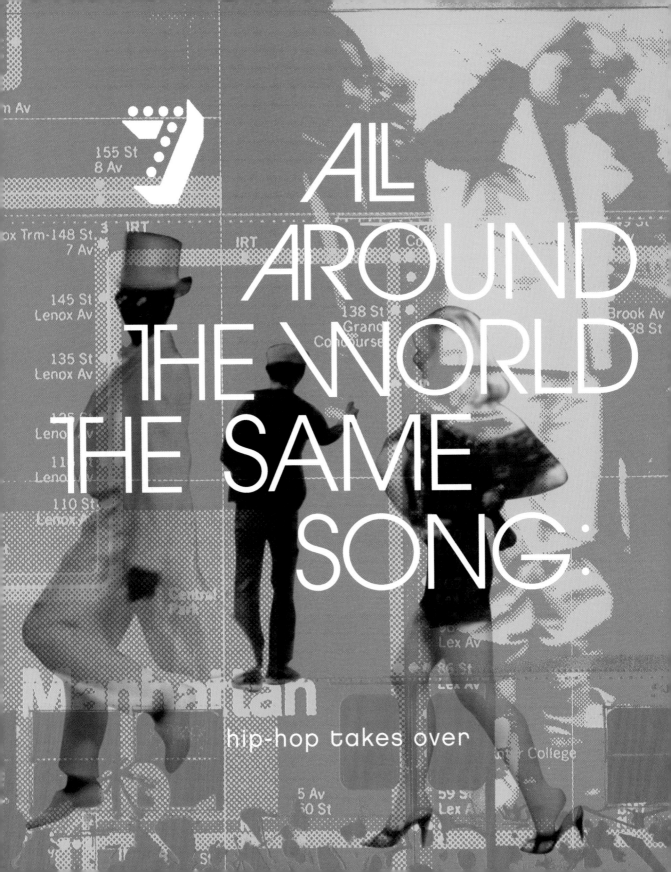

ALL
AROUND
THE WORLD
THE SAME
SONG.

hip-hop takes over

The fantastically painted subway cars coursing throughout New York City provided outsiders with the first visual evidence of the new culture blooming in the Bronx. By the time "Rapper's Delight" came out, the city's subway art had become famous—or infamous—but people outside the city had no idea what other aspects of the scene looked like. This changed in the early '80s, as b-boying became a media phenomenon and filmmakers documented the music, art, and dance of hip-hop culture. The film *Wild Style* brought the actual stars of the hip-hop scene to the screen, and the documentary *Style Wars* provided glimpses into the lives of graffiti writers. Hollywood jumped in with *Beat Street*, and suddenly "rappers" were movie stars and "break-dancers" were on the cover of *Time* magazine and featured in the opening ceremonies of the Olympic Games.

Kids around the world memorized the scenes in *Wild Style* and copied the dance moves and mural styles they saw on film and on TV. The Funky 4 + 1 had made a few forays downtown in 1980; by 1982 hip-hop had arrived in full force and was the hottest thing on the scene at hip clubs like the Roxy. There British expatriate Kool Lady Blue created a sensation booking DJs, MCs, graffiti writers, and b-boys in weekly celebrations of hip-hop culture. Soon a second generation of performers emerged. The crossover success of Run-DMC and L.L. Cool J ushered in a new sound and a new wave of performers, pushing the pioneers aside.

"it was like a
mini art world"

FAB 5 FREDDY (FRED BRATHWAITE): I started tagging up in the neighborhood in the mid-'70s. My first tag was BULL. We didn't have street numbers where I lived, but I thought the number thing was cool, so my number was 99-BULL99. There was another cat that I was really good friends with; his name was Herb, so he made his number HERB99.

BLADE: You wanted everyone to know who you are. Except for the police, of course. It was just writing your name and getting it out there and seeing it and running up and down through the train stations. You went to each train car and you hit each car.

FAB 5 FREDDY: The markers that were available at the time were kind of small, and we were trying to figure out different techniques. They came out with a marker called a "Uni-Wide," which had a particularly wide tip. The store that sold the Uni-Wide was a store called Pearl Paint, in downtown Manhattan. We were living in Brooklyn at the time, so we found out you take the A train to Canal Street and you walk a few blocks and there was Pearl Paint. When you got off that train you realized that all the major graffiti writers from other parts of the city were converging to get these markers. You would see the fresh tags from these markers everywhere. It was like the Hall of Fame.

I didn't meet Phase 2 at that time, but he was a legend to me; we knew about him. I knew about all the big guys, Blade...Stay High. We saw their tags on Canal, so we were like, "Wow! We're getting closer!"

HENRY CHALFANT: I started taking pictures in 1976. I had recently moved to New York, so I had a lot of friends in other parts of the world, and I was sending them pictures, telling them, "Look at what's going on here. This is an incredible phenomenon that's happening." After about three years, I ran into a kid on Intervale Avenue; he had a camera, and as a train would come in he was snapping shots as I was. We got into a conversation, and it turned out he was [writer] Daze's cousin, Nock. He said to me, "If you want to meet writers, go to 149th Street and Grand Concourse at the back end of the train station after school around 3 o'clock. The writers hang out there." So I went, and just as he said, there was a mob of kids sharing black books, talking about the pieces that were coming through the station, dissing people whose work was terrible and praising what was good. It was like a mini art world going on right there.

"Art vs. Transit" by DURO, SHY 147, and COS207, 1981 (© Martha Cooper)

Fab 5 Freddy under the Brooklyn Bridge, 1980 (© Charlie Ahearn)

Chris Stein, Nile Rogers, Flash, and Fab 5 Freddy—a snapshot of hip hop. Flash's radical reviving of Rodgers's Chic hit "Good Times" was picked up as the rhythm for "Rapper's Delight." Brathwaite introduced Stein and Debbie Harry to Flash, and Harry rapped the story on Blondie's hit "Rapture." (© Charlie Ahearn)

BLADE: You could be sitting there and you would see something pull in from five boroughs away, and it's just bang, this huge whole car. Writers would actually run across over the top of the trains, even though the police was there, just to get a picture with their little 126 camera. The cops then, if they saw a teenager with a camera, they would confiscate it, rip the film out, stuff like that.

CEY ADAMS: 149th Street and Grand Concourse—the Writer's Bench—that's where everybody hung out. You go there and you see people just sitting there waiting for their new train to roll out. It was just amazing to actually be in front of these people that you idolized—Blade, Comet, Lee, Phase 2...

When you would ride the subway, you'd see their names. That was our world. I didn't go to museums so I wasn't exposed to that side of the art world. This was our high art—graffiti—and these guys just did it better than anybody. It was the equivalent of going into the Museum of Modern Art and seeing a huge canvas on the wall. I mean, when a subway car goes by and it's completely covered, that's a beautiful thing. And I just wanted to do that; I wanted to be that guy.

making connections

FAB 5 FREDDY: Around '77–'78 I was reading some books, and I saw this whole thing about pop art, and I saw a connection between the styles and what was going on in graffiti, which at the time had become really developed. Obviously a lot of the inspirations were coming from comic books and advertising. I made a connection that this stuff going on was like art, too, and I could perhaps become a part of it and be an artist like these pop artists. Like a graffiti artist would want to get his name up, I wanted to get up but in a bigger arena, you know, on a bigger train if you will.

LEE: Fred found me at my old school. I don't know how. I thought Fred was a cop when he came to my classroom and said, "I want to speak with Lee Quinones."

FAB 5 FREDDY: Lee Quinones was a master painter, and he had been a part of the Fab 5—Fabulous 5 graffiti crew. They had a tradition of doing these incredible murals, particularly on the Lexington No. 5, and I wanted to become a part of that but then take it to another arena. Lee and some of the other cats allowed me to become a member, kind of like the last member of the Fab 5.

Braithwaite's Soup Train was a hip graffiti homage to Andy Warhol (note the reference to Glenn O'Brien's TV Party, where Braithwaite met Stein and Harry) (© Martha Cooper)

Rapture: Debbie Harry,
Fab 5 Freddy, and Flash, 1981
(© Charlie Ahearn)

the soup can train

FAB 5 FREDDY: That train—it was pretty much known as "The Soup Can Train"—was a part of my assault on the art world. A stepping-stone, a calling-card into pop culture, whatever you want to call it. It was basically to let graffiti people see something differ-ent in terms of imagery. It was like an homage/salute to Andy Warhol. It was also like a message to anybody that knew about contemporary art that people painting on sub-ways weren't the animals or monsters we were often depicted as in the press, that we were sophisticated in terms of what we were aware of as far as the art world or pop culture.

I did two versions of it. The funny thing is, the second version was during the time when graffiti was still really heavy on the subways, and then they had this thing called the "Buff," which was the acid bath that they would put the trains through to clean the graffiti off. It ended up ruining the surface of the trains...But the MTA allowed the sec-ond version of that train to run for at least three or four years. It was uncanny. Somebody must have liked it.

* * *

I had been making moves in the downtown area of Manhattan for a couple years, hooking up with people who had a like sensibility to what I was trying to do. I saw a connection between the people that were doing punk rock and the pop artists, and that had led me to hook up with Glenn O'Brien, who is the original editor of Andy Warhol's *Interview* magazine. Through that relationship, I met Chris Stein and Debbie Harry—Blondie.

CHRIS STEIN: Freddy took Debbie and me up to a Police Athletic League in the Bronx for this big sort of hip-hop convention. That was really exciting; it was just so fan-tastic. It grabbed me immediately as such a vital street form. And it was very parallel to what was going on in the punk scene.

FAB 5 FREDDY: We went up to the P.A.L. at 183rd and Webster in the Bronx. Glenn O'Brien came with us, Chris, Debbie...there might have been a couple other heads, and we went to this party, which was Mercedes Ladies...I think Cold Crush was there and a couple of other groups. I was really hoping that nothing would go down, because there was a real ill element that would hang out at the parties, like things could hap-pen, you know what I'm saying? But everything was cool. People bugged out seeing all these white people coming into the club.

CHRIS STEIN: "Rapture" was just about making a song that had a rap in it. It was totally that. A really odd note is that that song really was the first rap song that most people heard. Or most white people.

FRED BRATHWAITE: I actually used to tell Debbie, "Listen Debbie, you guys should make a record about me." And she would laugh, "Oh, Freddy, you're crazy!" So then they went off and made that record, and they called me over to listen. On comes this rap part, which I thought, "Oh, that's so sweet of them they just did like a special mix." So I was flattered, but I never really believed that it was going to be a record, that they were going to really release it, you know?

The Deadly Art of Survival
poster (© Charlie Ahearn)

the deadly art of survival

FAB 5 FREDDY: We had seen this poster in Lee's neighborhood for a film called *The Deadly Art of Survival*, and the poster would always captivate us. The cat on the poster was this local guy who was a kung-fu hero/teacher. Kung fu was really popular at the time—you'd go to Times Square to see kung-fu movies—and it just seemed like this must have been a really cool movie. And the guy who made it was Charlie Ahearn.

CHARLIE AHEARN: Years before I made *Wild Style*, I was making a super-8 movie, *The Deadly Art of Survival*, with Nathan Ingram, a local kung-fu teacher. I was casting these kids in the Smith Housing Projects in lower Manhattan where Lee Quinones lived. The total budget of the film was about $2,000, which was mostly to pay for pizza to keep the kids around. I saw all these incredible murals all over the place. I would ask these kids, "Who painted these murals?" and they'd look at me in wonder like, "You don't know who did these? Lee!" And I'd go, "Great, where can I find him?" And they'd go, "Well, we don't know. He's kind of hard to find. He's sort of a mystery."

One time Lee showed up. He was this really skinny kid with a big afro, and I said, "I'd really like to have you in part of this movie." And he'd say, "Bet." And I'd say, "Well, how can I get in touch with you?" And he goes, "Oh, I'll be around." And then he'd disappear.

FAB 5 FREDDY: I hooked up with Charlie Ahearn, I believe it was the spring of 1980. There was a show that had opened called the Times Square Show. I had met Diego Cortez, who was like a curator on the scene, not long before, and he said, "Oh you should definitely be in this show!" I mean almost anybody could be in it. You could literally just walk in there and say, "I'm an artist," and hang your work.

So me and Diego went up there to the Times Square Show, and those posters for *The Deadly Art of Survival* movie were up. I said, "That's that poster we saw on the Lower East Side." Diego introduced me to Charlie: "Charlie Ahearn is the guy that made this movie." And right away I started saying, "Hey, we should get together. I've got this idea for a film about this culture."

CHARLIE AHEARN: I was at the Times Square Show showing *The Deadly Art of Survival* when I meet this tall guy with dark sunglasses, Fab 5 Freddy. He said that he was good friends with Lee, and I said, "If you come here tomorrow to the Times Square Show, I could give you guys $50 to buy spray paint and do a big mural on the wall outside."

LEE: At the Times Square Show we did the paintings outside. Everybody was there— Kenny Scharf, Keith Haring. I thought it was odd that people were coming to Times Square to look at art.

FAB 5 FREDDY: Keith Haring was just starting out; he was kind of a fan of graffiti. I had just hung a couple of paintings in one of the rooms, and I was standing around the room. He came into the room and began to give me a lecture on who had made these paintings. And then somebody came in and said, "Oh, Fred!"...or "Fab!" And Keith looked at me, and it was like, "I just put my foot in my mouth." So we became good friends.

Kool DJ AJ with DJ Smalls
(Son of Hollywood), at the
Ecstasy Garage, 1980
(© Charlie Ahearn)

CHARLIE AHEARN: The Ecstasy Garage was only three or four blocks from where my twin brother John was living and making portrait casts of people in the neighborhood. I started taking pictures there, and then the following week I would set up two slide projectors over the DJs and show pictures of people at the previous week's jam. Mean Gene or DJ AJ would be on the wheels of steel, and Kevie Kev would be rapping about what was on the screen.

The Chief Rocker Busy Bee at the Valley, 1980 (© Charlie Ahearn)

wild style

CHARLIE AHEARN: I would talk to Fred about how we were gonna make this movie and how I'll rent a theater on 42nd Street and just run it twenty-four hours a day like a grind-house theater. The gangs used to come in the '70s to 42nd Street to see the kung-fu movies. So that was my ambition for the movie. And we came pretty close to that.

FAB 5 FREDDY: At that time people weren't seeing all these different elements as one thing, you know? It was like people doing graffiti were just doing graffiti. Rapping people were rapping. The break-dance scene would go on at hip-hop parties, but it was pretty much like a Latin thing, so there were Latin clubs that would happen where break-dancing would go on. So I had this idea to bring these things together, and Charlie was like, "This is cool."

CHARLIE AHEARN: Right after the Times Square Show, Fred and I went to this place in the Valley (North Bronx). It was my first jam, and it was at night in a very large dark park. There was a single light bulb over the DJ. We approached to meet some of the rappers that were up on stage. I was standing next to this guy, the Chief Rocker Busy Bee. He later told me that he was sweating bullets because he was holding a joint in his hand, and he thought I was a cop.

Busy says, "Hey man, what are you doing up here?" And I said, "I'm a filmmaker, and I'm trying to make a film about the rap scene." And he takes me by the arm and leads me right out to the middle of the stage to a microphone, and he puts his arm around me and says, "This is Charlie Ahearn. He's my film producer, and we're making a movie about the rap scene." So Busy Bee got first place in line, and everybody who was involved in the rap scene there came around me and wanted to get involved in the movie. It was that easy.

290

Charlie Ahearn directs the Fantastic 5 in the *Wild Style* basketball scene (© Cathy Campbell)

CHARLIE AHEARN: We were shooting the Cold Crush and the Fantastic scene at the Dixie Club. I see these guys and I thought, they look pretty hard; they'd be good gangsters. So I said, "Would you guys be interested in doing a scene where you play some stick-up kids?" Later we're outside on the street, and I hand the guy this pistol, which was, in fact, a starter pistol, but it looked like a real serious gun. And he says, "I can't use this. That's a pussy gun." And I go, "Well, that's the only prop we got." His car is parked like only four feet away from us, and he reaches under the front seat and pulls out this really, raggedy-lookin', old sawed-off shotgun. I was very impressed. I never asked him if it was loaded. And I didn't make up the lines, "A to the K, A to the motherfuckin' Z." They were lines that these guys had obviously been using for years. It was real.

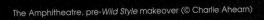
The Amphitheatre, pre-*Wild Style* makeover (© Charlie Ahearn)

Chief Rocker Busy Bee rocks the amphitheater in this climactic party (© Martha Cooper)

THE HIP HOP MOVIE HAS ARRIVED!!

RAPPING SCRATCHING BREAKING

WILD STYLE

NYC SUPER
RAPPING STARS
ON THE SCREEN!!
**COLD CRUSH BROS!
GRAND MASTER
FLASH! FANTASTIC
FREAKS!
CHIEF
ROCKER BUSY BEE
AND DJ AJ!!
RAMMELLZEE!
DOUBLE TROUBLE!
GRAND MIXER DST!**

THE WORLD FAMOUS BREAK
AND ELECTRIC BOOGIE DANCERS
ROCK STEADY CREW
AND **ELECTRIC FORCE!**
MUSIC BY **FAB 5 FREDDY**
AND **CHRIS STEIN** OF **BLONDIE**

HIGH POWERED GRAFFITI MASTERS
LEE, DAZE, CRASH, DONDI
STARRING 'LEE' QUINONES, FRED
BRATHWAITE, PATTI ASTOR,
'PINK' FABARA, 'ZEPHYR'

A FILM BY **CHARLIE AHEARN**
A FIRST RUN FEATURES RELEASE

OPENS NOVEMBER 23RD

Guild's **EMBASSY 3** B'WAY & 47 ST. 730-7262

THE EMBASSY
WILL BE SMOKING!!!!

Advertisement for *Wild Style* premiere at the Embassy Theater, 1983.

Ahearn filmed this 1981 show at the Amoitheatre for *Wild Style* but the sound was poor, leading him to film at the venue the following year.

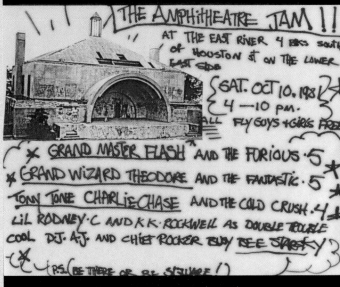

FAB 5 FREDDY: I can't really claim credit for coming up with the *Wild Style* story, per se, because Charlie did the writing. At the time, I was also painting and exhibiting and trying to do that as well. But we collaborated on all the ideas to a great extent, because it was basically just me and him.

My character was specifically to illustrate that there was a real link between graffiti and hip-hop. But that was also heavily inspired by the life of Phase 2, who had been this legendary graffiti character who then was very involved in the hip-hop scene, like doing fliers for all the key parties and stuff.

LEE: In the end, it became a genius piece because it captured the energy and innocence of all of us. It didn't really have a script, but we didn't have a script in real life. The film didn't call for acting because we were being ourselves. There's no Hollywood thing about it.

CHARLIE CHASE: That movie, Wild Style, the script was terrible, but to me, it was the best movie out of all the rap movies ever put out to this day, because in that movie, there were no actors. Whoever was DJ-ing was a DJ. There was a graffiti writer in the movie, and he was a graffiti writer. Not like today, where you have all these Hollywood actors doing these things. It's all commercialized now.

CHRIS STEIN: Wild Style was just so ahead of its time. I remember telling Charlie Ahearn, "As soon as this thing comes out, mark my words, Hollywood will eat it." And Beat Street came out within just months after it came out, which was a sappy, watered-down version.

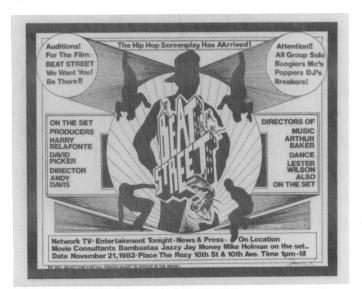

b-boys: the rock steady crew revives

ALIEN NESS: By 1979 b-boyin' was already passé; it was played. Nobody was doing it, nobody wanted to see it, and if it wasn't for Crazy Legs going around New York City and searching for people who still danced and asking the original leaders of the Rock Steady Crew—JoJo, Jimmy Dee, Jimmy Lee—if he could continue using the name...that's how the b-boy was kept alive.

CRAZY LEGS: I knew some of the Zulus, but my idols were other crews, like the [original] Rock Steady...The Bronx Boys was the first crew I was ever down with.

JOJO: BOM5 and Rip 7 were in the TBB [The Bronx Boys] at the time. I was a freelance b-boy. I'd help them out. We started hanging out, and we formed Rock Steady ...in 1977 with Jimmie D. We had one of the first b-girls; her name was Bunny Lee and she was Jimmy Lee's girlfriend. Jimmy was a member of Rock Steady. She got killed by mistake—she fell out a window. She was a true female pioneer.

I'm like the only survivor of [the original] Rock Steady. Everybody is either dead or in jail. I still can't find Jimmie D. Nobody knows where he's at. Jimmie D was always considered the Pres, but I taught him everything.

BOM5: Crazy Legs used to look through the window where me and my other cousin used to be breaking, at Islam's house. I'd sneak out of the house, spend the night breaking. A couple of times we saw Legs looking through the window, and we yell, "Go home! Go home or else we'll all get into trouble!"

FROSTY FREEZE: The first time I went to something in the park was 1977. Being from Manhattan, we had to see what was going on up in the Bronx, and my mentor Sundance took me and a couple of guys from the West Side with him to the Bronx. Sundance was big and loud and had cousins who were down with the Zulu Kings, who were the baddest dancers around. When they hit the dance floor, they were swift, with the shuffling and the footwork and the spins...the helicopters, the sweeps! They were bad! I said to my friends, "We got to go back to Manhattan and practice before we're ready for this."

Around 1980 there were different Hispanic b-boys on the Manhattan side, and I started hearing about Crazy Legs. I was freelancing—my crew, the Rock City Crew, had just stopped. B-boying was played out to me, but then again it was still in me, so I always used to go down if I see anybody else go down. My DJ, Louie Lou, was bringing his equipment out to the park over there on 84th Street, Columbus Avenue, and Crazy Legs happened to come in the park along with one of his boys from uptown. He'd just moved to Manhattan, way up on the upper Manhattan side. Everybody wanted to see us go down and battle each other. At first, Legs was getting the best of me, and then the tables turned; I was getting the best of him. Our styles were basically the same, but Legs introduced a little something different, like the backspin and the windmills. I had my own particular styles, like mainly freezes and doing stuff that just came off my head.

Me and Legs hooked up, and he asked me to be down with his crew, 'cause we respected each other's styles. We became Rock Steady in 1981, me and Crazy Legs. He went up against Ken Swift and his crew out in USA in Queens, and then I kind of brought everything together 'cause I was telling Crazy Legs, "If this is the crew that you want, I could talk to Ken Swift, Ty Fly, Doze, Kippy, Nelski, Gene-O," and that's when we became Rock Steady. We practiced together, we made up routines, we was just taking this breakin' to another level, until we met up with Henry Chalfant. Then the forces became stronger and bigger and better. We just advanced it from the b-boy side.

FABEL: The Rock Steady Crew has been the number one b-boy crew that has kept this thing alive, with all its various members. Crazy Legs, Ken Swift, Frosty Freeze, all of these guys throughout the years have helped preserve the closest that you're going to get to seeing the original style. They keep it alive.

graffiti rock

HENRY CHALFANT: I had a loft in SoHo. I had told the writers up at 149th Street that I had a studio and a lot of photographs of graffiti, so they began to visit the studio, and it became sort of like a salon for graffiti artists.

Right next door to my studio was a performance place called Common Ground. In March 1981, the guy who ran the place asked me to put together a performance in his space, based on my photos. By this time, I had met Charlie Ahearn and Fab 5 Freddy, so I said, "Well, I'll have some rappers come to part of the slide show, and maybe Fred could write a rap about graffiti."

Also, at this time, I had heard from my future partner, Martha Cooper, that she had come across a new dance called break-dancing. She was a photojournalist, and she kept listening in on police calls. She heard about a bust of a gang fight up in Washington Heights somewhere, and she rushed over there to see what was going on. When she arrived, there was some befuddled cops and a bunch of kids standing around trying to explain to them what they were doing. They weren't fighting. They were dancing.

That was Martha's next project—break-dancing—but that's all I knew about it. So I asked Take 1, who was one of the graffiti writers hanging out in my studio at the time, if he'd ever heard of breaking, and he said, "I know the best b-boys in New York." The next day, sure enough, he brought in Crazy Legs and Frosty Freeze from Rock Steady. I was just blown away by the amazing moves that they could do, so I said immediately, "Well, I'm having this performance. Do you guys want to be a part of it?"

FROSTY FREEZE: Take 1 brought us down to Henry's studio in SoHo. I thought Henry Chalfant was a graffiti writer, 'cause he had all these pictures of graffiti. We did a little demonstration in front of Henry, and Henry liked what he saw.

HENRY CHALFANT: I notified Marty that I'd found some actual breakers. She called in Sally Banes, who was a dance critic for the *Village Voice* at the time, and we had a session where Marty took pictures and Sally interviewed the guys. This was all leading up to the performance. It was the first article ever about breaking, in which Sally Banes talked about a new young subculture with their own art form, music, and dance forms. I think that's probably the first time that these three forms came together under the heading of hip-hop.

In any case, word got out because of the article, and it looked like the performance was gonna be a sell-out. People even came to the dress rehearsal, which is when I found out some things that I didn't know about the culture: how contentious and territorial it is, and how in spite of the attempt by people to say it's a mediation of violence and a way to lessen violence, it was often a buildup to it. What they had done is they had created a battle with their own members, calling one side Rock Steady and the other side Floormaster Dancers. Their own crew was divided up into two crews so that they could have a battle.

FROSTY FREEZE: Maybe two or three days later, we brought the rest of the Rock Steady Crew—myself, Crazy Legs, Little Crazy Legs, Ken Swift, Mr. Freeze, Ty Fly, Doze, Rip 7, and Lenny Len. So we split the crew into two groups, like we were demonstrating what a battle was all about. We were still under the name Rock Steady, but I took Ken Swift, Ty Fly, and Mr. Freeze on my side as the Floormasters. Crazy Legs, Little Crazy Legs, Kippy, and Take One were the Rock Steady Crew.

HENRY CHALFANT: The real rivals were still out there—the Ball Busters. Halfway through the dress rehearsal, the Ball Busters arrived, and half of my event crew hid behind the big speakers, and the other half got into words with them. There was a gun pulled; machetes were pulled to protect the DJ equipment. All hell broke loose. At that point, I called the police, but by that time the fight had run out into the street. Everybody chased each other down the street.

Nobody got hurt, but it was an eye opener for the man who had invited me to do the show. He said, "Sorry, Henry. I don't have insurance to cover this." So we had to cancel the show. But by this point, word had gotten out that there was going to be this show, so mobs showed up to see it. It would have been great if we could have done it.

Tony Silver, a filmmaker that I knew, saw the dress rehearsal, and he said, "Let's do a film together." For the first shoot, we pooled some money together just to get something on film to make a proposal. There was a battle that Rock Steady had with Dynamic Rockers at USA Skating Rink in Queens, and that was the first thing we shot for *Style Wars*.

FROSTY FREEZE: When I first seen my picture on the *Village Voice*, I went to the stationery store there, and the guy gave me, like, three or four copies. And then we read the interview inside, and that's how Bambaataa and them found out who we were, 'cause we mentioned that some of his b-boys had inspired us, the Zulu Kings. So after that, everything started happening pretty good for us. Our first real performance was downtown at Common Ground. This is when I first got to meet the graffiti writers, like Dondi, Futura, Zephyr, and all these other guys. Unfortunately, our show was cut short because of another rival group that wasn't into breakin'—guys called the Ball Busters screwed that up. But after that, we got publicity. We played on 20/20 at the time; we did Live at 5, a public service announcement with Kurtis Blow. We came out in the *New York Daily News*, the *New York Times*, which did an article on the show we were doing at the Lincoln Center, the Out of Doors of 1981.

the village VOICE

Cockburn Rejects the Pulitzer (P. 18)

VOL. XXVI No. 17   THE WEEKLY NEWSPAPER OF NEW YORK   APRIL 22-28, 1981   75¢

Revolt in Reagan's Backyard
Dispelling the Myth of a Reactionary Age

By Alexander Cockburn & James Ridgeway

The conventional wisdom today is that the election of Ronald Reagan last November ratified a conservative political tendency throughout the country, which politicians can only ignore at their peril. The myth of a new reactionary age has a self-reinforcing momentum. Democrats, claiming fealty to "the spirit of the times," vie with Republicans in cost-cutting rhetoric. "New liberals" jump into bed with old conservatism.

But the evidence to back the myth is wanting. Within months of the election there are signs, in local politics, that what the voters want is not a return to 19th-century frontier politics, but effective government which will help them materially and offer a vision of the future. These were the ingredients of a political program which Jimmy Carter's Democratic Party so signally failed to provide. (And to judge from polls on U.S. intervention in El Salvador, it does not seem that the voters much approve of resurgent cold-war adventurism either.)

An election in California last week offered an interesting inkling of what is really going on. There, in Santa Monica, a city of 100,000 wedged between the Pacific and metropolitan Los Angeles, the voters chose by a clear margin a highly progressive slate of candidates denounced by opponents as socialist agitators. The candidates came down strongly for the maintenance and indeed expansion of rent control against untrammeled development; they held their ground and finally prevailed against the right on the issue of crime, with a proposition to increase financing if necessary for community protection. And they took a strong position on the poisoning of the environment with toxic substances.

The official name of the group sponsoring this victory is the Santa Monicans for Renters' Rights, which itself was a political coalition of four organizations: the Santa Monica chapter of the Campaign for Economic Democracy, the statewide political organization started by Tom Hayden; the Santa Monica Democratic Club; the Santa Monica Fair Housing Alliance; and the Ocean Park electoral network. The overall coalition has about 3000 members who have contributed $5 or more.

The coalition won four seats to the Santa Monica *(Continued on page 10)*

THAI SHTICK
Mark Jacobson
(P. 15)

BALI HIGHS
Jan Hoffman
(P. 38)

MARTHA COOPER

Physical Graffiti
Breaking Is Hard To Do
By Sally Banes (P. 31)

Sarris on Stanwyck
(P. 43)

MAKING AGE LOOK EASY
Rickey on Astaire
(P. 44)

HENRY CHALFANT: I became sort of an informal manager, a role that I did not like and did not do well. But at the time, I was willing and happy to try to get something to happen for them. There was a big event—"Lincoln Center Out of Doors"—which I hosted, which led to another disaster. Rock Steady came with all their back—their crew— it's still the street. Dynamic Rockers came from Queens with all their back, and it was impossible for anybody in the audience to actually see the show because everybody got up on stage and surrounded the performances. There was no way of moving anybody away 'cause that was how it was done. That's how everyone did it, and too bad for the audience. It also degenerated into a kind of battle at the end, fist fights and that sort of thing.

Michael Holman came into the picture by the fall of 1981. He became Rock Steady's manager, doing it on a professional basis as I never had done. He put them in Club Negril on a regular basis, and then, following his relationship with them, Kool Lady Blue came into the picture, and she was the one who promoted the Roxy performances.

It became hard to have access to Rock Steady after they had managers promising them the world. We started out filming *Style Wars* with them, and the whole film was going to be more about breaking than it turned out to be, but when we got thwarted there, we just ran with the graffiti story line, which turned out to be a good move.

Flashdance

FROSTY FREEZE: In 1982 when we was all going to the Roxy, the director from *Flashdance* was there. I got a phone call from Kool Lady Blue, who was our booking agent and our manager in the Roxy, saying that they were wanting to do this movie *Flashdance*. So they did a lot of talking, and then we got to be picked as the cast members in that part of *Flashdance*. They picked me first, along with Crazy Legs, Ken Swift, and Mr. Freeze, who was doing the popping—Electric Boogie at that time was starting to come into the scene. So we filmed that scene in Pittsburgh. To me, that was the exposure that we really needed, because the movie was nationwide, you know? *Wild Style* was more of an underground movie; *Style Wars* was more of a documentary thing.

ALIEN NESS: I knew breakers back in the days, and stuff like that, but I wasn't really attracted to the breakin'; I was more for the DJ-ing and the MC-ing until *Flashdance* came out. When *Flashdance* came out, it was just like the next level. It was like, "Okay, I see this being done everyday on the block, but now I'm seeing it on a big screen." It was like everybody in the neighborhood, you had fifty, sixty, seventy-five kids at a time going to the movies and paying $2.50, which was expensive at that time for us, to watch thirty seconds of film—that one little scene with the Rock Steady Crew. That's really what set it off. Not just for me, but for a lot of b-boys nationwide. Nationwide.

302

Rock Steady crew practicing, 1981 (© Martha Cooper)

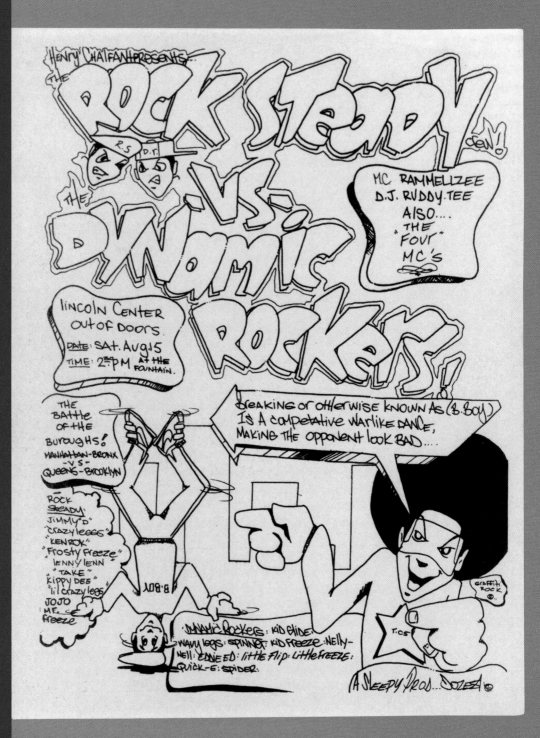

Frosty Freeze in park scene from *Wild Style*.
(© photo: Cathy Campbell)

The Lincoln Center battle, with the Rock Steady Crew's JoJo and Crazy Legs in the foreground (© Charlie Ahearn)

FROSTY FREEZE: After we filmed *Flashdance*, which was in October 1982, a guy Bernard Zekri from Celluloid Records put together this Europe One tour, which represented the Rock Steady Crew along with Afrika Bambaataa, Grand Mixer D.St., Fab 5 Freddy, Futura, Rammelzee, and the Double Dutch Girls. The Europe One tour was the first tour with the elements of graffiti, DJ-ing, MC-ing, to take that overseas. Me and Crazy Legs were the first b-boys to go on a tour around the United States; that was called the Kitchen Tour. So when we came back, that's when everything was happening so fast for us. We were young then, and we were enjoying that.

CRAZY LEGS: B-boying, it's the thing that blew up the whole hip-hop industry. People took to the visual aspect of hip-hop before they took to the spoken word. When we went to Europe...they didn't understand English in France, but the beat was slamming, and the dance and the graffiti, that all opened the door for rap. We all helped each other.

FROSTY FREEZE: We got the credit from that point, but there were other people before our time that just didn't get their recognition. I pay respect to those that paved the way for us. We knew it wasn't all about us.

Afrika Bambaataa spins at Negril, as Jazzy Jay and Fab 5 Freddy look on (© Lisa Kahane)

the downtown scene

AFRIKA BAMBAATAA: When hip-hop was coming up, punk rock was also coming up at the same time. So I started having this vision that I've got to grab that Black and white audience and bridge the gap. A lot of the Black community thought I was crazy as hell, but they didn't see what I was trying to do. I was trying to get that same audience like Sly and the Family Stone had, which was 50/50 of each audience.

In the early '80s, I started playing places downtown like the Jefferson, the Mudd Club, Negril, Danceteria, and eventually the famous Roxy Club, where all races and nationalities from around the world was coming. It was a time when a lot of people was nervous for us, saying, "Well, what's going to happen when these Blacks and Latinos start mixing with the whites downtown on the scene?" The media was pushing a hype like there was going to be racial violence and all this type of crap. But when I got down there, and I started playing all that funky music, you seen them punk people start going crazy! Slam-banging, jumping crazy, with the hip-hop people looking at them like, "What's this?" Then you see the hip-hoppers trying to do that punk dance and that thing where they're going side to side, and then the punks trying to do the rap steps and all this sort of stuff.

AFRIKA ISLAM: Kool Lady Blue is the lady who put it together, who brought the brothers down. Broke the prejudice barrier, let the brothers come out and be themselves. It was a place where dressin' up was cool and dressin' down was cool. Just come down wearin' what you wanted to. You didn't have to wear shoes to get in, you could wear your sneakers, jump off...it was a good atmosphere. Plus it was a big, open space, and that's what you need.

Everybody got a chance to display what they did best at the Roxy. It was a lot of peace, lot of harmony, lot of rich, lot of poor...It was a place where you could come out and do your own thing, no matter who you were. Crazy Legs and the Rock Steady Crew did the breakin', Futura and Fab 5 Freddy and Keith Haring and Doze and Dondi were the graffiti artists. D.St. at points...there were a lot of people involved. Madonna was down with the crew.

CEY ADAMS: The Roxy was on 18th Street and 10th Avenue, way over on the West Side. You'd go in, and there would be this long ramp, and they'd hang artwork along the ramps, so by the time you got in, it seemed like you'd been walking for two minutes just to get up the ramp. You'd go inside, and there was this huge room—I think it was a roller skating rink during the week; it was on the weekend that they'd do parties.

You'd have all kinds of people performing there, but usually it was a hip-hop act, and in addition they'd put this huge canvas on the wall, and they'd have graffiti artists come in and paint while people were rapping, or while they had like a break-dance exhibition. So it was interesting because you had these different things goin' on all at the same time. Now in addition to having people from the Bronx and Queens and Harlem and everything, you had all these white club kids who just loved being around the culture. That was when the marriage started to come together between rock and rap.

AFRIKA ISLAM: It was not just hip-hop; it was new groups. There was new underground bands, new punk bands. Everybody got a fair shot down there, 'cause the crowd was made up of everybody. People that are heavyweights in the industry now. We had everything in Roxy's from Parliament-Funkadelic to Trouble Funk to Herbie Hancock to David Bowie. UTFO, Whodini, Kurtis Blow...didn't matter.

AFRIKA BAMBAATAA: The Roxy was truly a world club. A lot of the stars was coming there, where they didn't have to be stars; they was just regular human beings. You could see Bianca Jagger or Mick or the people from Fame or Madonna before she blew up...everybody just partying all together under one roof. And the wilder we was onstage, the wilder the crowd was and the more the different races started coming to see us. The media just went crazy after that, showing the music bringing the people together. It did its job—a little peace, unity, love, and having fun. And "One Nation Under a Groove."

planet rock

FAB 5 FREDDY: I brought Bam to Club 57, where he played, and also this other downtown club called the Jefferson. The style at the time was...I think they called it New Romantic, the English kids were dressing up like pirates. That experience of Bam being downtown playing for those kind of kids inspired him to make "Planet Rock." He had always had records that a lot of the kids up in the Bronx wouldn't understand. He had everything from the Monkees to the Rolling Stones, you know the story. But he saw he could play for that kind of crowd and mix those kind of records in, and that helped inspire him.

AFRIKA BAMBAATAA: I used to run around to so many different record stores in the Bronx. I started hitting the areas of the Village and looking for obscure records, and I came across this album with these four guys on it, and I said to myself, "There's some weird-looking, robot-type of things." They almost looked like they were some Nazi type of thing, but I said, "Let me take this home, and see what's going on."

When I heard that group, I said, "What is this? This is so funky...these are some bad-ass white boys!" Once I heard the Kraftwerk, I said, "I've got to buy all this stuff!"

PHASE II

THE ROXY

Phase 2 with his homage to the Roxy, 198

Angie B and Double Trouble at the Roxy

A classic Negril show form 1982

Afrika Bambaataa in all his "Planet Rock" glory, ca. early '80s (Bob Gruen/Starfile)

And I started looking around, seeing that there was no Black group that was strictly electronic. I said, "We're going to be the first band to be electronic; I'm going to call my sound the Electro-Funk sound."

I met this keyboard guy by the name of John Robie, and I asked him, "Can you play the synthesizer as funky as the group Kraftwerk?" He said, "I'll tear them guys up!" I introduced him to our producer, Arthur Baker, and the rest is history—the birth of the "Planet Rock" sound, the Electro-Funk sound, which was the up-tempo style of hip-hop.

VAN SILK: Bambaataa changed the course of hip-hop music with "Planet Rock." He was wanting us to hear it for weeks. Flash had "Birthday Party" out, and Bam kept gettin' on the mic, "Soul Sonic Force has got a record that's going to change the hip-hop world. It's gonna change everything." That year at the Zulu Nation Anniversary, they got up on stage and said, "We're going to play our new record." When he put on "Planet Rock," it was like the ultimate record. That was the first time that the electronic drum machines were actually used on a hip-hop record, because all the Sugarhill records were recorded by live bands.

AFRIKA BAMBAATAA: When we made "Planet Rock," when we got into the Electro-Funk style of hip-hop, we was really trying to reach the Black, Latino, and the punk rock whites. But I didn't know that "Planet Rock" was going to cause some type of chain reaction. "Planet Rock" became the sound that sparked a lot of other musical categories coming out from the Electro-Funk: the Miami Bass to the Latin freestyle, Latin hip-hop, to the house music, hip-house, techno.

you were all of a sudden this hip-hop celebrity

CEY ADAMS: A lot of the art galleries were starting to show graffiti as "fine art," commercial art, pop art. You had all these famous painters from the '50s and '60s coming down to graffiti shows—Andy Warhol, Roy Lichtenstein, Robert Indiana. It was just an amazing thing to actually be in the same room with Andy Warhol and talking to him about graffiti. And then you find out that they're fans of graffiti artists the same way graffiti artists were fans of pop icons of the '60s and '50s. I guess they could identify with what we were doing because we were the young rebellious art of our time, and what they were doing was the rebellious art of their time, the pop art of the '60s. It was very similar in a lot of ways.

PISTOL: Graffiti sort of went the way of the '80s; it just started getting glamorous and more about marketing. Andy Warhol...I mean, God bless him, I loved the guy. I worked for *Interview* magazine for a little bit. He took graffiti and brought it into the public, brought it into everyone's living room, made celebrities out of them. And in a way it helped sell the artwork.

CEY ADAMS: These are kids from the Bronx; most people were dirt poor. It was a way of earning some money while doin' what you do. I mean it was a hobby for most people—the idea of getting paid was just unheard of. "You're going to pay me to do this?" [laughs] So coming downtown and fusing with the whole rock world, the white downtown club scene, was really interesting. You had real celebrities—this famous artist or this famous singer—and you were all of a sudden this hip-hop celebrity.

If you met a millionaire developer, it was nothin' for him to give you $500 to paint a wall. It was nothin' for a critic to say a few words about you, and all of a sudden you were in an art magazine, and then a dealer decides he's going to represent you. I mean that's really what it was all about. It was about finding that person who was going to be your ticket out of the ghetto.

downtown's up, uptown's down

VAN SILK: The progression of hip-hop, when it started coming downtown, it really bothered me because it became a money factor. These groups weren't promoting themselves; if it wasn't for the Van Silks, the Ray Chandlers, the Arthur Armstrongs, there wouldn't be no rap because there was nobody to promote it. We pay a group like the Fearless 4—I'm going to use them as an example—the $400 or $500; they go downtown and play, and when they come back, they want fifteen hundred. They forgot where they came from. We couldn't book them in the local schools like we wanted to because only so many people could come in the gym. We could handle $500; they wanted $1,500. You went under, because you couldn't charge $20 to get in. We were charging $5 or $6. The only group that could demand money without playing downtown was Grandmaster Flash, and we would pack three thousand people in the Audubon Ballroom with Flash back then in those days for $5.

So it goin' downtown with Blue as a promoter, which Afrika Islam was involved with, and Fab 5 Freddy...it was cool, the graffiti scene, the break-dancing scene. It was cool, but I personally didn't participate in it. I wasn't feeling it, because when they got tired of them downtown, they had to come back uptown again, and their price went back down.

318

Funk Box party in Bridgeport, Connecticut, with LL Cool J, 1985

FROSTY FREEZE: Everybody from uptown, the DJs, everything, started playing downtown. The downtown scene connected with the uptown scene. Everything was still going on up there, but people were coming downtown more, to Manhattan. The Bronx, the scene up there was sort of dying out in the Roxy's era.

SAL ABBATIELLO: The Roxy opened up in Manhattan, and now all of a sudden Disco Fever wasn't that in anymore. Now we're talking Manhattan, trendy...you got white people, rockers, Spanish and Black, and now it's getting national. The Fever was becoming just another neighborhood spot. Little by little, the violence started happening. I had a murder at the club. I had a problem with one of the gangsters in the street who was trying to shake me down, and I'm wearing a bullet-proof vest every night...In about six months to a year, everything was just falling apart. My workers were becoming addicted to drugs, and the clubs were closing up; everybody was going to Manhattan. None of those rappers were coming to the club anymore. It just wasn't worth it anymore.

The one bright spot that was happening for the Fever was that Warner Brothers wanted to do this movie *Krush Groove*. The Fever was one of the main scenes, and I thought this was gonna be an uplift, that this would bring attention to the club. They were breaking down after filming the last scene, and we were going to have a big party that night. People were saying, "You gotta hurry up. There's some people out there, and they're gonna shut you down." I'm going, "They can't shut me down. I have all the licenses." And they're going, "No, I'm telling you." So now I'm looking around. I see all these different men—white men—and I said, "It looks like all feds out there." It was ironic. *Krush Groove*...I thought it would give the Fever another ten-year life, but that's what got the club closed. Because it brought so much attention to the neighborhood. So sure enough, I didn't have a cabaret license. A dancing license. That's what they closed me down for, because I didn't have a dancing license. They put 150 people out of work, and that was the end of the Fever. We closed the last night of the filming of *Krush Groove*. And that was the end of that era.

the decline of the
old school

AFRIKA ISLAM: All of Russell's groups, from L.L. [L.L. Cool J] on, really got their break at clubs like Danceteria, the Roxy, Peppermint Lounge, and the Mudd Club. It's because the DJs of hip-hop were all in the Zulu Nation—Flash, Jazzy Jay, Bambaataa, and myself—we always played downtown in underground white-mixed clubs, and people like Kool Lady Blue let us play and get off the stuff that we wanted. When Russell approached me at the Roxy to play the first DMC joints—"It's Like That (and That's the Way It Is)," "Hard Times," "Rock Box"—it was no problem putting them on. I was the man in control. So it was just nice to be able to do it. You put the records on with no politics, and you put them on just to support another brother. So he basically broke his Rush/Def Jam Empire from Zulus supporting him on the turntables and putting it on the air. That's how it happened.

RAY CHANDLER: When we was coming up, Russell Simmons, he come out of Queens. He was doing all the college stuff. Our paths would cross at different clubs. I used to see his guys out promoting his shows. There was never no friction between him and me. There was even times when he would do a show in Queens with Kurtis, and the promoter there didn't want to pay. We'd go out there with some of the fellas, the Casanovas, and talk to them and say, "Take care of Kurtis".

One time we had a big party at the Hotel Diplomat. The Hotel Diplomat used to be the home of Russell Simmons and Kurtis Blow; it was where they gave all their parties. Huge. Hotel Diplomat held thousands of people. You weren't supposed to, but we had thousands come in. I wanted to make this the biggest party that ever hit Manhattan. We had Kurtis Blow that night. He and Russell used to do the college crowd, and I did the high schools, junior high schools. They had a little more sophisticated crowd. More cool out with the ladies. I had the rough crowd.

I needed the Furious to help me promote the party. I would get up early in the morning and hit all the schools. I said, "Give me an appearance." They refused. I said, "OK. I'm going to do all this work by myself. But don't ask me for one penny above what you supposed to get." Deal is a deal.

I went out there with my crew and promoted this stuff off the hook. Everybody in the city was at this party. Long Island, Staten Island, New Jersey, Poughkeepsie, Newberry...We went all over! Flash would come with me to help, but the Furious didn't want to get up in the morning in the cold to help.

We had a sold-out crowd. The Furious came to do the show, but after the show they wanted more money, 'cause they felt that the crowd was so big because of them. No. It was my promoting. I was adamant about not giving one penny more. It was a matter of principle.

Rodney Cee and K.K. Rockwell broke from the Funky 4 + 1 in the summer of 1981 and formed a duo called Double Trouble. They did several scenes in *Wild Style*, such as their a cappella "Stoop Rap" and their appearance in the Ampitheater in white gangster suits and plastic guns, pictured in this mural by the artist Daze.
(© Charlie Ahearn)

RAHIEM: The place was packed wall to wall. The walls were sweating. We got paid $40 apiece, and they were charging $20 to get in. It was Christmas Eve. Without exaggeration, I would say between 3,000 and 5,000 people were there. We were discussing with Ray backstage our plans for the next few shows, and Ray was saying how the group had to accept short money that night to ensure that we'd lock in this other date for another night. I'm the newest member of the group, and I wanna be heard just like everyone else, so I say to Ray, "We're in demand, and this is like sardine money you're paying us." I'm the youngest member of the group, saying this to Ray Chandler. I remember the look that he gave me: it was like he was an elephant and I was an ant. He lunged at me. And not only did he lunge at me, he didn't stop, he kept coming. I'm sweating bullets, because now I'm running all around a table in the room with Ray Chandler on my heels, and he wants to fight me! I'm a child! He's big! Melle Mel jumped in between us, and now Melle Mel's about to fight Ray. As soon as Mel was about to get into it with Ray, everybody rushed over to where Mel was—not to try and do something to Ray but to grab Mel and get him away from Ray. I've never gotten hit by Ray Chandler, but you could kinda do the math.

RAY CHANDLER: Me and Melle Mel was almost ready to have a fight. They was pulling him back. It was quite embarrassing cause I had my wife there. They had their family there. I wanted to discuss it later, but it got so bad that Mel jumped up and said, "We never gonna play for you! Never!" That was the break-off point. It caused a big dilemma 'cause Flash stayed with me.

* * *

JAZZY JEFF: Funky 4 + 1 broke up after "That's the Joint." Rodney and K.K. walked out of the group. We was traveling, we was touring, we was doing things, and me, Keith, and Sha didn't feel like that was our audience. We tried to maintain a good perspective of the type of clientele we had. We didn't feel like we had that much clientele if we went out on the road on our own. Rodney kind of took things a little too fast, and we felt he should have slowed down. We felt he tried to rush our success. Rodney felt we was worth more than what we felt we was worth. I think he just got misguided and tried to float when it wasn't time for us to start floatin'. He was in a feelin' by himself, and we felt K.K. was a follower, so K.K. followed along with him. And that's how we ended up breaking up. We was in my house when they walked out the door, and we didn't bother to look for them; we just left it.

SHA-ROCK: The Funky 4 was still doing things together; we'd perform together in different areas. Sometimes it would just be me, Jeff, and Keith-Keith that would do shows. We still had the name Funky 4, but it wasn't as though we were really together. It just somehow happened that we just dissolved. It wasn't that this was something that we wanted. Somehow Lil' Rodney Cee and K.K. was able to get out of their contract, and that's how they formed Double Trouble. Rodney Cee said, "I'm gonna get out of this, 'cause I have other things I wanna do." And K.K. said, "OK, I'm going with you." Me and Jeff and Keith wind up staying with Sugarhill Records because we thought that they were gonna do good by us.

REGGIE REG: The first couple of years with Sugarhill was great. We came out with "We Want to Rock." The next record was "Breaking Bells," and we did nice with that one, too. Then after "Breaking Bells," it was "On the Radio," which got even better. That was our first gold record on Sugarhill. After that, it's like, "We don't want no more advances. We want royalties now." We see this record as doing good and they tell us somebody bootlegged a lot of 'em. You know what I'm saying? So we checked that out and come to find out it was them! They bootlegged their own record. So we got a lawyer, and they closed Sugarhill down for awhile. Flash was already suing 'em. The Funky 4 was already suing 'em. Sugar Hill Gang was having problems with them. All the groups that was on Sugarhill like in '84 was having a lot of problems with Sugarhill. It was a lot of money, and nobody wasn't getting it but Sugarhill.

We left Sugarhill. A year later we came out with a record done by [producer] Teddy Riley called "The Crash Is Back." And on the flip side, DJ Red Alert had produced a different version of the "High Power Rap." We did it with some fly-by-night label. Teddy Riley wasn't signed yet, and Red Alert wasn't signed yet neither, so that record didn't come out 'til like seven years later. By that time, G-man had joined the police force. Barry joined the police force. Dave joined the police force. All the members of Crash Crew was either cops or city workers by then. 'Cause we was eighteen when we started, but we was becoming men then. We was having kids, and we could not sit around and wait for this hip-hop. We had already did our thing with hip-hop.

PARTYTIME
T LA ROCK & JAZZY JAY
SIDE A
PT 104
Def Jem
(ASCAP)
Street Studios
Ltd. (ASCAP)
STEREO
33 1/3 RPM
IT'S YOURS
(K. Keaton, R. Rubin)
Radio Mix (4:23) Inst. (4:34)
A S. U. R. E. Shot Mix, Produced by:
RICK RUBIN & Edited by: WEEMS
Recorded at: Power Play
Mastered by: HERB POWERS
at Frankford/Wayne
© & ℗ PartyTime Records 1984

SPECIAL K: When the movie *Beat Street* came into play, somehow it went from Treacherous 3 starring to us doing some "Santa Claus Rap." But what was good was that we was doing the soundtrack with ["Planet Rock" producer] Arthur Baker, and in the interim, we doing shows for this cat Rick Rubin. He's doing shows out of Hotel Diplomat, and we'd get gigs from him, and he started talking like he wanted to make a record. That's when he had Beastie Boys there doing some stuff, down to NYU in this dorm room.

I started hooking up with him. He gave me two tracks, and I wrote two songs. One was "I Have to Break Down," and the other was "It's Yours." I wrote "It's Yours" for my bro, T LaRock. I didn't do the role; I went back and got my brother. I was still on Sugarhill, getting paid. Rick Rubin was nervous as all outdoors; he kept wanting me to do the record. I told my brother to do it, and me, my brother, and Jazzy Jay, we collaborated. We went down to the studio, cut it, and I took the record. I was still working on the Beat Street soundtrack, and I overheard Arthur Baker saying that he was looking for a solo act. Bingo: I got "It's Yours" on the test press. Boom. "It's Yours" came out on Party Time, and you see the little logo of Def Jam there. Now, mind you, there was no Russell Simmons involved at the time. That was me and Rick Rubin's baby. I'm thinking me and Rick is cool; Rick is gonna look out for me.

I'm still working on the soundtrack for *Beat Street*, and Michael Holman came up with this idea for the Graffiti Rock, so we did that show, too, and Run-DMC and them was in the show with us, doing that little battle thing with Treacherous 3 versus Run-DMC. When Graffiti Rock had the party to celebrate its completion, Rick was like, "Yo, introduce me to Russell." Why not? Me and Russell was mad cool. I had took "It's Yours" down to his office, and Russell got on the phone, and it was on the radio that week. I'm still struggling with Sugarhill, and I'm like, "Well, this could be something." I put them two together, and now all of a sudden it's Russell Simmons and Rick Rubin. I missed the tag hard. That's just one of them things that happened to me in this business. I remember Rick calling me up all nervous, "L.L. Cool J, what do you think of it?" And if you listen to "I Need a Beat," it's the blueprint for "It's Yours." It's the same, just different drums. To this day, people think that Def Jam's first artist was L.L. Cool J...

REGGIE REG: When Def Jam came out, that was like the nail in Sugarhill's coffin. Sugarhill had the Treacherous 3, they had Mean Machine—the first Latino rappers— and they had Sequence. They had Spoonie Gee, they had Flash, they had us, and they was getting ready to sign Doug E. Fresh. They had the Funky 4, they had the Sugar Hill Gang. They had the best. They had everybody. But they wouldn't change.

Def Jam was a newer, fresher label. They weren't doing the old stuff that Sugarhill was doing...what Sugarhill wouldn't stop doing. We used to plead with them, "Yo, we need a drum machine. Forget about that live drum player you got there; we need a 808 (drum machine). We need to make it electronic." And they just didn't want to change.

They didn't want to make the videos, and they didn't want to hire DJs to make music for them, which was everything Def Jam and Russell Simmons and them was doing. They was taking it to the next level, and Sugarhill wasn't going to that next level 'cause of their greed. They didn't want to pay the price. They wanted to get that money, just how they was getting it.

The guys on Def Jam—Run-DMC, L.L., and them—we wanted to do what they was doing. At the time, we were like right neck-and-neck with them. If we was doing what they was doing, we'd probably still be out there with them. I remember Run-DMC opening up for us at a show in Broadway International. They came up there with 40-ounces and hats on backwards and stuff, and we was not allowed to do stuff like that on Sugarhill. We couldn't. We couldn't curse on Sugarhill. After that, Sugarhill was just wack. Def Jam was what was going on.

GRANDMASTER CAZ: Run-DMC was the cutoff point between us and hip-hop after that. That was the end of the era for Grandmaster Flash and the Furious 5, for the Cold Crush, for the Funky 4+1, for the Fearless 4s and for the Fantastic 5s and all that. That was the end of our era, when Run-DMC and them came into the game. Because we had taken hip-hop from its bare necessities, from a baby, from being just in the park with speakers and stuff and plugging into light poles, up to doing shows in leather outfits with fur shit hanging off of us. We took hip-hop as far as it could go without it changing into something else.

If we'd have went any farther where we were going with it, it wouldn't have been hip-hop anymore, so I think it was a good thing that Run-DMC and them came. It simplified the whole process. Let's take this back: the cats who came after us, they couldn't fill our shoes. They couldn't say, "Okay, we're going to take it from here. We got the boots, we got the leather stuff like they got." They couldn't do that. They're like, "Look, we're going back, we're going to put on the sneakers, the jeans. We're going to look just like we look when we're at a party." So that was a good thing. That was a good thing for hip-hop.

SAL ABBATIELLO: Run did his first show at the Fever. They were kids, and their outfits were so hysterical. They had these plaid, checkered jackets on with these hats, and everybody was laughing at them because the whole scene was leather and fringes and sparkly and rhinestones—made outfits—and they came out with these plaid jackets. But you knew it was something special, and that's when rap took the change. They made, "It's Like That" and "Sucker MCs," and Russell kept saying, "Yo, you heard my brother's record?" and I'm going, "No." He goes, "It's the biggest record in the Fever!" 'cause Russell's motto was always "It wasn't a rap record until it went around in the Fever."

BILL ADLER: The key to Russell Simmons's success is, "I'm not going to water it down. I'm not going to whiten it up. This is going to be pure and uncut. This is what these young Black kids are bringing to the party. This is their ticket, okay?" And fifty years ago, you couldn't have imagined that they'd get over that way!

When rap first emerged, the only really big crossover artist who was Black was Michael Jackson. And he was clearly not the Black guy next door. He's a very exotic character; he's a brother from another planet. These rappers were much more everyday. And it was Russell's genius to broker them to the mainstream as they were. They didn't have to be white. They didn't have to have white mannerisms. They didn't have to speak standard English. None of that. And even so, they were going to get over. And more than that, Russell's point was that it was because they were authentic and true to themselves that they would get over. And he was right.

DMC: At a time when hip-hop was becoming really popular in all the five boroughs in New York, Bambaataa, Grandmaster Flash, everybody started dressin' up 'cause they had a little bit of money. The Cold Crush would just come to the parties as is and do their performance. And the performance became the attention-getter and not how good you looked, how many curls you had in your hair, how many braids you had in your hair. It was just about the beats and the rhyme. To Run-DMC, it was like, "Oh, you mean to tell me we don't gotta dress up?" They showed us what to rap about, how to rap, how to represent yourself with your title, to make it royal...but they also showed us come as you are, you know what I'm sayin'? And when Run-DMC first came out, that was the reason why people related to us—even the rock 'n' roll kids, the white kids. They could relate to us because we was just like the guys on the corner they saw, or the guys they went to school with, or the people they worked with. You know, we had on Lee jeans, shell-toe Adidas, Pro-Keds, Pumas, Kangol hats, sweatshirts, whatever was just common at the time, not the fly gear, not the British walkers and the Playboys and the leather coats, but the common gear. People looked at us and could relate to us. The Cold Crush showed me that what my mother bought me was cool. We don't have to go to the leather guy and get costumes made up to look like Superman or to look like the stars of the day 'cause we are the stars. We're normal guys, but we're good, and this is who we be. This is who we are.

CHARLIE CHASE: When Run-DMC first came on to the scene, they blew up so fast! I felt like...these guys didn't earn theirs, man. I put too much effort into this, and I was frustrated. I was angry. Yet these guys will give us props straight up and down for their start. We inspired them. A lot of people give them more props than they deserve, but they give us the credit for helping inspire them; they give credit where credit is due.

I was frustrated for a long time, but what finally made me say, "You know what, man? You gotta give it to 'em," was when they took hip-hop to that other level. You could actually say they picked up where we left off. There was a next level there, and I guess we just couldn't do it. But they had the new vibe, plus they had Russell Simmons behind 'em. I knew Russell Simmons when all he had in his office was a desk and nothing else. There was echo like crazy in there, it was so empty. But at this point in time, you have to give it to them.

REGGIE REG: We met L.L. when he was auditioning for Russell Simmons and them. We was right there in the office, and he was like, "Yo, Crash Crew, my grandma got your record. Yo, I like that one 'Breaking Bells,' and I want to do it over." At the time, we were like, "Yeah kid, sure..." And sure enough, he did it. He did it good. I'm proud, you know what I'm saying? It's not like he really took from us, but we know where his mind was at when he came up with these records. Like "Rock the Bells"—we came up with "Breaking Bells." "I Can't Live Without My Radio"...it could just be the words, but knowing L. personally, I know that we had a little influence in that record with "On the Radio."

I can't take total credit because I didn't really invent anything. I'm on the bandwagon of hip-hop culture, which is that everything has been done before. You can't really be mad at a cat who just makes your stuff better. That's just how everything is. Everything has been done. You just make it better. Like the wheel came, then the car. You can't get mad at that.

A young L.L. Cool J on the bill in early '85

332

EPILOGUE:

no boundaries

More than twenty-five years—that's how long hip-hop has dominated pop culture, and that's an eternity in a landscape that discards last year's next-big thing before we grow accustomed to her face. Hip-hop dominates global youth culture and has had a pervasive influence on dance, fashion, and graphic design. And it was all created by the pioneers in this book. Yet if you ask most people who call themselves hip-hop fans to name an "old school" performer, chances are they'll name Run-DMC or L.L. Cool J. This shouldn't really surprise us, as it's an old story in popular music. Despite Busy Bee's statement that the Fantastic 5 "were like the Beatles," the fact is they were a lot more like Hank Ballard and the Midnighters: front-runners whose music and historical importance is appreciated by the historian and the knowledgeable fan, but who are just music trivia for the mainstream consumer.

For today's teenagers, the music of Def Jam—the artists who supplanted the true old school—is their parents' music. The sound and feel of hip-hop have been transformed three or four times since the mid-'80s, which makes it that much more remarkable that young people around the world now turn out in droves to hear Kool DJ Herc or Afrika Bambaataa DJ a major rave. Late-night television watchers in the late '90s saw Grandmaster Flash DJ-ing as the musical director of the Chris Rock show. Grand Wizard Theodore is still active and revered as a guest performer and judge of "turntablist" competitions—affairs put together by worldwide organizations devoted to a musical idiom that these pioneers created out of whole cloth. Many of the artists we've been following are still active and looking forward to their next break; others have moved on to other fields of endeavor or just moved on. Their collective accomplishments have changed our culture immeasurably, and their example of the will to create in the face of neglect and adversity is surely one of the most inspiring artistic legacies of the twentieth century.

(D.ST.) DXT: I realize that when I was at Bambaataa's parties, I was one of those guys who would never say anything. I would just stay in the back and dance. I would close my eyes and go off. I didn't know shit about African culture, but for some strange reason when we heard those beats and those rhythms something happened.

Bambaataa was the Mecca of the energy source, Bambaataa was the witch doctor...there would be a certain moment when the records would play; at that point it would be this tribal thing and everybody would just do it. That's some deep shit. What was that? How can I use that information to grow? That's the true purpose of what we have to do.

Hip-hop culture, if you truly understand it, is profound. It is an energy source that has an effect on the entire planet. I've been everywhere, Russia, Cuba, Japan, you name it. And everywhere that I have gone I have seen hip-hop. That energy has spread itself around the globe. Every culture on this planet now has some sort of interaction with this energy. You have to ask yourself, "why?"

AFRIKA BAMBAATAA: I see a lot of people today who are excited almost like back then. Back then it was more in its fresh mode, but now when I go to different countries you see all the different rappers. Before, a lot of the rappers from different countries used to try to rap in English, and I used to tell them, "No, no—rap in your own native tongue. You will be more successful because you can rap about your own problems or your own party-type moments," and now you have a lot of stars who have blown up in France and Germany—Germany has a crazy large hip-hop scene—and England now with the drum and bass and the jungle scene.

And a lot of these people are becoming stars in their own right, speaking their own native tongues. The excitement that you see a lot of places outside of America, it's more true to the hip-hop culture than America itself.

FAB 5 FREDDY: I was recently down in Brazil, meeting rappers there and really getting an in-depth look at their scene, and a lot of it is amazing to me because it's replaying in some ways what happened in the early '80s as hip-hop became a force in American culture. You see the similarities, yet the complete differences, you know? You see that in France. You see that in Cuba.

I've recently been down in Cuba with a lot of rappers there, and you see them grasping on to a lot of the purer aspects and things that are very similar to hip-hop in its earlier form here. It's very refreshing for me, to see these things play out again, to see hip-hop serve different functions and different roles for people.

Like in Brazil, which has the second largest population of people of African descent on the planet. They have a very advanced form of apartheid, if you will, where people of color are so far down on the economic totem pole. Now, in the last seven to ten years, hip-hop has become a raging force, with similar scenarios to what happened here, where you have artists with no airplay, no video play, selling platinum. And the best of these artists, the artists in the forefront, are all speaking about the situation that people of color are living in, in Brazil. It is forcing the society as a whole now to take a look that they've never taken before. So that's interesting, seeing how hip-hop's playing out in different areas.

WHIPPER WHIP: We go to Japan—this is like fifteen, twenty years later they're seeing us—I took Grandmaster Melle Mel's place in a venue that he wasn't able to go to. I wasn't even on the poster; they just had it scratched out: "In Mel's place we got Prince Whipper Whip," and there's guys with Wild Style posters in the front, and they're like, "Yo, sign my posters!" And Wild Style albums! It's like, "It's the first time we've seen you in fifteen, twenty years." It felt great; it was incredible. In Japan they call us heroes, 'cause we're the first thing they know about hip-hop. And they dig back deep. When you dig to the root of hip-hop, what're you gonna find? Us! You're gonna find the pioneers that set it off. And who never gets paid? The pioneers that set it off [laughs].

GRANDMASTER CAZ: I'm a DJ and I'm an MC, and I'm hip-hop. I mean, rap is one thing; hip-hop is something else. Hip-hop is the entire culture, and rap is just one element of it. It's the most exploited and the most marketable element, but it's only one element. I mean DJ-ing is a whole world in itself. It might not be as marketable as an industry, but it's just as important an element in the culture. So is graffiti. Graffiti is just as important in the culture of hip-hop. B-boying. What the media calls break-dancing, we sell a few products with it here and there. We can only take it this far; we don't know what to do with it. So b-boying is not a multibillion-dollar industry because they don't know how to market it that way. But rap? MC-ing? Oh yeah, it just went through the roof. But it's only one element of the culture. And the culture is more important than any one of its elements. The culture as a whole.

DJ DISCO WIZ: I don't think that people know how to go to a party and really have a good time anymore. Because when we did it, it was about having a good time, and we did it for free. Hip-hop never gave me a cent. I never earned a dollar from hip-hop. But what I gave to hip-hop is priceless. You understand? I put my kids through college. I'm going to be a grandfather. And I never got a penny from hip-hop. What I did, I did it from the heart. And that's my legacy that I leave. What I gave to hip-hop I gave to them.

THEODORE: When I first started doin' it, I didn't do it for the money. I did it for the love, ya know? That shows when people see me or see the Fantastic perform: you see that we are really into it because we really love it. You have a lot of guys today that's into it just for the money, and that's not real. When you do something, you have to love it in order for you to put your 110 percent into it. That's what I do.

JAZZY JEFF: We didn't do shows then; we did all-night parties. A show was like something where you get on and you get off. We did parties. We was onstage all night, which is what rappers do not do anymore. They come in there, do a record, and they're gone.

REGGIE REG: Twenty-five, thirty years ago when hip-hop was started with Kool Herc and them, everybody was like, "It's gonna play out. It's gonna play out just like bicycles and skateboards." And they was wrong. They was very wrong.

What I would like people to remember about the Crash Crew is that we was like Wu Tang of the '70s. You know what I'm saying? We all started like ten to fifteen years old deep in the projects, in Lincoln Projects. We pooled our money together. We came out with a record. It was a beautiful ride to be in on the beginning of hip-hop. It was good to be a part of that and still to be remembered like twenty-five, thirty years later.

TONY TONE: We used to do parties, and they used to cost girls $2, guys $3, to get in to see who they wanted to see all night. Now they paying $30, $40, $50 to see somebody on stage for twenty minutes. As far as the gangsta rappers, it's always been some kind of gangsta rappers, but in a different form. A lot of people are talking, and you have these kids listening to them and trying to live what they saying on the records. We was living it, but we wasn't saying it on the records—we was trying to tell people to have fun and enjoy life. So it's changed, some for the good and some for the bad. I still love it. I started in it when I was like sixteen and I'm forty-two now, and I'm still doing it. I'm still able to catch the beat.

DMC: The Cold Crush was about the heart; that's what they personified. They had the essence of hip-hop. And that's why everything Run-DMC does is just an emulation of them. And I'm not embarrassed to say that. The reason why we're def, 'cause we're out to beat the Cold Crush, not just back then, every day—because the thing that they did is untouchable.

TONY TONE: "Tony Tone never leaving the girls alone...." I used to be on the train, sitting there, and I would hear people saying it. I would look at them, and they would look at me like, "Is that really you?" And I'd just shake my head, like, "Yes, it's me." So it's good, it's good. I didn't make the money that artists are making now, but I ain't bitter about it. Jay-Z's got a record out now sayin' his price is inflated because of what they did to the Cold Crush. Hey, life is life. I love hip-hop!

SHA-ROCK: It's like, "Listen: I started this. I started this from the streets." We paved the way, but we never reaped the monetary benefits, the fame. It was our fault, because as teenagers we didn't know to learn the business. We made it easier for the next generation to be able to just explode from it, because at that point the world was ready for it. There was no limitations.

BUSY BEE: We old school, if that's what you want to call us, but we wasn't old fools. If you've got a skill to rap, now you can make you some money. You can live off of that now. At that time, we didn't even think this was going to happen, but it happened. Rap is going to go on forever now. We in London, Germany, Portugal, Tokyo. I mean, where can you go where there's nobody rappin'?

SHA-ROCK: We never felt like it was a fad. If you were there from the beginning, then you knew that this was real, this is a part of history. You can choose to listen to it, or you can choose not to listen to it, but this is just history. It's just like blues, just like jazz. It's just the way that it is.

ART ARMSTRONG: These kids that developed rap—they were true pioneers. I think they were pioneers on the terms of jazz artists or blues artists. They followed the same pattern without even knowing it. They developed a skill of battling each other because reputations were made and lost in those battles. Same as in jazz. They developed the art of making their own flyers. They developed a lot of promoting, without any blueprint being laid out for them. So I think it should be recognized that they were real pioneers.

EASY AD: They say it's a democratic society, but it's not. There's a rich and a poor separation. So out of the poor we grew the art form called hip-hop. This is our baby. We birthed this. It was a message to everyone all over the world. A record can go a long way. It's like the telephone; you can reach out and touch people. Hip-hop was reachin' out and touching people, not only in the ghetto. So now it's come to where it's not a baby anymore; it's like a full-grown man or woman. Now it's about economics. It's about money, it's about exploitation, like any other music. I mean you go back into the '40s and '50s and the '60s, bebop music and all that; companies exploited the artists like they do today. It's just on a larger level.

GRANDMASTER CAZ: We have one thing in common, everybody that lives where hip-hop started, and that's that it's impoverished. It's the ghetto. We the ghetto people. There's basketball courts in the parks, and that's free. That's why we so good at basketball, because that's all we got, you know what I'm sayin'? We reach within ourselves to pull out something creative, and when hip-hop came to the front, it appealed to every kid because everybody could do it. All you had to do was just want to do it. It was somethin' that you could be a part of, and you didn't need accessories. To be a b-boy all you have to do is dance. All you got to do is just hear the music and learn the moves, create your own. There was no wrong or right; everything that was done was somethin' new. That's why it was exciting.

GRANDMASTER FLASH: I always knew that...for those who never heard this music, that if they had a chance to hear this, they would have no choice but to love this. Because unlike all the other genres of music, there are no boundaries to hip-hop. We can lyrically describe and talk about anything that we want to. Musically, we could almost use anything. We don't have to sing in key. We don't have to have a bridge or a chorus. It doesn't matter. This particular style of music...is it.

GRANDMASTER CAZ: Hip-hop is my life. It's what I've done since I was a kid. My whole entire adult life has been dedicated to it, and I've still got stuff to bring. I've still got rhymes in my head and in my heart. There's more to do.

THEODORE: I am hip-hop. My everyday life is hip-hop: what I do, what I say, the way I dress, the kind of music I listen to, seeing the graffiti on the walls all the time ...it's like my everyday life. It's in my blood. If you was to cut my veins, a bunch of music notes and records would just start pouring right out, ya know? It's just my life.

340

Grandmaster Flash, Kool DJ AJ, DJ Baron, Kool DJ Herc, Grand Wizard Theodore, Easy AD, Tony Tone, and Kevie Kev at an EMP oral history shoot, Harlem, 1999 (© Martha Cooper)

acknowledgements

This book began with a series of filmed interviews I did in the process of developing the Experience Music Project's Hip-hop Nation exhibit. These interviews continued over a three-year period as part of EMP's Oral History Program, and will carry on into the foreseeable future. As we developed EMP's exhibit program I had the sense to know that we couldn't open a museum at the cusp of the new millennium without acknowledging the centrality of hip-hop to our global popular culture. I also had the enlightened and generous support of EMP's founders, Paul G. Allen and Jody Allen-Patton, whom I can't thank enough for supporting me in this and numerous other projects. What I did not have was direct knowledge of hip-hop culture, or contacts with the insiders and artists whose aid I would need in gathering the materials and knowledge to put the exhibit together. So I have a lot of people to thank.

I need to acknowledge people in three categories. Starting at the beginning: Reebee Garofalo introduced me to Bill Adler; Bill—either directly or indirectly—introduced me to pretty much everybody else. He also conducted a number of the interviews that are excerpted here. I couldn't have put together the exhibit or this book without his help. A number of other people who are interviewed here regularly provided me with assistance and reality checks: Henry Chalfant, Tony Tone, Grandmaster Caz, DJ Disco Wiz, and Fabel Pabon. Van Silk, Darnell Williams, Arthur Armstrong, and Kool DJ AJ all provided invaluable insight and/or contacts and materials. A few people whose names don't show up in the text provided crucial assistance at one point or another: Michael Gonzales, Martha Cooper, Dana Heinz-Perry, Erni Vales, Cey Adams, Elliott Wilson, Zephyr and Lady Pink. Among other things, Martha Cooper was the person who told me that Charlie Ahearn had all these great photographs that nobody had ever seen…

On the business side, I need to thank Sarah Lazin for helping me shape the original proposal and finding us a publisher and an editor who saw the potential in this project. That editor—Andrea Schulz—moved on before we finished the project, but not before working hard and long to help shape the book you have in your hands. A special thanks to Ben Schafer, who picked up where Andrea left off, to Alex Camlin, who massaged the ideas of two opinionated authors into a coherent book design, to Stanley Smith, who prepared all the digital images, and to Mickey Brady, who helped organize them for publication.

On the content side, a heartfelt thank-you to all of the people who granted us interviews. My co-author Charlie Ahearn has already inspired a couple generations of hip-hop artists and fans through his wonderful film Wild Style; this book is in some ways a continuation of that remarkable legacy, and I thank him for bringing so much insight, emotion, and knowledge to the development of this book. In addition to a wealth of incredible photos and a bunch of great interviews. Speaking of people who have helped educate the world about hip-hop, thanks to Nelson George for his inspirational work over the years and for consenting to write the introduction to this volume. My friend and colleague Jacob McMurray helped organize and conduct many of the interviews, corrected the transcripts, and provided invaluable research, intellectual, and psychological support. Van Silk provided us with a number of interviews he did back in the early '90s that helped fill holes in my and Charlie's work. My wife, family, colleagues and friends put up with me while I obsessed about this topic for a couple years, and then for the 10 weeks or so that I was locked in the basement editing all of it together. When I wasn't tethered to my laptop I was on the phone with Charlie, who tolerated my periods of euphoria and despair. To all of the interview subjects that we contacted and couldn't hook up with, the people we couldn't find and the people who wouldn't talk: the job's never done; it's not too late. If someone had told me a year ago that this book would come out without including interviews with (insert at least a dozen names here) I would have told them they were crazy; if someone had told me five years ago that I would have had the opportunity to speak with all of the wonderful people whose voices appear in this book, I would have told them they were crazy. Hopefully y'all think we did pretty good with what we got. Lastly, in the immortal words of the Crash Crew: "Debie Deb rocks the house!"

Jim Fricke

This book was conceived in Jim Fricke's office in November 2000 as we poured over EMP's collection of early party flyers and imagined them along-side personal stories of those times. Jim's spontaneous enthusiasm and enduring trust laid the foundations for this project to exist. Thanks, Jim.

I want to thank many people who have helped to connect me to their world along the way. Nathan Ingram, who has been not just a martial arts teacher but a hero to me and his community for over twenty five years. Lee Quinones, who inspired me with his murals. Fred Brathwaite who shared a simple idea with me which became the Wild Style movie. My brother John who made art of the people of the Bronx. My wife Jane Dickson for her eye and her guidance. Busy Bee, Grand Master Caz, Rodney Cee, Kevie Kev, Flash and so many other hip hop pioneers who invited me to their jams and into their homes.

I am grateful to Marty Cooper, Henry Chalfant and Jack Stewart who helped to preserve subway art for the future. Steve Hager who first put the hip hop story together in a book.

I am indebted to everyone who shared their stories with me. Blade, Baron, Bom5, Burn, Busy Bee, Caz, D.St., Crazy Legs, Flip Rock, Frosty Freeze, Joe Joe, K.K. Rockwell, Kevie Kev, LEE Quinones, Lucky Strike, Melle Mel, Pee Wee Dance, Rahiem, Theodore, Tony Tone and Ray Chandler. I would especially like to thank Caz and Tone for their support in this project.

Charlie Ahearn

**discography:
breakbeats**

It's Just Begun Jimmy Castor
It's Just Begun (RCA, 1972)

Give It Up, Or Turn It Loose James Brown
Sex Machine (King, 1970)

Get Into Something The Isley Brothers
Get Into Something (T-Neck, 1970)

Get Ready Rare Earth
Get Ready (Rare Earth, 1969)

Melting Pot Booker T & the M.G.s
Melting Pot (Stax, 1971)

Apache Incredible Bongo Band
Bongo Rock (Pride, 1973)

Take Me to the Mardi Gras
Bob James *Two* (CTI, 1975)

Bongo Rock Incredible Bongo Band
Bongo Rock (Pride, 1973)

Good Ole Music Funkadelic
Funkadelic (Westbound, 1970)

Bra Cymande
Cymande (Janus, 1972)

Listen To Me Baby Huey
The Living Legend (Curtom, 1971)

The Breakdown (Part II) Rufus Thomas
Did You Heard Me? (Stax, 1973)

The Mexican Babe Ruth
First Base (Harvest, 1972)

Heaven and Hell Is On Earth 20th Century Steel Band
Warm Heart, Cold Steel (United Artists, 1975)

Scorpio Dennis Coffey
Evolution (Sussex, 1971)

I Know You Got Soul Bobby Byrd
I Need Help (King, 1970)

Different Strokes Syl Johnson
7" single (Twilight, 1967)

Dance To The Drummer's Beat Herman Kelly & Life
Percussion Explosion (Electric Cat, 1978)

Get Up and Dance Freedom
Farther than Imagination (Malaco, 1979)

Mary Mary The Monkees
More of the Monkees (Colgems, 1967)

Soul Makossa Manu Dibango
Soul Makossa (Atlantic, 1972)

Daisy Lady 7th Wonder
Climbing Higher (Parachute, 1979)

Ain't No Half-Steppin' Heat Wave
Too Hot to Handle (GTO, 1976)

Jam On The Groove Ralph McDonald
Sound of a Drum (Marlin, 1976)

Think (About It) Lyn Collins
Think (About It) (People, 1972)

Rock Steady Aretha Franklin
Young Gifted and Black (Atlantic, 1972)

Hihache Lafayette Afro-Rock Band
Voodounon (Makossa, 1974)

The Champ The Mohawks
7" single (Pama, 1968)

Scratchin' Magic Disco Machine
Disc-O-Tech (Motown, 1975)

Hook & Sling Eddie Bo
7" single (Scram, 1969)

Shack Up Banbarra
7" single (Atco, 1976)

Ashley's Roachclip The Soul Searchers
Salt of the Earth (Sussex, 1974)

Trans-Europe Express Kraftwerk
Trans-Europe Express (Capitol, 1977)

Stand Sly and the Family Stone
Stand (Epic, 1969)

Johnny The Fox Meets Jimmy The Weed Thin Lizzy
Johnny the Fox (Vertigo, 1976)

Good Times Chic
Risque (Atlantic, 1979)

Walk This Way Aerosmith
Toys in the Attic (Columbia 1976)

Say It Loud—I'm Black and I'm Proud James Brown
Say It Loud, I'm Black and I'm Proud (King 1969)

Honky Tonk Woman The Rolling Stones
7" single (ABKCO, 1969)

I Can't Stop John Davis and the Monster Orchestra
Night & Day (Sam 1976)

Catch A Groove Juice
12" single (Greedy 1976)

Planetary Citizen Mahavishnu Orchestra / John McLaughlin
Inner Worlds (Columbia, 1975)

Indiscreet D.C. LaRue
Tea Dance (Pyramid, 1977)

Conga Lafayette Afro-Rock Band
Malik (Makossa 1976)

Razor Blade Little Royal & the Swingmasters
7" single (Tri-Us 1971)

Brother Green (The Disco King) Roy Ayer's Ubiquity
Mystic Voyage (Polydor, 1975)

Hot Shot Karen Young
12" single (West End, 1978)

discography: early hip-hop records

1979

You're My Candy Sweet b/w
King Tim III (Personality Jock)
Fatback Band (Spring)

Rapper's Delight
Sugarhill Gang (Sugar Hill)

We Rap More Mellow
The Younger Generation [`Furious Five] (Brass)

Superappin'
Grandmaster Flash and the Furious Five (Enjoy)

Rappin' and Rocking the House
Funky 4 Plus 1 (Enjoy)

Christmas Rappin'
Kurtis Blow (Mercury)

Spoonin' Rap
Spoonie Gee (Sound of New York)

Funk You Up
Sequence (Sugar Hill)

1980

Zulu Nation Throwdown Part 1
Afrika Bambaataa and the Cosmic Force (Paul Winley)

Zulu Nation Throwdown Part 2
Afrika Bambaataa and the Cosmic Force (Paul Winley)

Freedom
Grandmaster Flash and the Furious Five (Sugar Hill)

The Breaks
Kurtis Blow (Mercury)

To the Beat, Y'All
Lady B (T.E.C.)

The New Rap Language / Love Rap
Treacherous Three / Spoonie Gee (Enjoy)

The Body Rock
Treacherous Three (Enjoy)

High Power Rap
Disco Dave and the Force of the 5 MCs [Crash Crew] (Mike and Dave)

Vicious Rap
Tanya Winley (Paul Winley)

Adventures of Super Rhyme (Rap)
Jimmy Spicer (Dazz)

1981

Jazzy Sensation
Afrika Bambaataa and the Jazzy 5 (Tommy Boy)

That's the Joint
Funky 4 Plus 1 (Sugar Hill)

Can I Get a Soul Clap / Fresh Out the Pack
Grand Wizard Theodore and the Fantastic Five (Soul On Wax)

Feel the Heartbeat
Treacherous Three (Enjoy)

The Birthday Party
Grandmaster Flash and the Furious Five (Sugar Hill)

The Adventures of Grandmaster Flash on the Wheels of Steel
Grandmaster Flash (Sugar Hill)

Genius Rap
Dr. Jekyll and Mr. Hyde (Profile)

Dancin' Party People
Little Starsky (Golden Flamingo)

Apache
Sugarhill Gang (Sugar Hill)

Rapture
Blondie (Chrysalis)

It's Nasty (Genius of Love)
Grandmaster Flash and the Furious Five (Sugar Hill)

1982

Looking for the Perfect Beat
Afrika Bambaataa (Tommy Boy)

Planet Rock
Afrika Bambaataa & Soul Sonic Force (Tommy Boy)

Change the Beat
Fab Five Freddy (Celluloid)

It's Magic
Fearless Four (Enjoy)

Rockin' It
Fearless Four (Enjoy)

Grand Mixer Cuts It Up
Grand Mixer D. St. with the Infinity Rappers (Celluloid)

The Message
Grandmaster Flash and the Furious Five (Sugar Hill)

Breaking Bells (Take Me to the Mardi Gras)
Crash Crew (Sugar Hill)

Weekend
Cold Crush Brothers (Elite)

Making Cash Money
Busy Bee (Sugar Hill)

"Funk Box Party" The Masterdon Committee (Enjoy)

Magic's Wand
Whodini (Jive)

Renegades of Funk
Afrika Bambaataa & Soul Sonic Force (Tommy Boy)

The Roxy
Phase II (Celluloid)

1983

Punk Rock Rap
Cold Crush Brothers (Tuff City)

Beat Bop
K-Rob vs. Rammelzee (Tartown)

New York, New York
Grandmaster Flash and the Furious Five (Sugarhill)

You Gotta Believe / Lovebug Starski Live at the Fever
Lovebug Starski (Fever)

Play That Beat Mr. DJ
G.L.O.B.E. and Whiz Kid (Tommy Boy)

All Night Long (Waterbed)
Kevie Kev (Sugarhill)

Problems of the World Today
Fearless Four (Elektra)

White Lines (Don't Do It)
Grandmaster Melle Mel (Sugar Hill)

It's Like That / Sucker MC's
Run-DMC (Profile)

Rockit
Herbie Hancock Featuring Grandmixer D. St. (Columbia)

Wild Style (soundtrack LP)
Various artists (Animal/Chrysalis)

1984

Fresh, Wild, Fly and Bold
Cold Crush Brothers (Tuff City)

8 Million Stories / A.J. Scratch
Kurtis Blow (Specific)

It's Yours
T. La Rock / Jazzy Jay (Partytime)

I Need a Beat
LL Cool J (Def Jam)

Rock Box
Run-DMC (Profile)

Just Having Fun
Doug E. Fresh (Enjoy)

index